Cold War Narratives

ANDREA CAROSSO

Cold War Narratives:
American Culture in the 1950s

PETER LANG
Bern • Berlin • Bruxelles • Frankfurt am Main • New York • Oxford • Wien

Bibliographic information published by die Deutsche Nationalbibliothek
Die Deutsche Nationalbibliothek lists this publication in the Deutsche Nationalbibliografie;
detailed bibliographic data is available on the Internet at ‹http://dnb.d-nb.de›.

British Library Cataloguing-in-Publication Data: A catalogue record for this book is
available from The British Library, Great Britain

Library of Congress Cataloging-in-Publication Data

Carosso, Andrea
 Cold War narratives : American culture in the 1950s / Andrea Carosso.
     pages cm
 Includes bibliographical references and index.
 ISBN 978-3-03-431270-7
 1. United States–Civilization–1945- 2. United States--Social conditions–1945-
 3. Cold War–Social aspects–United States. 4. Popular culture–United States–History-
 -20th century. 5. Cold War in mass media. 6. Discourse analysis, Narrative–United
 States. 7. Conformity–United States–History–20th century. 8. Dissenters–United
 States–History–20th century. I. Title.
 E169.12.C2783 2012
 973.921–dc23
                            2012044442

Cover illustration: from iStockphoto © by PictureLake
Cover design: Didier Studer, Peter Lang, Bern

ISBN 978-3-0343-1270-7 pb.   ISBN 978-3-0351-0515-5 eBook

© Peter Lang AG, International Academic Publishers, Bern 2012
Hochfeldstrasse 32, CH-3012 Bern, Switzerland
info@peterlang.com, www.peterlang.com

All rights reserved.
All parts of this publication are protected by copyright.
Any utilisation outside the strict limits of the copyright law, without the permission
of the publisher, is forbidden and liable to prosecution.
This applies in particular to reproductions, translations, microfilming, and storage
and processing in electronic retrieval systems.

Printed in Switzerland

Contents

Introduction	7
CHAPTER 1 America in the Cold War Years	15
CHAPTER 2 The Affluent Society	39
CHAPTER 3 Building the Suburban Nation	59
CHAPTER 4 Projecting America Through Television	83
CHAPTER 5 Gray-Flannel-Suit Nation	103
CHAPTER 6 Beats, Rebels and the Other 1950s	129
CHAPTER 7 Reshaping Race in America	159
CHAPTER 8 The Age of Rock 'n' Roll	171
Notes	191
Index of Names	215
Acknowledgements	221

Introduction

> People don't see the world before their eyes until it's put in a narrative mode.
> (Brian De Palma)

In 1955, Robert Frank, a 30-year-old Jewish Swiss émigré, crisscrossed America in a second-hand automobile for almost one year, with a Leica camera and a Guggenheim Fellowship "to see what is invisible to others," as he later wrote.[1] Taking pictures of ordinary people, barber shops, jukeboxes, gas stations, and funerals, capturing the vacant, empty spaces of America's urban fringes and open lands, its rituals of exclusion, the aching loneliness, Frank seized an unaesthetic vision of drabness, gloom, and isolation. Frank's photos revealed a face of America that was a far cry from the current, pompous postwar rhetoric of a nation at the highest point of its economic prosperity.

In 1959, after several U.S. publishers had turned down his photos, Grove Press published *The Americans*, Frank's book of 83 carefully chosen snapshots from over 20,000 negatives he took during those journeys. Initially a flop, the book is now regarded as a landmark of modern photography. Many of the photos in *The Americans* were shot in the Deep South, where Frank documented the absurd rituals of racial segregation – the segregated buses, the segregated social functions. Others offered commentaries on the alienation of urban life, exposed the widespread isolation of postwar America's society, pondered on its obsession with automobile culture. Others still commented on the hollowness of the country's patriotic ostentation. In memorable shots, Frank underlined the distance between the people and their leaders: an unevenly hung poster of President Eisenhower next to a faceless mannequin dressed in a tuxedo in a barren store window; a man playing a tuba at a political rally whose head, and identity, vanished behind the instrument; recurring shots of the American flag so prominent in the foreground as to conceal the individuals behind it; a photo entitled "City Fathers – Hoboken, New Jersey," showing a row of tuxedoed men during a parade whose un-civic looks engaged questions on the status of America's institutions.

Published at the closing of a decade that saw, according to widespread consensus, the inception of what *Time* publisher Henry Luce had heralded in 1941 as "the American Century," *The Americans* struck an eerie note amidst the Cold War rhetoric of the United States as a land of benign democracy and generalized affluence. Many resented Frank's approach: the editors of *Popular Photography* denounced it as "an attack on the United States," full of "spite, bitterness and narrow prejudices;" others dismissed the photos as "badly framed" and "willfully obscure;" others still claimed they were "unpatriotic."[2]

The Americans appeared at one of the most disquieting periods in American history, at a time when the United States presented "two obvious public faces to the world."[3] On the one hand, there was the face of prosperity – America as the Land of Opportunity, a beacon of freedom, a nation enthusiastically celebrating its newly-won well being. This was America under the reassuring spell of the television sitcom, enjoying the purported glamour of the suburban home and its endless array of never-before-seen appliances, where consumption was understood as a close synonym of happiness. It was the America in which dad was the breadwinner and mom the homemaker, and home and car-ownership appeared to be natural facts of life. On the other hand, there was the face of unease and anxiety. The 1950s was the era of the Cold War and the constant threat of nuclear annihilation, when nuclear fallout shelters were constructed in public buildings and schools; it was the America of McCarthy's crusade against "un-American activities" and of the Hollywood blacklists, a country in which racial segregation was largely legal and the division between economic and social classes was beginning to widen.[4]

Official statistical data reflected that ambivalence. As Bremner and Reichard have pointed out, new developments in almost every area of American life resulted in new institutional arrangements and relationships. Demographic changes were decisive: a massive postwar baby-boom increased the population from an estimated 140 million in 1945 to 180 million in 1960, an increase of almost 30 percent. The number of children aged 14 or younger in America grew from

33.5 million in 1945 to 56 million in 1960.[5] Accordingly, family, child rearing, education and juvenile unrest became prominent in American society, as a highly visible "youth culture" dominated the latter part of the decade. The non-white population grew at an even higher pace than the national average and the migration of hundreds of thousands of African-Americans from the South to the industrialized North, East, and West further accentuated the problem of racial discrimination, which ceased to be a "regional problem" of the Deep South and emerged to national attention.

The country's population expanded mostly in urban settings. The 1960 census listed 212 Standard Metropolitan Statistical Areas, with a total population of more than 112 million – or over 60 percent of all Americans. This metropolitan population included the burgeoning suburbs, which transformed America's urban geography while polarizing race separation, as whites fled to the new suburban subdivisions, leaving blacks and other minority groups behind in the decaying inner cities. The economy as a whole underwent sweeping transformations. Under the growing dominance of large industrial conglomerates, the postwar era was very prosperous, with average annual earnings for all workers more than doubling while inflation remained low. This pushed most Americans towards a pattern of intensive consumption, which taxed the country's natural resources significantly and increased American dependence on imported energy sources – particularly petroleum.

Despite the generally upbeat spirit in the country, inequalities also deepened. While the ratio of families earning under $3,000 per year declined significantly during the decade, the percentage of nonwhites under the poverty level continued to be twice that of whites. Likewise, women, entering and remaining in the work force in greater numbers, continued to experience job frustrations and extensive discrimination by employers.

Culture also reflected that pattern of ambiguity, embarking on parallel routes: one spreading exaltation of the newfound postwar economic prosperity and one suggesting doubt or discontent toward the growing middle-class conformity which, many felt, was embracing the status quo in an exceedingly passive mode. If televised America appeared upbeat, care-free, and uninterested in the country's growing tensions, certain books, films and music forms – mostly appealing to the tastes of youths and minority groups – elaborated critical alternatives to that suburban imaginary which fulfilled adult fantasies of social mobility and consumption.

Intellectual life reflected that double path as well. On the one hand, American intellectuals gave up the rebellion and radicalism of the previous decades and embraced a more sedate, high-modernist intellectualism. The thinkers gathering around magazines like the *Partisan Review* and *Commentary* – a large group of liberal public intellectuals including, among others, philosopher Sidney Hook, literary critic Lionel Trilling, and social critic Norman Podhoretz – grew, in the words of Kevin Mattson, "fat and comfortable during the Cold War."[6] Others however, from within and without the liberal establishment, such as C. Wright Mills, Paul Goodman, Arthur Schlesinger, and John K. Galbraith, expressed discomfort at the growing tensions and inequalities of the Cold War era, best summarized in the opening sentence of Schlesinger's 1949 book *The Vital Center*: "Western man in the middle of the twentieth century is tense, uncertain, adrift. We look upon our epoch as a time of troubles, an age of anxiety."[7]

The American 1950s were indeed an "age of anxiety," whose master rhetoric, however, was mostly aimed at countering that discomfort with intimations of national wholeness and prosperity. In other words, 1950s America was pervaded by conflicting and contradictory narratives, whose convergence within a continuum of either idealized presentation of a prosperous and confident nation, or within a troubled agenda of fear, rebellion, and inequality appears problematic and inappropriate. The 1950s call for the superimposition of divergent images, designating post-World War II America as a distinct culture in which, as Warren Susman has argued, "triumph was accompanied by [...] a new self-consciousness of tragedy and sense of disappointment."[8]

The purpose of this book is precisely to look at some of those conflicting representations of the early Cold War, i.e. at the way in which American culture has been shaped by that superimposition of divergent images of itself. My starting premise is that meaning is generated precisely in the linguistic articulation of narratives, which, according to Alan Nadel, broach "the fissure between event and history"

Introduction 11

and allow individuals to "construct a self."[9] Defined by Jean-François Lyotard as "the quintessential form of customary knowledge," narratives are the principal way in which we make sense of the world by inserting events within a succession that "accounts for […] what we see."[10] Setting out from the principle that narratives are, as Roland Barthes has emphasized, "the very stuff of which history is made," I will look at accounts of the Cold War in the perspective, suggested by Nadel, that they are not "opposite of facts," but rather "their source and their condition of possibility."[11]

I will therefore investigate some the leading narratives of the American 1950s in an effort to make sense of the consistencies as well as the tectonic shifts that American culture underwent in the postwar years. My inventory will trace a trajectory that begins with the triumphal accounts at the end of World War II and ends with the contested tones of public and private uneasiness as emerging in key-texts ranging from David Riesman's *The Lonely Crowd* to the Nixon-Khrushchev "kitchen debate," from Betty Friedan's *The Feminine Mystique* to rock 'n' roll's contestation of the suburban imaginary. In short, I will discuss the diversity of cultural forms that largely dispel earlier one-dimensional narratives of the 1950s as age of consensus, aka the "tranquillized fifties."

Which raises the question: "When do the 1950s exactly begin and end?" One of the weaknesses of decade-by-decade analysis is obviously the fact that the calendar alone is inadequate to map out significant cultural trends and shifts. Scholars have repeatedly argued the viability of the notion of the 1950s as a "distinct era" in American culture, and have suggested possible alternatives to its exact periodization.[12] One of the earliest periodizers of the 1950s, historian Eric Goldman, identified the period from 1945 to 1955 as "the crucial decade," in which America finally broke with its nationalist-isolationist tradition in foreign affairs.[13] More recently, scholars have tended to see the 1950s in terms of a "long decade" spanning from the end of World War II to sometime in the early 1960s: some have set 1960 as a calendar end to the 1950s, others have extended the 1950s until the end of the Kennedy presidency.[14]

I tend to subscribe to the "long decade" theory, since representations of the American 1950s can come into full focus only if read against the larger narrative of the Cold War, whose inception predates January 1, 1950. Therefore, in the first chapter I discuss that "long" decade's political context, both domestic and international, retracing the leading narrative of the Iron Curtain and America's efforts at securing its own space while facing the challenges of world decolonization. I follow the Truman Doctrine's "natural" deployment in Korea and elsewhere as well as the domestic repercussions of the Red Scare, as epitomized by the HUAC investigations and the concurrent red-baiting hysteria. I end with America's witch-hunt revival under senator Joe McCarthy and the many ambiguities of the Rosenberg trial. In the second chapter I study the other face of the Cold War, when sustained military spending and the alignment of positive economic indicators converged to create the most extraordinary economic boom in American history, one that gave rise to the "affluent society." Named by John K. Galbraith, the affluent society stood at the cross-roads of a national myth of prosperity and the harsher realities of class and racial exclusion, as the U.S. focused – as Galbraith made clear in his less than celebratory account – on individual well-being and neglected social progress.

My third chapter studies the new social and geographical conditions under which the newly-won affluence was deployed: as inner cities became contested spaces of racial and social division, white Americans fled to the suburbs, initiating what is arguably America's most unique contribution to the invention of modernity. Mirroring, and purporting to defuse, Cold War anxieties, the suburbs were the defining sites of the middle-class consensus and my study focuses on contrasting cultural narratives of their inception and social role. This chapter also leads me to analyze the agency of family as emerging from Cold War discourse, as well as the emergence of specific narratives that capitalized on and helped reinforce the Cold War-era middle-class consensus, at the center of which I place the inauguration of Disneyland as the most emblematic example.

The fourth chapter focuses on the spreading of television culture in 1950s America and discusses the emergence of television as the natural medium for the formation and fostering of a suburban culture. In the chapter, I discuss the way in which the leading genres and strategies of American television forcefully took hold of America's domestic imaginary in the early postwar years. My fifth chapter brings

Introduction 13

all intimations of the Cold War consensus home with an analysis of postwar conformist narratives: starting from leading metaphors of conformity, such as David Riesman's notion of "inner-directedness" and William Whyte's conception of an "organization society," I analyze the problematic roles of men and women as players on the newly-defined stage of America as a privileged space of social consensus.

My final chapters study dissenting voices to that consensus narrative, pointing out the emergence of identitarian discourses in the decade. I focus on the renewed space of youth, especially adolescence, as privileged area of dissent and rebellion from the middle-class status quo and on the emerging civil rights movement, seen as another powerful area of destabilization of the white consensus. Besides the more canonic narratives of that dissent (which include Salinger, the Beats, and the classic "rebel" movies), I also study the emergence of rock 'n' roll, understood as the most vibrant area of dialogic convergence between white and black culture in America. After pointing out the merging of conditions that enabled the rise of rock 'n' roll at mid-decade, I study Elvis Presley's contradictory subservience to the middle-class consensus agenda as well as his aural and visual challenge of that consensus, in what I call, after Leerom Medovoi, his "Fordist counterimaginary."

In September 1957 Robert Frank met Jack Kerouac, a fellow naysayer whose novel *On the Road* was just about to be published after almost a decade of rejections by publishers. Like Frank, Kerouac had seen and documented another side of America that the country did not yet seem to be ready to see. Kerouac wrote an introduction to *The Americans*, in which he praised, in his typical style, Frank's pictures for "the humor, the sadness, the EVERYTHING-ness and American-ness," – images that he regarded "as pure [...] as the nicest tenor solo in jazz." In his own way, Kerouac provided a compelling narrative for Frank's vision of early Cold War America. According to Kerouac, Frank had been able to convey "that crazy feeling in America when the sun is hot on the streets and the music comes out of the jukebox or from a nearby funeral." Kerouac praised Frank's shots for their unmediated authenticity, a virtue of which televised alienation was depriving the nation: "Anybody doesnt like these pitchers dont like potry [sic], see?

Anybody dont like potry go home see television shots of big-hatted cowboys being tolerated by kind horses."

And yet, Kerouac's and Frank's visions diverged. Reviewing *The Americans* for the *New York Times*, Gilbert Millstein commented that Kerouac's introduction was "fine descriptive reading, but rather too optimistic for Frank's photographs," since "[Kerouac] sees a different America than Frank does."[15] Millstein probably stated the obvious: narratives always add to meaning and never remain neutral to a zero degree of signification. Like Kerouac's misreading of Frank, the Cold War narratives I present in this book do not claim convergent vision, but would like at least in part to fulfill a sliver of the praise Kerouac bestowed upon Frank: "To Robert Frank I now give this message: You got eyes."[16]

CHAPTER 1
America in the Cold War Years

> From Stettin in the Baltic to Trieste in the Adriatic an iron curtain has descended across the Continent.
> (Winston Churchill, *Sinews of Peace* speech. Fulton, Missouri, 5 March 1946)
>
> In America any man who is not reactionary in his views is open to the charge of alliance with the Red hell.
> (Arthur Miller, *The Crucible*)

Stettin to Trieste: The New World Order

The vast transformations of the United States during the 1950s took roots in the previous decade, as World War II finally came to a close and a new world order came into place. The U.S.-Soviet wartime alliance that brought an end to the war in 1945 suddenly collapsed with the end of the conflict, or arguably even before, with the victors going their own ways, in the postwar era, shaping their blocks of influence. These blocks lay on both sides of the "Iron Curtain" which, according to Winston Churchill's famous speech of 1946, had descended across Europe "from Stettin in the Baltic to Trieste in the Adriatic." The world that opened up after the fall of Nazi Germany in Europe and the defeat of Japan in the Pacific was polarized around two irreconcilable views of the way societies should function: capitalism/democracy on one side, and socialism/communism on the other. The uneasy wartime alliance between the U.S. and the Soviet Union, often referred to as a "shotgun marriage," quickly deteriorated into an economic and military standoff which rapidly brought the two former allies against Nazism to cast themselves in stark contraposition to one another, beginning a forty-year long confrontation which came to be known as the

Cold War and which repeatedly brought the world to the brink of nuclear annihilation. Although nicknamed "the long peace," the Cold War era was by no means peaceful.

The United States emerged from the war as the most powerful nation in the world. Unlike its ally, the Soviet Union, it emerged unscathed from the war, which had taken place away from its national boundaries. Hence, its economy was immediately able to display stability and dynamism. Moreover, the U.S. emerged from the war as the sole atomic power, a dominance that would both influence the making of the postwar world order but also cast long shadows of impending doom upon that newly achieved order.

The war not only put the United States in a position to dominate much of the world, but "created conditions for effective control at home:" higher prices for farmers and higher wages for workers generated enough prosperity for enough of the population to insure against (or be able to resolutely curb) the threat of social unrest that had so much characterized the crisis of the 1930s.[1] Harry S. Truman, who had succeeded F. D. Roosevelt after his death in April 1945 and was later re-elected to a second term in 1948, presided over the country at a time in which the specter of a widespread communist threat cast a Cold War mantle of crisis both abroad and at home. Some historians view that crisis context as instrumental in the recovery of the American industrial machine after the depression of the 1930s.[2]

The Truman Doctrine and International Decolonization

By 1947, tension had risen to high levels in the international political climate, as the two superpowers were striving to carve out areas of influence around the world, especially in Europe and in Asia. Americans feared communism not only internationally, but also at home, as fierce labor disputes in the winter of 1945/46 racked a nation already under stress by housing shortages, continued rationing, and inflation. In 1946, a Republican-controlled Congress passed the highly contested Taft-Hartley Act, a piece of legislation aimed at curbing "unfair labor practices," i.e. limiting union activity. Concurrently, amidst intimations of widespread domestic subversion, Congress granted the House Un-American Activities Committee (HUAC) broad powers to investigate breaches of national security at home, especially when concerning members of the Communist Party of the United States or their so-called "fellow travelers."[3] It was the beginning of the Red-Scare, a campaign of fear and suspicion of communist infiltration in the country that soon turned into vicious witch-hunts that significantly curbed civil liberties in the United States for more than a decade.

Pressured by the changing climate at home and abroad, Truman, who had alternated, during the first years in office, between a rhetoric of conciliation and one of confrontation with the Soviet Union, embraced a much firmer tone in a speech before Congress of March 1947. In the speech he called for U.S. intervention in helping "free peoples to maintain their free institutions and their national integrity against aggressive movements that seek to impose upon them totalitarian regimes," a political course soon dubbed as the Truman Doctrine. Truman clearly addressed the gulf that at that point divided East and West, giving shape to two irreconcilable, "alternative ways of life:"

> One way of life is based upon the will of the majority, and is distinguished by free institutions, representative government, free elections, guarantees of individual liberty, freedom of speech and religion, and freedom from political oppression. The second way of life is based upon the will of a minority forcibly imposed upon the majority. It relies upon terror and oppression, a controlled press and radio; fixed elections, and the suppression of personal freedoms.[4]

The Truman Doctrine introduced a new vision of the global agenda of the United States, in which "totalitarian regimes imposed on free peoples, by direct or indirect aggression, undermine the foundations of international peace and hence the security of the United States." Emerging at a time when the United States had become the dominant world power, the Truman Doctrine declared a new U.S. policy centered on "support[ing] free peoples who are resisting attempted subjugation by armed minorities or by outside pressures" and aimed at containing Soviet expansion around the globe. The Truman Doctrine set off a long course of U.S. military interventions throughout the world, in a "containment" effort which would then escalate in the following years and decades, later culminating in the Vietnam War, America's most comprehensive Cold War engagement to contain communism and seek global stabilization.[5]

The bipolar worldview that stood at the basis of containment politics emerged within a larger framework of rising nationalisms across the globe, which the Truman Doctrine sought explicitly to address. The widespread retrenchment of colonial empires at the end of World War II triggered a global readjustment of influence on the international scene: within this context, the Cold War backdrop merged nationalist uprisings and imperialist ambitions by the global powers, as "first" and "second" world powers tried to carve their influence in the emerging "third-world," calling for the preservation of democracy *vis-à-vis* dangers of totalitarianism on the one hand and avoiding the spreading of exploitative capitalism on the other. As it turned out, the U.S. foreign policy displayed contradictions when facing the complex scene of global decolonization: faced with the pressing question of how to manage the end of wartime occupations, the United States on the one hand sided for nationalists when it came to pressure the Soviet Union to give up the war-occupied territories, but supported colonialism while helping its European allies to regain power over South-East Asia.[6]

As the Truman Doctrine was officially launched in 1947, in that same year the U.S. administration also launched the Marshall Plan, a thirteen-billion dollar aid package aimed at both re-igniting the Western European economy after the destruction of the war and at creating and enforcing American political and corporate control over Europe. According to historian Randall B. Woods, the Truman Doctrine and the Marshall Plan combined constituted the "U.S. declaration of Cold War:" a promise "to provide economic and military aid to those nations threatened by international communism."[7]

In 1948, the U.S. and its allies – now close to coming together under the umbrella of the North Atlantic Treaty Organization, NATO – set out on their first and perhaps most resonating test of containment policy: the Berlin Airlift. In late June the Soviet Union blocked all land access to the "divided city," in an attempt to starve West Berlin, force the Western allies out of the city, and establish four-power governance over all of Germany which would have blocked the formation of a pro-Western government in the country. In response, the United States and its allies orchestrated a spectacular relief operation in which 13,000 tons of supplies (especially food, fuel, and medicines) were airlifted to the city daily for 324 days, until the Soviets agreed to restore overland access.[8]

Through the 1950s, the Truman Doctrine remained a bulwark of American foreign policy, with an intervention in Lebanon to protect the pro-American government from being overthrown by revolution (and to keep an armed presence in that oil-rich area) and, most notably, with the Korea campaign of 1950–1953.

The HUAC and the "Witch-Hunt" Malaise

If the Truman Doctrine was the instrument for containing communism abroad, the HUAC served the same purpose on the home front. Established in the 1930s to combat fascism, the HUAC was charged, beginning in 1945, with the task of investigating widespread allegations that communist agents were threatening American democracy from within.

In 1948 Alger Hiss, a former State Department official, was put under investigation for espionage following the testimony of a former communist party member, Whittaker Chambers. To many, the case against Hiss appeared specious (it hinged on facts that were prior to the war) and the verdict appeared as an outright revival of "witch-hunting" on American soil. In February 1950, Joseph McCarthy, an hitherto unremarkable first-term senator from Wisconsin, began his infamous anti-communist crusade when he claimed to "hold in [his] hand" a list of 105 "known communists" working in the State Department. The first of several public exploits by the senator, McCarthy's allegations – together with the passing in the same year of the McCarran Act, which mandated tighter government control over communist organizations – raised the stakes of the Cold War inside the U.S., by creating an atmosphere of internal suspicion and fear which would shape the first half of the decade.

The first conspicuous target of the HUAC was Hollywood, which investigators alleged had been infiltrated by communist agents – screenwriters, producers, directors, and even actors – who not only tainted American films with propaganda, but in fact were conspiring to overthrow the U.S. government. Within a public campaign of enemy-baiting and public defamation, the Hollywood industry was the perfect witch-hunt target, because it guaranteed resonance for the campaign at all levels of society. The HUAC specifically targeted Hollywood in the early phases of the hearings by claiming that it was a cesspool of subversive radicalism, all the more dangerous since it was the factory of the American Dream. As a symbol of "dangerous" radicalism, Hollywood was only the tip of an iceberg, but it had the potential like nothing else to captivate the nation's attention.[9]

The anti-Hollywood campaign began in November 1946, when the *Chicago Tribune* ran an article claiming that Hollywood was ruled by three families – the Warners, the Goldwyns, and the Mayers – all of Russian origin. The implication was simple enough: these families had "communism in their blood" and therefore the Screen Writers' Guild (the writers' trade union as well as core of the Hollywood dream factory) was controlled by communists. This started a campaign in which anti-communism and populism quickly converged: because the film industry bosses were Jewish, America's repressed anti-Semitism came quickly to the surface as many people were ready to link allegations of the Jewish hegemony over Hollywood with threats to American freedom.

Public opinion became persuaded that such an equation had a legitimate foundation the moment the HUAC began investigating these allegations. In September 1947, forty-one witnesses were subpoenaed to appear in front of the Committee (most prominent among these were high-power Hollywood conservatives such as Walt Disney, Gary Cooper, and John Wayne), nineteen of whom declared their intention to be "unfriendly," i.e. to refuse to answer the key questions: "Are you or have you ever been a member of the Communist party?" and "Can you name any individuals that you believe in your opinion are communists?" Of these, eleven were called in front of the Committee, and although one of them, German émigré Bertolt Brecht, left the country immediately after his appearance, the other ten – who were either screenwriters or producers and soon became known as "The Hollywood Ten" – defied the HUAC and refused to testify, leaning on their constitutional First Amendment right of free speech.[10]

The Hollywood Ten were cited for contempt of Congress and fired from their jobs, initiating the infamous, unofficial "Hollywood blacklist," which kept as many as 400 people from working in the Motion Picture Industry throughout the 1950s. Two of the Hollywood Ten even spent jail time for refusing to answer during the HUAC hearings. Although the film community stood up to the intimidation (actors and directors – John Huston, Humphrey Bogart, Lauren Bacall, Danny Kaye, and Gene Kelly among them – rallied in Washington to protest; Ira Gershwin hosted a historic fundraiser at his house), the crusade inevitably eroded the quality of Hollywood movies. Directors became afraid to say anything controversial and this contributed to the decline of Hollywood during the 1950s.[11]

As Carl Solberg has explained, at the opening of the 1950s, communism was no longer a target for Americans; rather, it had become a weapon: "McCarthy never cared much about how many communists he unearthed or whether the hapless individual he publicly tortured was or was not a Russian espionage agent."[12] During its heyday in the early 1950s, the HUAC interrogated Americans about their communist connections, held them in contempt of Congress if they refused to answer, and distributed to the American public millions of pamphlets carrying titles such as "One Hundred Things You Should Know About Communism" and replete with warnings such as: "Where Can Communists Be Found? Everywhere."

The HUAC campaign proved undoubtedly successful: fearful of communists, Americans were ready to endorse drastic action against them, both at home and abroad, and anti-communism became a hot commodity. Mickey Spillane's 1951 hard-boiler *One Lonely Night* sold three million copies to Americans eager to read its hero, Mike Hammer, claim: "I killed more people tonight than I have fingers on my hands. I shot them in cold blood and enjoyed every minute of it […] They were Commies […] red sons-of-bitches who should have died long ago."[13] Red-Scare blockbusters spanned the whole range from the comic strip super-hero *Captain America*, which warned: "Beware, commies, spies, traitors, and foreign agents! Captain America, with all loyal, free men behind him, is looking for you," to longtime FBI director J. Edgar Hoover's *Masters of Deceit* (1958) and *A Study of Communism* (1962), whose plain, highly readable style targeted communists and the Communist party as a devious, ambiguous, ever-shifting "enemy," whose destruction was one crucial responsibility of America's Cold War effort.[14]

The War in Korea

The War in Korea of 1950–1953 catalyzed much of the agenda of Truman's second term in office and remains a textbook case of postwar containment policy in action. Despite his "Fair Deal" re-election platform calling for increase in the minimum wage, an extension of Social Security benefits, repeal of Taft-Hartley, a federal health insurance plan, civil rights legislation, federal funds for the construction of low-cost housing, and a guaranteed income for farmers, Truman's presidency was haunted by the specters of the Cold War and by internal pressures to move resolutely in the containment arena.

After the defeat of Japan at the end of World War II, both the United States and U.S.S.R. had sent troops into Korea to fill the vacuum left by the Japanese decolonization. The nation was divided in two parts along the 38th parallel. On June 24th, 1950, the armies of communist North Korea swept across their southern border and invaded the pro-Western half of the Korean peninsula. Within days, they had occupied much of South Korea, including the capital, Seoul. Almost immediately, the U.S. committed itself to the conflict as Truman declared that he wanted "a unified, independent and democratic Korea."[15]

Although the U.S. engagement in the region (under a U.N. mandate) covered a four-year span, most of the conflict was over by mid-1951 when, after the U.S. troops had regained control of the 38th parallel (by early Fall of 1950) and made military progress to the north within few weeks, soon were pushed back to the 38th parallel by China's entry into the conflict in October of that year.

In order to preserve the post-World War II status quo in Asia, the United States committed a total of 6.8 million troops overall to Korea, before, during, and after the war; approximately 30,000 Americans died and another 105,000 were wounded or missing. Contrary to common assumptions, the Korean war was no "small bush-fire war" and the bloodshed was enormous: an estimated total of 1.8 million soldiers died – 1.4 million of them on the Korean-Chinese side – for a war that both sides, upon the June 1953 armistice, declared neither victory nor defeat.[16]

Although inconclusive, the Korean campaign affirmed the U.S. full commitment to its containment policy within the framework of postwar decolonization. For some, the American Century began precisely in the wake of this war and it has been argued that it was the Korean War, not World War II, that made the United States a world military-political power, because it was during the Korean War that America's full-fledged "imperial" commitment to contain communism on a global scale actually began.[17]

The Korean War sparked economic recovery at home, by injecting new government funds into the American economy. But although it was instrumental in fueling the economic boom of the same decade, the war also dealt major blows to American morale. Filled with pride after the moral and military triumph of World War II, Americans found it hard to accept that the country had appeared incapable of successfully bringing home what had originally looked like "a minor border skirmish." The substantial loss of American lives, paired with the hardships and inconclusiveness of the Korean War, led public opinion to feel that "something must be deeply wrong – not only in Korea, but within the U.S. as well."[18]

Eisenhower, "Man of the Hour"

This climate of turmoil at home and fighting abroad had put the American people in an "ugly mood" and many Americans came to view the Truman administration as the culprit of their Cold War anxieties.

Americans also blamed Truman for the highly traumatic "loss of China," which had turned communist following Mao Zedong's rise to power in 1949. In March 1951, Truman announced he would not run for re-election and the Democratic party pitted Governor Adlai E. Stevenson of Illinois against the GOP candidate and war hero Dwight D. "Ike" Eisenhower. Stevenson was, according to historian Randall B. Woods, "a man of refined taste [...] intelligent, polished, sophisticated, literate, and self-deprecating. He was also wealthy, divorced, and cosmopolitan – a thoroughly modern man who was filled with self-doubt."[19]

Eisenhower's firm control over his own "emotional pull," which Vance Packard lauded in *The Hidden Persuaders*, proved impossible for Stevenson to beat.[20] Propelled by the powerful "I like Ike" slogan and by a campaign that for the first time used advertising research for building a "presidential image," Eisenhower used his universal World War II popularity as the "man of the hour" (as well as the inadequacy of the Democratic opposition) to win a landslide victory in 1952, ending twenty years of Democratic control of the White House. Eisenhower won again in the following election of 1956, once again showing pre-eminence on the persuasion front in the first campaign to fully exploit the potential of television for political advertising.

Eisenhower's eight-year tenure coincided with the peak of an unprecedented economic boom, which began around 1949 and would continue with only brief interruptions for almost twenty years. The least experienced politician to become president in the twentieth century, Eisenhower was also, in Alan Brinkley's words, "among the most popular and politically successful presidents of the postwar era."[21] A staunch anti-communist in the international arena, he nevertheless always sought the most restrained measures possible: domestically, he was a moderate, and never gave in to the pressures from the right wing of his party to dismantle the welfare policies of the New Deal. To his cabinet, Eisenhower appointed wealthy corporate lawyers and business executives and consistently called to limit government spending and encourage private enterprise, although these propositions often resulted contradictory.[22] Charles Wilson, for example, president of General Motors, who became secretary of defense under Eisenhower, was a firm supporter of "a permanent war economy," and a believer that "what [was] good for our country [was] good for General Motors, and vice versa."[23] Indeed, the interdependence of government and business intensified: by the 1960s, the jobs of 7.5 million Americans, one-tenth of the workforce, directly depended on the military budget, which in turn stimulated huge investments in many industries, especially the steel and chemical industry.[24]

Fearing and Loving the Bomb

Historians concur on the fact that one secret of America's limitless economic expansion during the 1950s was increased government spending in areas such as schools, housing, veterans' benefits, welfare, interstate highway construction and, above all, military buildup.[25] After the Hiroshima and Nagasaki bombings of August 1945, the U.S. had continued its relentless development of nuclear technology for military purposes. Nuclear buildup became entwined with the Cold War scenario when, in 1949, the Soviet Union successfully tested Joe 1, its first nuclear bomb, and the race for pre-eminence in the development of nuclear weapons took center stage.[26]

On the American side, nuclear deployment was aimed at, in Miller and Nowak's nice turn of phrase, "waging peace:" a path that involved neither demobilization from the war nor total militarization and was centered on the principle of "national security."[27] A broad concept, "national security" accounted for the United States' postwar purported necessity to build up as much destructive capability as possible – a strategy that soon produced the effect of building a culture of nuclear proliferation that "oddly combined horror and hypnotic appeal."[28] Much more than a national security program, nuclear development became ingrained in post-World War II American culture, with an impact that transcended its specific military contingency: from the eerie fascination with all things "atomic" to the relentless campaigns for the buildup of an efficient civil defense strategy, the bomb came to modify the everyday behavior of American citizens in many ways.[29]

Nuclear testing by the American military continued without interruption throughout the 1950s: 122 nuclear bombs were exploded by the U.S. between 1951 and 1958, mostly in the Pacific and in the Nevada desert. In 1952 a new thermonuclear device, the hydrogen bomb (also known as the H-bomb) – hundreds of times more powerful than the A-bomb which had been used to end World War II – was successfully tested (and replicated by the Soviets two years later). In order to defuse fears of nuclear proliferation, the U.S government adopted widespread "information" campaigns centering on the claim that increased nuclear testing aimed at the development of a "clean bomb" and that the tests posed no threats to the local populations.

Americans felt powerless when faced with the reality of a nuclear dawn and generally rushed to dreams of domesticity, religion, and material conformity, as I will discuss in later chapters of this book. Many scientists protested the nuclear buildup: J. Robert Oppenheimer, the lead scientist of the Manhattan Project, was particularly vocal in this respect.[30] Popular culture was quick to capture the new collective nuclear psychosis, in science fiction novels and comics predicting a world populated by genetic monsters of all sorts: *Godzilla* (although originally a Japanese creation, it had large distribution and success in the United States following its release in 1954), a huge mutant created by nuclear fallout, was symptomatic of a host of new fictional monsters which included *The Blob*, *The Incredible Shrinking Man*, and *X the Unknown* (in fact, a British creation). Films were no less prominent in depicting nuclear aftermaths of various sorts, in releases such as *Panic in Year Zero* (Ray Milland, 1962) and *The World, the Flesh and the Devil* (Ranald MacDougall, 1959).

Faced with dissonant intimations of a fearful and a reassuring nuclear future, Americans responded to the Cold War nuclear buildup with a combination of anguish and readiness for civic duty. By appealing to the idea of a "manageable fear," government propaganda made it possible for the American public to not only endorse atomic development, but also recover an all-American sense of self-reliance against the possibility of atomic warfare. By 1957, the aircraft industry was the nation's biggest single employer and economic progress was in large measure the consequence of increased military spending. At the close of the decade, the United States nurtured in excess of

40,000 so-called "prime" defense contractors as well as hundreds of thousands of lesser ones.[31] Military expenditure amounted to $45.8 billion – 9.7 percent of the national budget; and when, in 1962, the United States claimed – after further increases in military spending by newly elected President John F. Kennedy – nuclear superiority over the Soviet Union, this amounted, as historian Howard Zinn has claimed, to having built up "the equivalent, in nuclear weapons, of 1,500 Hiroshima-size atomic bombs, far more than enough to destroy every major city in the world – the equivalent, in fact, of 10 tons of TNT for every man, woman, and child on earth."[32]

The Atomic Cafe

In the 1950s, the Cold War became a "vested interest" for the United States, which on the one hand provided justification for military buildup during peace time and on the other accounted for a significant portion of the country's economic boom, precisely because it demanded intense production from the military industry.[33] According to historian Joyce Nelson, the Cold War was in fact the result of economic expediency. Associating economic growth with a "permanent war economy," the U.S. deliberately set out on a path of national and international tension after World War II which was instrumental in developing its all-too-powerful "military-industrial complex," against which President Eisenhower warned in his farewell address of January 1961:

> This conjunction of an immense military establishment and a large arms industry is new in the American experience. The total influence – economic, political, even spiritual – is felt in every city, every State house, every office of the Federal government. We recognize the imperative need for this development. Yet we must not fail to comprehend its grave implications. Our toil, resources and livelihood are all involved; so is the very structure of our society. In the councils of government, we must guard against the acquisition of unwarranted influence, whether sought or unsought, by the military-industrial complex. The potential for the disastrous rise of misplaced power exists and will persist.[34]

According to Nelson, atomic buildup was a consequence of economic need and was camouflaged by non-existent concerns of national security. In Nelson's view, the United States government tapped post-World-War-II fears of a continuing conflict and set up public campaigns to fabricate a "communist threat," which would eventually empower the country's big corporations to expand their business interests in highly profitable military-related areas of business. As the United States military confiscated Japanese footage of the Hiroshima aftermath in mid-1946, "documentary material that might have alerted the North American public [...] to the real dangers of radiation itself," it concurrently launched so-called "Operation Crossroads," a massive public campaign to show that there were no visible effects on living beings exposed to atomic tests.[35]

The reassuring propaganda footage produced by the U.S military upon the lunch of "Operation Crossroads" is presented in one of the early sections of the 1981 documentary *The Atomic Cafe*, produced by Jayne Loader, Kevin Rafferty, and Pierce Rafferty, a film aimed at capturing the ambiguities of America's approach to nuclear buildup. Edited according to the canons of early 1960s "direct cinema" – with no narrative commentary, following the belief that images alone are better suited to convey original factuality – *The Atomic Cafe* weaves its narrative by juxtaposing hard-to-find post-World War II archival material and brilliantly manages to re-actualize the key themes of Cold War rhetoric. Addressing crucial moments of post-World War II American history, *The Atomic Cafe* focuses especially on the Red Scare hysteria and on the civil defense propaganda of the early containment years.

As footage unfolds of President Truman defining the Korean War as "necessary [...] for American freedom," of Richard Nixon holding before the cameras the State Department tapes that led to the indictment of Alger Hiss, of early Levittown desolation and Dwight Eisenhower's "I Like Ike" 1952 presidential campaign, *The Atomic Cafe* develops its central discussion of the bomb and its practical and cultural impact. We watch the surreal public statements by the pilots and crew of the Enola Gay bomber plane just back from the Hiroshima mission, eerily claiming that dropping the first nuclear bomb had been a "routine operation." Just as eerie to today's ears, the "Crossroads" propaganda on the safety of nuclear tests in the Pacific of the mid-to-late 1940s and 1950s is presented as a striking demonstration of the manipulative nature of nuclear rhetoric.

The documentary aims to show how little postwar Americans knew about the consequences of nuclear radiation and the way in which the government, as well as the popular media, played a central role in directing people's conflicting feelings of trust and fear of the bomb. The clips assembled in *The Atomic Cafe* document the unwavering belief in science pervading the decade and how this was instrumental in "selling the bomb" to the American public, in a dual strategy of half and concealed truths. As propaganda films and booklets appearing in the U.S. during the 1950s, bearing titles such as "You Can Survive" and "Atomic Attack," encouraged Americans to purchase Geiger counters and build fallout shelters, a famous nine-minute civil defense cartoon entitled *Duck and Cover* used a familiar Disneyesque pattern of alternating cartoons and live footage to reassure about the survivability of a nuclear attack. The cartoon's protagonist is an anthropomorphic turtle named Bert, who goes about his daily business while remaining "very alert" to impending danger. As a sudden crisis unfolds, embodied by a monkey holding a stick of dynamite hanging on a string, Bert is unharmed because of his promptness to "duck and cover," as the government campaign instructs him to do. The soundtrack extols the virtues of Bert's civil defense alertness:

> There was a turtle by the name of Bert
> and Bert the turtle was very alert;
> when danger threatened him he never got hurt
> he knew just what to do...
> He'd duck! And cover!
> He did what we all must learn to do
> You! And you! And you! And you!
> Duck, and cover!

Shown in schools as the cornerstone of a civil defense public awareness campaign, the *Duck and Cover* film established the containment-era official orthodoxy: that a nuclear attack could strike at any time without warning, that citizens should be ever ready for it and, most of all, that with simple preventive measures it could be survived, even within the limited capabilities of home-made defense measures.

Atomic Spies: The Rosenbergs

Nuclear anxieties connected with the Soviet Union's successful deployment of the A-bomb in the late 1940s were at the root of one of the darkest hours of Cold War-related hysteria in America, which brought to the conviction and execution for nuclear espionage of Julius and Ethel Rosenberg in June 1953. A lower middle-class Jewish couple from the Bronx, both members of the Communist party, the Rosenbergs were indicted in 1950 of A-bomb espionage following the arrest of Klaus Fuchs, a German refugee and physicist who had worked for the Manhattan Project in 1944 and had later confessed of passing nuclear information to the Soviet Union during the war. The U.S. government claimed that the Rosenbergs had received secret information from Ethel's brother, a machinist who had worked in the Manhattan Project in New Mexico, and passed it on to the Soviet Union through other secret agents.

Appearing from the start as an "exemplary" case which combined America's ingrained anti-Semitism and anti-communism, the Rosenberg trial was the most debated event in early 1950s America. Everyone took a stand and when Eisenhower declared that "the action of these people has exposed to greater danger of death literally millions of our citizens" it was clear that its symbolic value had transcended the boundaries of legal process and that the Rosenbergs had become the metaphor of a nation in the throes of the Red Scare.[36] In *Class and Culture in Cold War America*, George Lipsitz has noted that even before McCarthy left-wing militancy did not play well with American culture: during workers' strikes throughout the 1940s "those who refused to testify on the basis of their constitutional rights, or who claimed that they had insufficient time to obtain counsel, found themselves ridiculed by the Congressmen and spotlighted in the newspapers as non-cooperators suspected of communism." Lipsitz has contended that it was Truman's manipulation of the diplomatic tension between the United States and the Soviet Union that "transformed a relatively minor fear into a national obsession."[37]

The Rosenbergs were convicted in 1951 and executed in the electric chair two years later amidst intense media scrutiny involving the Cold War, Jewishness, communist militancy in America and the private fate of the couple's two young children. Their conviction raised the stakes of America's anti-communist crusade, since it brought into the United States not only the (at least alleged) evidence of communist infiltration in the country, but also the fear of being suspected of communism, in other words the culmination of an intensive five-year campaign "to root communism and all the individuals, ideas, and organizations associated with it out of American life."[38]

By 1950, the stereotype, relentlessly promoted by FBI director J. Edgar Hoover, that "any member of the Communist party is an active or potential Soviet espionage agent" had gained currency in the country, thus establishing the association between being a communist in the United States and being involved in anti-American activity.[39] The policies and practices of the Communist Party of the United States, the catalyst of a significant stream of sympathy for socialism across the country in the previous decades, did little to arrest the notion that it constituted an outright danger for the nation: renowned for its secrecy, lack of internal democracy, and above all its loyalty to the Soviet Union, the Communist party was an easy target for Hoover and his allies, who were able to intensify anxieties surrounding communism by criminalizing it.

Scapegoating rapidly led to the distortion of Constitutional guarantees and when alleged communists turned to the Fifth Amendment (the Constitutional provision granting freedom to remain silent to avoid self-incrimination) because of a fear that anything they might say would then be used against them, those same guarantees became in turn a weapon against the defendants. Historians agree that the Rosenbergs' defensive strategy, revolving around strictly "taking the Fifth," contributed in no small way to their conviction, as it generated a wide publicity campaign developing the notion that people who refused to answer questions about communism were implicitly admitting their guilt.

Blanche W. Cook has argued that the Rosenberg trial was a political one from its very beginning, a witch-hunt reminiscent of the Salem trials of the late seventeenth century, in which the highest priority was to persuade the accused to recant and confess committing the crime. The Rosenbergs always refused to plead guilty and in so doing were gradually abandoned to their own destiny both by public opinion, which came to perceive them as guilty, but also by the Communist Party of the United States and large segments of the organized political left, whose silence and fear was the prelude to their political demise in America. Ultimately, the Rosenberg trial was turned into an exemplary case, not because of an overwhelming testimonial evidence against the couple, but rather as a consequence of the nationwide anti-communist consensus, a fabricated political climate that sanctioned the couple's execution as well as the firing, jailing, and punishing of thousands of other political enemies.[40] Their guilt became, in J. Edgar Hoover's famous definition, the "Crime of the Century" and, according to many commentators, the result of a well orchestrated propaganda effort aiming at representing communists as actual threats to national security in a Cold War scenario.[41]

Literature and the Cold War

American writers' response to the Cold War and the Red Scare was rich and multi-faceted, as several of them took issue especially with the McCarthy era. In Ralph W. Ellison's *Invisible Man* (1952), the African-American narrator/protagonist is disillusioned with the Communist party and more generally with Marxism.[42] A testimony of the early Cold War years, the novel is caught in the dilemma of an individual who refuses to denounce "the Brotherhood" as a godless plot against America, but rather seeks philosophical justifications for his own (and its author's) disenchantment with the Party. Ellison depicts American communism as a controlling hierarchy with its rigidities and cruelties, an organization made of smart individuals who strip down their own intelligence to the point of mouthing a revolutionary rhetoric that is completely disconnected from the condition of the suffering classes.[43] Moreover, beyond discovering that the Communist party is incapable of delivering on its promises of social justice, the *Invisible Man* also realizes that the confidence with which Marxist dogma asserted that historical and psychological contradictions would be resolved was ill placed.[44] In the novel, Ellison most of all denounces the McCarthy era's drive toward uniformity and advocates a pluralistic and autonomous frame of mind that rarely emerges elsewhere in that age. David Castronovo has defined it as "a protest against ideologies," whose style and intellectual pose "blasts the conventions of its time and ours."[45]

Another testament to the political climate of the McCarthy years is found in Arthur Miller's drama *The Crucible*, which was published in 1953 and premiered on stage in January 1954 in England, at the height of the Red Scare crisis in America. *The Crucible* is a historical play based on the 1692 events of the Salem Witch Trials, one of the most obscure and least edifying episodes of American history, when dozens of women were brought to trial for witchcraft in colonial Massachusetts between February 1692 and May 1693. At the center of the drama is a study of the madness that plagued New England in the late seventeenth century. In arguing that the Salem witch-hunts were rooted in both rational (social or economic) as well as irrational causes (the human psyche and its ability to degenerate into both individual and mass hysteria), Miller draws explicit analogies between Colonial and Red Scare America, describing both of them as "the children of a history which still sucks at the devil's teats."

Zooming in on the Red Scare situation, Miller denounces the bigotry of both Cold War fronts:

> At this writing, only England has held back before the temptations of contemporary diabolism. In the countries of the communist ideology, all resistance of any import is linked to the totally malign capitalist succubi, and in America any man who is not reactionary in his views is open to the charge of alliance with the Red hell. Political opposition, thereby, is given an inhumane overlay which then justifies the abrogation of all normally applied customs of civilized intercourse. A political policy is equated with moral right, and opposition to it with diabolical malevolence. Once such an equation is effectively made, society becomes a

congerie of plots and counterplots, and the main role of government changes from that of the arbiter to that of the scourge of God.[46]

The fate of John Proctor, the play's tragic hero, seems to closely mirror that of Miller himself: like Miller, who was called to appear in front the of HUAC and asked to name names of communists known to him, John Proctor is asked to give names of people he had seen at the meeting and refuses to answer the question "as I would not violate what on the spur of the moment I said was my sense of myself." No metaphor of Red Scare hysteria could be more explicit and the analogies between the play's seventeenth century event and the ongoing witch-hunts of communists were immediately perceived by the critics.[47]

Turning to other genres, two other notable works of the 1950s elaborated the decade's impending Cold War fears. Jack Finney's *The Body Snatchers* (published in 1955, later reissued as *Invasion of the Body Snatchers*, and turned into a widely popular movie in 1956) was a chilling sci-fi tale of aliens who emerge from pods in the guise of humans whom they have taken over and was widely interpreted as an allegory of America's fear of a takeover by Communists. A similar apocalyptic scenario was evoked in Ray Bradbury's *Fahrenheit 451* (1953), a dystopian novel presenting a future American society where books are outlawed and firemen burn any house that contains them.

If 1950s narratives had to mobilize allegory to thematize the Red Scare, E.L. Doctorow's *The Book of Daniel*, published after the fact in 1971, has enjoyed a much freer hand in reviving the horrors of Red-bating. The novel, loosely based on the trial and execution of Julius and Ethel Rosenberg, follows the couple's tribulations through the lens of the fate of their children, before, during and after their execution. Spanning three decades, from the late 1940s to the late 1960s, the narrative is presented as the outcome of the findings of Daniel, one of the Rosenbergs' two children in the novel, who devotes his young-adulthood to the academic study of McCarthyism and of his parents' predicament. In a postmodern play of metanarratives, Doctorow's book is in fact the "Book of Daniel," i.e. the result of Daniel's quest into his own as well as America's collective troubled past. The novel revolves around the fictional personae of two McCarthy-era communists, Paul and Rochelle Isaacson – the Rosenbergs' fictional proxies – and their two children, Daniel and Susan. Alternating settings in the late 1940s, early 1950s, and mid-to-late 1960s, the narrative is filtered through the subjective memory and non-conclusive historical research of the narrator, Daniel Isaacson, whose focus on personal memory, childhood recollections, and attempted final closure to his personal trauma drives him through his quest. His study delves into the conspiracies that led to his parents' conviction and execution and tries to understand in what way the Red Scare hysteria became responsible for the alienation of a large generation of Americans.

This alienation takes several forms. By frequently setting up resonances, in a typically postmodern pastiche of voices, between the main narrative and the Biblical *Book of Daniel* (in the Bible, Daniel is the prophetic interpreter of dreams and visions; here Daniel is ultimately unable to make sense of his own family's tragedy), Doctorow analyzes the alienation of Jews in American society, which for the Isaacsons doubles up in the further alienation of their left-wing politics, locking them into a community of peers which will be the primary source of their demise. They are also alienated by their American Dream, i.e. their belief in the fairness of the American legal system, as well as in their faith in the Communist party, which withdraws support as soon as their case turns sour.[48]

In his fiction, Doctorow has changed some of the historical facts: the Rosenbergs are called Isaacsons; their two real-life sons become son and daughter in the novel and the crucial witness against the Rosenbergs has shifted from a family member to a family friend, Selig Mindish. This well fits Doctorow's declared agenda, careful to distinguish "between the historical Rosenbergs as putative spies and the *idea* of the Rosenbergs embodied in the Isaacsons, complicitous victims in their own radical martyrdom."[49] As Paul Levine has well noted, the novel is not so much about the Rosenbergs but rather about "the *idea* of the Rosenbergs," and what happens "when all the antagonistic force of a society is brought to bear and focused on one or possibly two individuals."[50]

Structured in four parts, the novel's narrative moves fluidly and rapidly between 'the present' (1967, when Daniel is writing the book we are reading) and – through flashbacks – the early Cold War years, covering a multiplicity of subplots, which make it both a *Bildungsro-*

man – the story of Daniel Isaacson's struggle for manhood – and a *Kuenstlerroman* – the story of a writer (Daniel himself) discovering his identity and his fundamental conflict with the society around him. John Parks has argued that *The Book of Daniel* is three stories in one: the story of a survivor as narrated by a survivor – a boy whose parents were executed for treason, struggling for a narrative that will reconnect him to his own as well as America's dark history; a story of revenge – a son's obligation somehow to redeem his father's and mother's unjust executions; and a historical metanarrative in which a graduate student delves into historical research in order to exorcise history.[51]

Daniel's attempt to come to terms with his own family's history is a mirror of America's attempt to come to terms with the hysteria of the McCarthy era: alluding to the Biblical prophecy, Daniel Isaacson's quest is framed in the prophet Daniel's larger struggle against exile and persecution. Daniel comes to understand that his story cannot be told in a straightforward, linear, chronological manner, and a postmodern narrative enables him to attempt an alternative interpretation of the past. John Parks has pointed out that *The Book of Daniel* is "a virtual pastiche of genres – family stories, autobiography, essays, excerpts from newspapers and trial transcripts, letters, conflicting historical analysis, dissertation, biblical quotations."[52] Narrative viewpoint shifts abruptly: the story is told from Daniel's perspective, but it switches back and forth between first and third person – a device allowing the reader to face the story from both an emotional first person perspective and a more "objective" third person point of view, thus affording grown-up Daniel the opportunity to ponder his parents' innocence.

Doctorow has described the genesis of the book of Daniel as an effort to discover his story and characters in the process of writing:

> I started to write the book in the third person, more or less as a standard, past tense, third person novel, very chronologically scrupulous. And after one hundred pages I was terribly bored. That was a moment of great discomfort in my life, because I thought if I could really destroy a momentous subject like this, then I had no right to be a writer. That moment, when I threw out those pages and hit bottom, was when I became reckless enough to find the voice of the book, which was Daniel. I sat down and put a piece of paper in the typewriter and started to write with a cer-

tain freedom and irresponsibility, and it turned out Daniel was talking, and he was a sitting in the library at Columbia, and I had my book.[53]

This is how Daniel's book, the narrative rising out of his voice, and his despair, in the time-span of its writing from Memorial Day in 1967 to the spring of 1968, becomes *The Book of Daniel,* a much wider narrative of a nation's engagement with the Red Scare and its unending trauma. In one of the closing sequences of the novel, Daniel finally tracks down a now senile Dr. Selig Mindish, his father's once closest friend turned main accuser. Mindish, who has fled to Los Angeles and spends most of his time in the fairy-tale universe of Disneyland, refuses to answer the crucial question as to the true reasons of his betrayal, thus casting Daniel's quest for truth back to the bottomless pit of unresolved guesswork – a fitting ending for this journey into one of America's darkest hours and a reflection of how the traumas of McCarthyism were to shape the country's troubled history for decades to come.

CHAPTER 2
The Affluent Society

> In every aspect of material plenty America possesses unprecedented riches and [...] these are very widely distributed among one hundred and fifty million American people.
> (David Potter, *People of Plenty*, 1954)

> Of what stuff is the new nation made? It is made of wealth and the things that wealth has brought.
> (*Newsweek*, 12 December 1955)

The Postwar Economic Boom

Amidst tensions and fears of a developing new world order, the United States enjoyed in the 1950s what historian Alan Brinkley has defined "a booming, almost miraculous, economic growth that made even the heady 1920s seem pale by comparison."[1] This golden age of abundance was largely the result of two major factors. On the one hand, a sudden, extraordinary national prosperity, which profoundly altered the social, economic, and even physical landscape of the country. On the other, an increasing sense of national purpose amid the anxieties of the Cold War, which encouraged Americans to be even more approving of their own society.

Between 1945 and 1960, GDP in the United States grew by 250 percent, from $200 billion to over $500 billion, while unemployment and inflation remained at favorably low levels throughout the decade. Meanwhile, the American economy completed its transformation from a simple production economy, centered on satisfying basic human needs such as food, shelter, and clothing, to a consumer economy, in which it was assumed that those basic needs had been attended to and that the task ahead was to stimulate and expand consumption in an incessant drive to increase production and raise profits.[2] At the same time, the United States crossed the line from being an industrial to being a postindustrial country: by 1956 more workers were involved in white-collar than in blue-collar jobs, while more and more of those jobs were being made available by few large corporations rather than by smaller companies: the age of oligopolistic markets (i.e. the domination of a business or industry by a few companies) had begun.[3]

In this period, the national birth rate reversed a long pattern of decline with the so-called baby boom, which began during the war and peaked in 1957. The U.S. population rose almost 30 percent between 1945 and 1969, from 140 million 180 million, fueling consumer demand. The rapid expansion of suburbs helped stimulate growth, increasing demand for new homes and household appliances as well as for new roads and new automobiles which would make those suburban homes reachable. The number of privately owned cars more than doubled in the decade.

Brinkley has pointed out that the economy grew nearly ten times as fast as the population in the thirty years after the war. As a consequence, the average American in 1960 had over 20 percent more purchasing power than in 1945 and more than twice as much as during the prosperous 1920s. One crucial consequence of this was the emergence of an ever larger, more powerful, and more self-conscious middle class, which shaped its own culture around a growing absorption with consumer goods.[4]

American Media Embrace the Boom

When *U.S. New & World Report* claimed in 1956 that "about everybody in America today is well off," it was certainly overstating the case: official data placed the number of Americans living in poverty in the 1950s at approximately 30 million, making it explicit enough that many were excluded from the American Dream of affluence.[5] However, that headline also reflected an upbeat sentiment that dominated economic journalism throughout the decade, whose consensus – at once economic, sociological and ideological – converged on the idea that the United States was rapidly growing into a land of ever-rising abundance, thanks to a new, and uniquely American, economic system in which almost everyone was a member of a prosperous middle class. The role of American media in setting the mood for the booming 1950s can hardly be overstated, as paper and broadcast outlets took on an ever-growing booster role in spreading the word of America's postwar boom, reporting the country's emergent prosperity in tones that escalated "from fearful amazement between roughly 1946 and 1948 to wondrous superlatives between 1953 to 1957."[6]

Throughout the decade, the media projected an image of America immersed in a "new era" of an improved version of capitalism where the business cycle allowed everyone to be rich. A Cinerama film produced by *Life* magazine immediately after the war and entitled *The New America* rapidly became a key domestic and foreign propaganda tool. It declared that, because of its economy, postwar America was a new world which could be measured by its economic achievements, which in turn were the result of a new version of capitalism, a "people's capitalism" which, the film claimed, was no longer ruthless or exploitative, but rather called upon workers, corporations and government to cooperate in improving living standards for all.[7]

The New America was one of many accounts to locate the centerpiece of America's new capitalism in the home-owning and stock-owning average citizen, who now held the means of production in an economic system that was no longer subject to depression, recession, or the instability of the boom-and-bust cycles. As a result, citizens could now engage in limitless mass consumption, demonstrating without any shadow of a doubt that the American people had achieved the highest standard of living of any society in the history of the world, and that America had now become an "affluent society."[8]

The Affluent Society

The term "affluent society" appeared for the first time in the title of a landmark study by prominent Canadian-American economist John Kenneth Galbraith, published in 1958.[9] An instant best-seller, *The Affluent Society* was not so much a celebration of the country's newly-achieved abundance, but rather a critique of the way in which the economic boom had failed to promote social justice.

The Affluent Society argued that America after World War II, while undergoing increasing material production, had lost sight of the need to redistribute the benefits of that wealth among society at large. Galbraith pointed his finger at America's oligopolies for focusing exclusively on increasing their wealth by creating artificial consumer needs that would trigger more production and more consumption. America, claimed Galbraith, was at the same time neglecting the improvement of public services, such as better roads and schools, as well as better management of natural resources.

Galbraith framed his discussion within a larger analysis of capitalism and the changing dynamics of production in the twentieth century. He explained that the concept of "production" as understood in classic economic thought, based on nineteenth-century European economic theory and consistent with a world characterized by widespread poverty, was no longer viable in post-World War II America. Rooted in the idea of production as satisfaction of need, classical economic theory was, in Galbraith's view, no longer suited to account for the unprecedented phenomenon of mass affluence which characterized American society in the second half of the twentieth century.

What had changed in the transition from the nineteenth to the twentieth century, according to Galbraith, was the role of industrial production. Traditional economic theory postulated that production was a mechanism to address a "sense of urgency" in society: past societies had produced goods in order to meet basic social needs, such as food and clothing. According to that theory, as more goods were produced, more social needs were met, and consequently the urgency to increase production would decline. This concept, defined by classic economics as the theory of "diminishing marginal utility," carried with itself an assumption that the more available goods become, the less people are prepared to pay for them, consequently decreasing (rather than increasing) the urgency to produce more goods.

Galbraith's theoretical insight derived precisely from the observation of the fact that, in the post-World War II "affluent society," the theory of diminishing marginal utility had not come to fruition. He observed that under conditions of increasing affluence and in a situation in which goods had been made widely available, people nonetheless craved more goods, which placed production once again as the critical agent in the economy. Galbraith lamented that in the twentieth century, and especially after World War II, production was still central to the economic cycle, because it had somehow managed to refocus consumer demand from a dependency on want (lack of food, lack of clothing, etc.) to a dependency on desire, i.e. the fact that production was now geared to satisfying consumer cravings:

> [Y]esterday the man with a minimal but increasing real income was reaping the satisfactions which came from a decent diet and a roof that no longer leaked water on his face [...] Today, after a large increase in his income, he has extended his consumption to include suede shoes and a weekly visit to the races. But to say that his satisfactions from these latter amenities and recreations are less than from the additional calories and the freedom from rain is wholly improper.[10]

According to Galbraith, in the postwar era the system of production had resorted to creating a "dependence effect" among consumers by creating "unnecessary" wants, which were no longer "original with the individual," but rather the fruit of "the process of production by which they are satisfied."[11]

Galbraith saw the race to increased production as a missed opportunity for postwar America, and appealed to re-focusing the nation's priorities towards the expansion of the "New Class," that portion of the population that no longer engaged in "work *qua* work," but rather favored leisure, perceived work as self-satisfaction, and valued education as the basic index of social progress.[12]

Persuading Consumers

As the desire-based economy forced manufacturers to concentrate not only on making the goods but also, in Galbraith's words, on "making the desires for them," advertising rose to unprecedented prominence in the 1950s.[13] During the decade, gross revenues in advertising went up 75 percent, faster than the growth of GDP, personal income, or any other economic indicator, and the potential for growth seemed unlimited.[14] Advertising agencies grew in size by expanding their market research, merchandising and publicity departments and Madison Avenue, where most of the larger companies were headquartered, became synonymous with glamour and hubris.[15]

An entire mythology developed around the advertising business during this period, of "Mad Men" (all, rigorously, white males) working long hours, cashing hefty pay-checks, abusing large expense accounts, and lavishly indulging in drinking and smoking. The advertising profession came to be perceived as a condensation of creativity, wit, and boldness, with a penchant for unashamed fraud. In Hitchcock's *North by Northwest* (1959), Cary Grant plays a dapper adman who is mistaken for a spy. Towards the beginning of the film, he says to his secretary: "In the world of advertising there's no such thing as a lie. There's only the expedient exaggeration."

Among the well-established giants of the profession, some of the newer, smaller firms on Madison Avenue led the so-called "creative revolution" of the 1950s, which essentially amounted to the invention of modern advertising. Believing that "advertising is fundamentally persuasion and persuasion happens to be not a science but an art," new agencies such as Doyle Dane Bernbach blazed new trails in the way ads were developed, by keeping agencies small and having copywriters and art directors work side by side – a practice that was considered taboo by the older firms, in which company hierarchies and division of labor were the primary concern.[16] Doyle Dane Bernbach rose to advertising fame in the late 1950s for its historic North-American Volkswagen Beetle campaign, in which the tiny (especially by 1950s American standards) German vehicle was pitched to American consumers with killer punch lines. One of these, "The only water a Volkswagen needs is the water you wash it with," referred to the then-frequent need in automobiles to top up radiator water, especially during long journeys. "Lemon," another famous slogan, playfully emphasized the carmaker's impeccable quality control, suggesting that an apparently spotless vehicle (as displayed in the photo ad) had been withdrawn from sales following excruciating quality checks. But the boldest of all was the "Think small" slogan, which challenged buyers to "think small in the land of the large, where the automobiles were the size of buses" as advertising historian Mark Tungate has noted.[17] Doyle Dane Bernbach's "subversive" approach drove Volkswagen sales in North America beyond those of any other foreign competitor, making the Volkswagen campaign a textbook example of the power of clever advertising and placing the Beetle on the short-list of all-American products.

Madison Avenue's "racy but dangerous" reputation was confirmed in its aggressive – and less than earnest – approach to tobacco advertising in the 1950s. As tobacco consumption began to decline in 1953–1955 in the wake of emerging scientific evidence linking smoking to health hazards, tobacco corporations resorted to Madison Avenue to defuse consumer fears. The story of the Avenue's "tobacco wars" remains a textbook case of how successful advertising campaigns can be in changing consumer behaviors. One typical counterattack strategy by the tobacco industry against health concerns was the promotion of filter smoking, which was advertised as safe, often through print and television ads in which actors posing as doctors guaranteed, cigarette in hand, that filter smoking was risk-free. One ad for a filter brand claimed that "all the tars and nicotine trapped in the filter are guaranteed not to reach the throat." However, in spite of the fabricated medical endorsements, filter smoking clashed with deeply ingrained smoking habits which associated masculinity with unfiltered cigarettes.

In 1955 Philip Morris marketed a new filter-tipped cigarette called Marlboro, which it had originally designed for women. Amid rising health concerns, the company decided to extend the new Marlboro brand to male smokers as well, although they knew it would take unprecedented persuasion for a filter brand to break into the male consumer market. Philip Morris brought its account to Chicago-based Leo Burnett, an agency priding itself of operating away from the mundaneness of Madison Avenue and of employing copywriters who "spit on their hands before picking up the big black pencil."[18] Burnett created the historic Marlboro Man campaign, associating the Marlboro brand with the rugged individualism of the frontiersman. The extraordinary and lasting success of Marlboro testifies to how effectively Brunett was able to exploit widespread Cold War anxieties for commercial advantage: at a time when many Americans feared losing their individualism to the norms of suburbia and amid fears of atomic annihilation, the myth of the cowboy, celebrated by Hollywood in a thousand films, was a powerful signifier placing Marlboro right at the heart of core meanings of smoking: masculinity, adulthood, vigor, and potency.[19]

Hidden Persuaders

One voice critical of persuasion-driven consumerism in the 1950s was advertising theorist and pioneer Vance Packard (1914–1996), whose best-selling *The Hidden Persuaders* (published in 1957) exposed the pervasive manipulation of society in the race to sell all sorts of commodities, from consumer products to candidates for political office, and questioned the ethics of extreme consumption as such. *The Hidden Persuaders* warned of the manipulative nature of advertising and explored the growing use of consumer research and psychological techniques, including depth psychology and subliminal tactics employed by advertisers to shape expectations and induce consumer desire.

Packard showed how advertisers had understood that at the core of consumerism lay human behavior and its unpredictability: consumers were essentially irrational, and marketing techniques had learned to account for it. One crucial weakness that advertisers exposed and took advantage of was the fact that consumers did not really know what they wanted and were unlikely to tell the truth about what they liked, hence could not be trusted to behave in a rational way.[20]

As consumption in post-World War II society no longer served to fulfill basic needs and purchasing became leisurely and discretionary, advertisers slowly learnt how to tap the human subconscious in order to make valid marketing decisions, by developing a three-level theory of the human consciousness loosely based on Freud. According to the theory, consumption-related decisions were mostly of a subconscious nature and success in advertising was based on probing the human psyche in order to understand what consumers really wanted, not what they said they wanted.

In *The Hidden Persuaders* Packard studied the work of "depth approach" guru Ernest Dichter, who argued in 1951 for the inescapable connection between MR (motivational research) and psychology, and exhorted advertising firms "to recognize themselves for what they actually were – one of the most advanced laboratories in psychology."[21] Packard placed Dichter, an Austrian-American psychologist known as the "father of motivational research," at the root of an "uneasy and ambiguous alliance" between social scientists and advertising firms, who used psychologists to help them "manipulat[e] human motivations and desires and develo[p] a need for goods with which the public has at one time been unfamiliar – perhaps even undesirous of purchasing."[22]

Psychologists instructed merchandisers on how to tap what Packard described as the "eight hidden consumer needs," which were located in people's most crucial psychological drives: quest for emotional security, reassurance of worth, ego-gratification, need for creative outlets and love objects, sense of power, and sense of roots. In *The Hidden Persuaders* Packard discussed how advertisers in the 1950s more aggressively targeted women, the symbolic center of the household and the member of the family responsible for food purchases. He exposed to yet unknowing consumers how marketing research studied women's "uncontrolled reactions" inside supermarkets and came to the conclusion that, upon entering a store, women fell into a sort of hypnoidal trance caused by the enormous availability of products. By placing "high-profit impulse items" in ways that they "would be the most surely noticed," stores could successfully tap into a woman's unconscious.[23]

A subsequent chapter of *The Hidden Persuaders* entitled "Politics and the Image Builders" discussed the way in which advertising techniques had, by the mid-1950s, come to affect political debate. The "I

Like Ike" campaign of 1952 was the first political campaign to be televised, shifting the focus of the debate "less on speeches and more on appearances." Packard pointed out how, as television became the prominent medium of political communication in the following presidential campaign, Eisenhower was first to hire TV advisers and make-up consultants to help him shape a successful public image. Packard's concern that "the idea that you can merchandise candidates for high office like breakfast cereal [...] is the ultimate indignity to the democratic process," questioned, possibly for the first time, the uneasy relationship between consumption and democracy.[24] In arguing that the 1952 campaign had for the first time focused on the "I don't know" voters (the so-called "undecided"), Packard pointed out how the democratic process had become focused on the voter as an "irrational purchaser," whose choice did not derive from "independence" of mind or rational behavior, but rather, in Dichter's words, on "snotty little reasons such as not liking a candidate's wife."[25]

Mad Men

No narrative better captures the ethos of the Madison Avenue advertising industry in the 1950s than the AMC television series *Mad Men*. Created and produced by Matthew Weiner, *Mad Men*, which premiered in 2007 to immediate critical acclaim, is set in the fictional agency Sterling Cooper (no commas, as with Doyle Dane Bernbach) at the turn of the 1960s. The first episode accurately sets its chronology as the protagonists discuss the possibility of handling Richard Nixon's campaign against John F. Kennedy in the 1960 presidential race. In a later episode, the same protagonists are distraught as they watch coverage of JFK's assassination in Dallas on television.

As a caption at the opening of the first episode explains, *Mad Men* was named after "a term coined in the late 1950s to describe the advertising executives of Madison Avenue ... they coined it." The series well captures what South and Carveth have defined "the morally ambiguous atmosphere of corporate and family life" of 1950s

The Affluent Society 49

America, and de-mythicises it by addressing "many uncomfortable truths," from the prevalence of drinking and smoking, to the systemic sexism, racism, and homophobia, that most nostalgic exploitations of the 1950s have typically repressed.[26]

Pivotal figure in *Mad Men* is creative art director Don Draper (played by Jon Hamm), whose suppressed wartime past casts a long shadow over his overachieving present. Inhabiting a life that is "real but not true," and in many ways reminiscent of Gregory Peck's divided hero in *The Man in the Gray Flannel Suit*,[27] Don is the firm's creative heart, and many of the episodes, especially early in the series, linger on his inexhaustible talent and acumen by portraying him as someone who is constantly, "unashamedly selling, whether it be a product, his agency, or himself."[28] In the first episode of the first season ("Smoke gets in your eyes"), the Sterling Cooper men are faced with the textbook case of the Lucky Strike tobacco campaign. As Don flounders in the seemingly impossible task of promoting tobacco in the face of scientific evidence and media campaigns emphasizing its health hazards, junior account Peter Campbell pitches an idea based on pseudo-Freudian research (a tongue-in-check reference to Dichter's theories) asserting that the public's tendency to smoke cigarettes is a response to a death wish – research Don had previously discarded as ludicrous. Outraged by the proposition of a campaign associating their product with death, the Lucky Strike executives are ready to abandon the meeting, disdainfully rejecting Campbell's pitch: "That's your slogan? 'You're going to die anyway. Die with us'? [...] What the hell are you talking about? Are you insane? I'm not selling rifles here. I'm in the tobacco business. We're selling America." At this point Don picks up the pieces in a last-minute epiphany, prompted by one of the tobacco executives' casual remarks:

> DON DRAPER: The Federal Trade Commission and *Reader's Digest* have done you a favor. They've let you know that any ad that brings up the concept of cigarettes and health together...
> TOBACCO EXECUTIVE: Well, it's just gonna make people think of cancer. Yes, and we're grateful to them.
> DON: But [...] if you can't make those health claims, neither can your competitors.
> EXEC: So we've got a lot of people not saying anything that sells cigarettes.

> DON: Not exactly. This is the greatest advertising opportunity since the invention of cereal. We have six identical companies making six identical products. We can say anything we want. How do you make your cigarettes?
> EXEC: We breed insect-repellent tobacco seeds, plant them in the North Carolina sunshine, grow it, cut it, cure it, toast it...
> DON: There you go. [Don draws the "It's toasted" slogan on the blackboard]
> EXEC: But everybody else's tobacco is "toasted."
> DON: No. Everybody else's tobacco is poisonous. Lucky Strike's... is "toasted."

As Sterling Cooper secures the account, Draper glosses on the key philosophy behind his breakthrough: "Advertising is based on one thing: Happiness. And you know what happiness is? Happiness is the smell of a new car. It's freedom from fear. It's a billboard on the side of the road that screams with reassurance that whatever you're doing ... it's okay. You are okay."

Unlike contemporary TV series in which, according to TV critic Will Dean, the story is secondary to the editing, and all is "winking lights and trick shots and musical montages telling you what to think," *Mad Men* takes a step back and relies on a tranquility and poise where, in Dean's words, "every scene has a pay-off; every line has momentum."[29] Aesthetically, *Mad Men* is reminiscent of 1950s movies in its details of period reconstruction, including *The Man in the Gray Flannel Suit*, from which it derives much stylistic detail. Most of all, *Mad Men* captures in full the ambiguity of America's new "persuasion culture," which unabashedly promotes consumerism amid a society hard at work debating its suddenly achieved abundance and its consequences.

A Consumers' Republic

The delicate linkage between consumption and the foundations of the democratic process has been recently explored by historian Lizabeth Cohen, who has argued that in the 1950s economic abundance became tied with ideas of political freedom as the United States turned into a "Consumer's Republic." According to this amended vision of democracy, an integrated conception of affluence as a precondition as well as a mirror of freedom "became almost a national civil religion."[30]

Among the quickest to capitalize on the linkage between American democracy and consumer freedom were the popular media, which consorted in shaping an image of the decade which readily associated affluence with national greatness. In a widely quoted article of October 1956, *Fortune* magazine bragged:

> Oh, what a country [...] never has a whole people spent so much money on so many expensive things in such an easy way as Americans are doing today. Their appetite, as Hamlet put it, grows by what they feed on. In the exhilarating process of exchanging cash (or a signature) for goods and services, they even seem to be laying to rest the specters of "saturation" and "oversaving."[31]

Like other similar pieces, this article described a nation caught in an astonishing age of abundance, where consumers were constantly buying more for less. As the market became saturated with goods year after year, people kept on buying "newer, improved products that were easier to handle, that produced cleaner laundry, washed more dishes and glasses, and housed more frozen steaks."[32] Consumption had become more than the mere satisfaction of an unconscious drive, as the advertisers would have it.

According to Cohen, mass consumption had turned into a vision entrusted "with delivering not only economic prosperity but also loftier social and economic ambitions for a more equal, free, and democratic nation."[33] In particular, an ideology of consumption as good citizenship emerged in the 1950s, which linked the endless purchase of goods on the one hand to the Cold War rhetoric of capitalist plenty versus socialist penury, and on the other to a sense of moral duty to keep the economic boom from exhausting itself. This historically new conception of the "consumer as citizen," and its reverse, "the citizen as consumer," emerged in post-World War II America, and exponentially grew throughout the 1950s, based on the idea of the United States as an "abundant society," in which it was each citizen's duty to contribute to keeping up that abundance. In this context, Walt Disney's introduction in 1947 of Scrooge McDuck, the misanthropic and greedy antihero who selfishly wallows in his own wealth, signaled a shared national intent to defend the ideology of consumption, as it served as a cautionary tale of the dangers of a society in which citizens resist their duty as consumers.

The first academic elaboration to explicitly link America's exceptionalism to its material wealth, productive capacities, and economic growth appeared in the middle of the decade, as David Potter's *People of Plenty. Economic Abundance and the American Character* was published in 1954. By elaborating on the way in which the American concept of inexhaustible plenty, originally connected to the description of the land, ended up shaping the peculiarly American developments of social status and political democracy, *People of Plenty* argued that American political forms were the result, not the cause, of the country's abundance. Potter posited economic abundance at the root of the creation of a culture of mobility and equality where advertising, which he understood as the quintessential institution of abundance, was as important as the church and the school in shaping the American character and American democracy.

As the language of growth, prosperity, free enterprise, and consumption increasingly supplemented the language of political liberalism and religion, suggesting that individual psychological fulfillment and meaning were to be found in prosperity, growth, and consumption, President Eisenhower hailed working-class Americans as members of the respected and prosperous middle class, in a culture which had come to regard expansion of wealth and expansion of freedom as irrevocable and interdependent processes.[34]

The post-World War II expansion of consumer credit (fueled especially by the increased issuance of credit cards) came to be interpreted not only as an instrument to expand consumption, but a tool in its own right to expand democracy. As people bought more in the 1950s because access to installment payment was no longer restricted to major purchases but it now covered all kinds of commodities, they were encouraged to overcome the previous generations' Calvinist fears of being in debt through the new image of the good citizen-consumer. In its "Hard Look at Consumer Credit," published in 1955, *Life* magazine identified a "revolution in consumer purchasing," where "instead of saving for years to afford major purchases, consumers buy on credit and enjoy the goods while they pay for them."[35] One simple word, "while," defused age-old fears: debt no longer meant breaching the protestant work ethic, but more practically it meant improving one's own well-being.

Corporations Triumphant

As American consumers indulged a sentiment of newly won citizenship in consumption, American manufacturing enjoyed an unprecedented expansion: the combined availability of abundant natural resources, an educated workforce (after the war, the government gave all returning veterans the opportunity to return to school through the Servicemen's Readjustment Act of 1944, commonly known as the "GI Bill"), increased government spending, and increased consumption further stimulated the growth of the economy.

No factor better reveals the changing climate of the American economy in the 1950s than the apotheosis of the large industrial conglomerate, the corporation. In a country where a newly-created affluence was leading to major social transformations rooted in the relocation of living space (the rise of suburbia) and a newly-earned idea of individual mobility, Detroit's "Big Three," GM, Ford and Chrysler, had a large role in capturing that country's new industrial ethos. Automobile historian Stephen Fox has shown that in the 1950s the most heavily advertised products were automobiles and General Motors replaced Procter & Gamble as the leading national advertiser. In 1956 the largest individual advertising budgets were spent by Chevrolet (a GM brand, at $30.4 million), and Ford ($25 million), trailed by a string of other automotive brands: Buick, Dodge, Plymouth, Mercury, Chrysler, Pontiac, and Oldsmobile. Coca-Cola, at $10.9 million, was the only non-Detroit company in the top 10 advertisers that year.[36]

The automobile industry was of mammoth dimensions: one of every six jobs in America could be related to car manufacturing.[37] At the beginning of the 1950s, approximately fifty million vehicles were registered in America and three out of five American families owned a car. By the time the decade ended, the ratio of car-owning families rose to four in five and the number of registered vehicles rose to seventy-four million: there were more cars in the United States than in the rest of the world put together. Accounting for fleet turnover, this meant that approximately seventy million cars were sold in America during the 1950s: ninety-nine percent of these were American, and General Motors alone sold half of them. Because the price of vehicles during the decade rose to twice the rate of the wholesale cost index, there is no doubt that GM was the number one manufacturer in the most profitable business of the decade.[38]

GM became so rich and powerful that the collective psyche of the nation came to identify it as much more than a corporation. According to David Halberstam, "it was like a nation onto itself, a separate entity, with laws and a culture of its own."[39] GM based its own corporate culture and image on specific values: loyalty, team work, and an "other-directed" sense of the organization as prevailing over the individual.[40] Its bosses were part of a breed unto themselves: white, mostly Protestant and raised in the small towns of the American heartland, educated in the nation's public colleges (and not in the Ivy-league schools), they fit an intellectual model that was new for the country: nowhere near the genius of a Henry Ford, they had a powerful knack for the organization and for fitting within one. In Halberstam's words:

> they were square and proud of it, instinctively suspicious of everything that was different and foreign [...] They were conservative, insular, and nationalistic [...] Everything about them reflected their confidence that they had achieved virtually all there was to achieve in life.[41]

At GM, industrial culture was hierarchical and the bosses were worshiped like half-gods, revered by their employees who, in the utmost form of emulation, "tended to take all signals" and "share all attitudes and prejudices of the men above [them]."[42]

GM's longstanding CEO Alfred P. Sloan, who steered the company into its post-World War II triumphs, established standards and industrial practices based on efficient internal division of labor and an unprecedented attitude to marketing automobiles as quintessential staples of the American Dream.[43] Sloan became GM's mythical figure, endowing the company with a new "family-like" image, distinct from its aloofness in the previous era, while embracing a rejuvenated corporate image capable of luring buyers to its products, which were now marketed as symbols of upward mobility and eternal youth.[44] At the core of this idea lay GM's "brand diversification," the revolutionary notion that each "consumer segment" could be marketed as a portion of the American Dream, as well as a vision of the next goal on their upward race.[45] To this end, GM developed five concurrent brands – Chevrolet, Pontiac, Oldsmobile, Buick, and Cadillac – each targeted at a different market segment and each carrying with itself the assumption that its buyer was on track to soon reach for the next rung of the mobility ladder. With brand diversification, Sloan also introduced the annual styling changes and so-called "planned obsolescence," the deliberate designing of automobiles to fall out of fashion after a certain period of time – a process George Walker, head of styling at Ford, summarized as such: "we design a car to make a man unhappy with his 1957 Ford long about the end of 1958."[46] Within an ever growing economy, planned obsolescence was supposed to boost sales indefinitely.

If Sloan's rigid corporate discipline and attention to marketing were decisive components for GM's success in the 1950s, the maverick creativity of some of its top engineers and designers were the other variable in GM's equation for success. Nowhere is this more true than in the history of the 1955 Chevrolet, a new design by legendary engineer Harley Earle that the company hoped would capture the burgeoning youth market.[47] Within General Motor's large archipelago, Chevrolet regarded itself as the heart and soul of the company – and there was certainly merit to the claim. Chevrolet was responsible for approximately seventy-five percent of GM's profits, as it was the division that specifically targeted the entry-level market.

Based on a brand-new, powerful as well as light V8 engine created by engineer Ed Cole and suggesting the speed of a fighter-bomber, the 1955 Chevrolet became an American icon, symbolic of a country in the throes of an unparalleled prosperity which, it appeared, had become available to all. By giving "the average guy [the feeling] that he was driving a Cadillac," the V8 allowed GM to crush Ford's predominance in the entry-level automobile market and became a key factor in reinforcing GM's corporate leadership in the decade.[48] The 1955 Chevy ads captured the sense of endless possibility that Chevrolet stood for, as the car branded itself in the short list of certifiably American things which could not be duplicated anywhere in the world, a "winner" which delivered the "pure pleasure of bossing around a car with Chevy's rapid-fire reflexes – plus the solid feeling of stability [...] at the wheel."[49]

The expanding automobile culture in the 1950s spawned a huge industry relying on the American longing for mobility, which included fast food restaurants (the McDonald's fast food concept emerged in San Bernardino, California, in the early 1940s, and by the end of that decade began to be merchandized as a franchise across the American continent), drive-in venues, especially movie theaters (although pioneered in the early years of the depression, the drive-in theater was one of the staples of 1950s culture), motels (Holiday Inn, the first motel chain, was founded in the early 1950s). It even included churches (the first drive-in church was conceived by "Christian capitalist" preacher Robert Schuller, founder of the Crystal Cathedral in Garden Grove, CA in 1955) and, of course, the suburban home, with its spin-off commodities such as kitchen furniture and appliances, which quickly found a place on every American consumer's wish-list.

A distinct symbol of comfort, better living and endless postwar progress, the American kitchen became one of the central sites of Cold War rhetoric. Appliances were the first consumer good Americans aspired to as soon as the depression ended, following the U.S. commitment to become an "arsenal of democracy" by contributing weapons to the war effort after the fall of France in June 1941. As Congress appropriated large funds to armament production – which immediately translated in new jobs and new money available to American families – kitchen stoves and refrigerators went to the top of wish list of American consumers. Once the war was over, production of appliances burgeoned with the introduction of an ever-growing range to gadgets. American families owning a mechanical refrigerator increased from 44 to 80 percent between 1940 and 1950 and the sale of household appliances mobilized the transaction of billions of dollars. Sales further soared in conjunction with suburban home building, where built-in state-of-the-art appliances were one strong selling point for the new subdivision homes.[50]

One figure that came to symbolize the kitchen-appliance frenzy pervading the country in the postwar years was declining B-movie actress Betty Furness, who was hired to do short live commercials on

CBS's *Studio One*, a TV show of which Westinghouse was the sole sponsor. Betty Furness gained immediate, unprecedented success, which turned her from a struggling entertainer into the pan-American "Lady from Westinghouse." Furness harnessed most of the qualities sought for by the new TV-viewing public: she was attractive, but not in a way that made women (who were the prime targets of her commercials) jealous; she appealed to the whole family, and had an intuitive sense about her role. Furness became "the all-American wife in the all-American kitchen," exuding confidence that she could handle anything in a way that made household chores, if not downright obsolete, "at least easy and glamorous."[51] Kitchen appliances quickly became, through this public-relations icon, symbolic of a nation increasingly immersed in new fantasies of privacy and family "togetherness." Dishwashers, toasters and vacuum cleaners became allegories of much larger transformations of domesticity in the postwar years, at the core of which lay the mass migration of white, middle-class Americans from cities to suburbs. The next chapter will tackle that delicate transition and its implications.

CHAPTER 3

Building the Suburban Nation

The suburban homebuyer is not buying a house, he's buying a way of life.
(William J. Levitt)

By the time they had lived seven years in the little house on Greentree Avenue in Westport, Connecticut, they both detested it.
(Sloan Wilson, *The Man in the Gray Flannel Suit*)

Levitt and Sons

Fears of a nuclear buildup as well as a quest for social homogeneity and domesticity after the turmoil of the war fuelled wide-ranging transformations in post-World War II America. Endowed by the GI Bill with hitherto unknown resource for consumption, returning veterans built families and fled *en masse* from the cities, drawn to the new, affordable housing developments that were springing up outside the major urban areas.[1] Commonly defined as "suburbs," these new sprawling subdivisions promised to fulfill the long-standing modernist project of fusing proximity to urban jobs and rural retreat, city and country life all at the same time. In the meantime, they shaped specific roles for men and women within a newly conceived sense of domesticity.

The suburbs and their culture were not new to America: from the first "commuter suburbs" dating back to the early decades of the nineteenth century, to the Victorian streetcar and garden suburbs later in that century and the bungalow buildings of the 1920s,[2] Americans have heeded the call to escape the corrupting urban sphere since at least Jefferson's famous exaltation of agrarian life: "Those who labor in the earth are the chosen people of God [...] whose breasts he has made his peculiar deposit for substantial and genuine virtue."[3] Before World War II, however, the absence of government and mortgage assistance made earlier suburban expansions less inclusive: the late nineteenth- and early twentieth-century suburbs often housed wealthy commuters and the lower income labor that served them; and although the 1920s bungalow developments attracted more middle-class residents, they only housed a small portion of the overall population. What changed the whole playing field after World War II was the combination of at least three factors: steeply rising marriage rates and the baby boom, creating a social demand for more homes; the newly-won affluence, transforming the American middle classes into consumers; the GI Bill, endowing returning veterans with the mortgaged capital which most of the time made it cheaper to buy a suburban home than to rent.[4]

The newly affluent middle class of post-World War II America found the suburbs particularly appealing: unlike inner city apartments, homes away from the cities were affordable, safe, spacious and modern. They were fitted with everything technology had to offer, from indoor plumbing to central heating, from fully equipped kitchens to automatic stoves, refrigerators, and washing machines. Besides, suburban homes guaranteed safe distance from the degrading urban environments of postwar America, where growing racial tension and the economic disruption caused by white flight itself were taking a heavy toll on living standards. All these factors put postwar Americans on the move, giving rise over the course of just a few decades to the largest combined population relocation in American history.

As a consequence of that relocation, the population of many of the nation's largest cities – New York, Chicago, Philadelphia, Detroit, Baltimore, Cleveland, Washington, Saint Louis, and several others – decreased, in spite of the persistence of the "Great Migration" of blacks from the rural South to the industrial cities of the north, and postwar relocation of white farmers to America's urban areas. Those Americans leaving the cities were not abandoning the urban areas altogether: rather, they were relocating to what historian Kenneth T. Jackson has called the "crabgrass frontier," the country's new suburban subdivisions. The relocation was extremely rapid: by 1960, there were more Americans living in the suburbs than living in central cities, and the margin of difference further widened in the following decades, so that by the end of the century two Americans in three lived in the suburbs.[5]

The reasons behind the flight to the suburbs were manifold: the new capital made available by the GI Bill and the affordability of the suburban developments were certainly crucial. But there were also psychological factors rearing up, which included the underlying atmosphere of post-World War II America, plagued by constant Cold War intimations of deceit and atomic annihilation and by escalating racial tension in the inner cities. Against the backdrop of the early Supreme Court decisions, such as the desegregation of public schools of 1954 threatening to end long-held tenets of white hegemony, white Americans sought a sense of security in the fantasy of a new suburban idyll, where restrictive covenants and redlining practices established codes of separation, both imaginative and demographic, which turned the suburbs into "a zone of protected whiteness over and against the racially marked zones of both the country and the city."[6] In the Cold War environment of rising, generalized fears, moving to the suburbs soon came to be perceived not only as a bargain and an avenue to homeownership and commodity abundance, but also as a way of retreating to a space that was at the same time removed from Cold War anxieties and racially homogeneous, a sheltered space of private quiet against the turbulence of the public sphere. Suburbia catered to the informal, family- and child-centered lifestyles to which young parents aspired in the postwar period. Ridding couples of the day-to-day obligations of extended family and ethnic community, relocation allowed the new American family to direct their focus inward, while at the same time providing illusion of engaging in an ever-broader rhetoric of postwar nationalism based on achievement and consumption, which linked their social status as Cape Cod and ranch house owners to a greater American good.

The mother of all American suburbs was a development built just after the war in Hempstead, Long Island, some thirty-five miles away from midtown Manhattan. Known as Levittown, after the name of its builders, Abraham, William and Alfred Levitt, it opened in 1947 and became the template for suburban development in America, not only because it was the first postwar suburb to be built, but especially because it set many of the standards of suburban building, based on standardization of design, assembly-line execution, and cost-cutting efficiency. Kenneth T. Jackson has described the process well:

> The formula for Island Trees, soon renamed Levittown, was simple. After bulldozing the land and removing the trees, trucks carefully dropped off building materials at precise 60-foot intervals. Each house was built on a concrete slab (no cellar); the floors were of asphalt and the walls of composition rock-board. Plywood replaced ¾-inch strip lap, ¾-inch double lap was changed to 3/8-inch for roofing, and the horse and scoop were replaced by the bulldozer. New power hand tools like saws, routers, and the nailers helped increase worker productivity. Freight cars loaded with lumber went directly into a cutting yard where one man cut parts for ten houses in one day.
> The construction process itself was divided into twenty-seven distinct steps – beginning with the laying the foundation and ending with a clean sweep of the new home. Crews were trained to do one job – one day the white-paint men, then the red-paint men, then the tile layers. Every possible part, and especially the most difficult ones, were preassembled in central shops, whereas most builders did it on site. Thus, the Levitts reduced the skilled component to 20–40 percent. The five-day work week was a standard, but they were the five days during which building was possible; Saturday and Sunday were considered to be the days when it rained. In the process, the Levitts defied unions and union work rules (against spray painting, for example) and insisted that subcontractors work only for them. [...] The firm made its own concrete, grew its own timber, and cut its own lumber.[7]

Between 1947 and 1949, the Levitts built some 6,000 homes (at peak production, the daily output was at thirty units) and the related services (school, post office, phone service, and streetlights), which they initially rented to returning GIs. Then, in 1949, the Levitts turned their attention to the growing ranks of middle-class homebuyers and began manufacturing larger, more modern homes called "ranches." Within four years from the start of construction they had turned out some 17,000 essentially identical houses, on identical plots of land, mandating stringent regulations on the use of the land by the new homeowners and restricting sales to "acceptable" (i.e. white-only) buyers.[8]

Addressing criticism that the homogeneity of architecture and landscape design could evoke fears of mounting social conformity, the Levitts understood that the success of their large-scale homeownership project depended on building homes that would respond to the needs and the symbolic projections of their customers.[9] Exercising nearly complete control over the landscape, they forged the first embodiment of American suburbia through a set of architectural ideas and shapes which reflected the new white middle-class aspirations to privacy, proximity to nature, and material comfort. Buyers were offered a selection of exterior shapes, which ranged from row-houses and two-family twin houses to ranch houses and the two-story colonial, each design carrying specific social and class connotations.

The catalyst of the middle-class suburban dream was the single-story "ranch" house, the promised land of most would-be suburbanites. Based on Frank Lloyd Wright's 1930s design for his utopian Usonian home, ranch houses responded to postwar needs.[10] Laid out on a single level and featuring low-pitched roofs, deep eaves, picture windows, and strong horizontal lines, the ranch house offered more living and storage space, ensured a living environment built for privacy and informality and allowed parents to concentrate on their children. Besides the practical advantages, ranch houses also fulfilled a symbolic function, in their receptiveness to some sort of nationalistic overlay, as though living in the suburban ranch house equaled fulfilling the destiny of the modern American lifestyle. Urban historian Clifford E. Clark has argued that in the 1950s the ranch house was the ultimate "reaffirmation of the American Dream of prosperity and security." The ranch house identified a "new ideal of the family," based not on style but on function: it needed not be beautiful, but rather practical for the large family.[11] In a way it evoked a sort of idyllic California lifestyle, replete with connotations of an easy, stress-free way of living. It emphasized a new relationship between home and nature, indoor and outdoor – an impossible proposition in the city. A "structure which fraternizes with nature," the ranch house promoted fantasies of a return to a more authentic existence, away from the noise, dirt and impersonality of cities.[12]

Inside, the typical ranch house was divided into three zones. A private zone, including bedrooms, multiple bathrooms and closet space – now a must-have for a consumption-prone middle class. A public zone, which included the living-room – typically open, sometimes sunken, "clean looking" and modernly furnished – and a playroom. There was also a mixed private/public zone, consisting of the kitchen, typically U-shaped and rich with never-seen-before electric appliances, and a multipurpose space. The dining area was usually an extension of the cooking area, making it easy to serve the food. The back or side door, which was often the favorite entrance, opened into the kitchen.[13]

The ranch house was one of several set architectural templates which the Levitts and other developers offered to their customers, and which also included the Cape Cod, intimating fantasies of New England colonial life, the "split level" (both typical of the more upscale suburbs), as well as the row-house and the two-family twin house (typically chosen by a lower-middle class clientele).[14] Regardless of design, however, the suburban home created an image of the postwar American family where "self-indulgence was glorified," convenience prevailed over style, and comfort took predominance over beauty. It was cost-effective and spacious; it was efficient, convenient and, most of all, instrumental to creating a new image of family life, based on integration of male and female family members and increased interactivity among them.[15] Writing about suburbia, urbanist William Whyte noted that people were moving to it because, besides the space, the amenities, and the ideal environment to raise a family, the suburb had become charged with the crucial symbolic value of delivering "a social atmosphere of striking vigor" – an asset its developers capitalized on when marketing the new suburbs not simply as "housing," but rather as "happiness."[16] An ad for Park Forest, a suburb outside Chicago which opened in 1948, made that connection explicit:

> A cup of coffee – symbol of Park Forest. Coffeepots bubble all day long in Park Forest. This sign of friendliness tell you how much neighbors enjoy each other's company [...] Come out to Park Forest, where small-town friendships grow – and you still live so close to a big city.[17]

The ad's evocation of "small-town friendship" was a code-word for the suburbs' crucial asset: their class and race neutrality. By literally placing distance between their residents' jobs and their private lives, privileging consumption over production, and each catering to a specific price-range bracket of the population, suburbia erased class differences. This was not because society had suddenly become classless, but because suburban homogeneity rendered class invisible.

Likewise, racial difference "vanished" in the suburbs, through a combination of discriminatory practices which ensured that African-Americans would be banned from the suburban dream. Among these infamous exclusionary practices were "redlining," where banks and the Federal Housing Administration (the governmental agency responsible for insuring the mortgages) systematically refused mortgages for racially mixed urban neighborhoods while almost automatically churning out loans for white suburban buyers, and the enforcing of "restricted covenants" in suburbia, explicitly barring nonwhites from buying property.[18] Although segregation-inspired restricted covenants were banned as unconstitutional as early as 1948, Jackson has argued that the suburban developers and the Federal Housing Administration were always very keen on avoiding "inharmonious racial or national [i.e. ethnic] groups."[19]

Amidst the widespread suburban consensus, several critical voices emerged. Urban theorist Lewis Mumford was among the most outspoken: in his book *The City in History* (1961), Mumford complained that the suburbs resulted in a conglomeration of "uniform, unidentifiable houses, lined up inflexibly, at uniform distance, on uniform roads, in a treeless communal waste." Mumford was especially critical of the dull homogeneity of the suburbs, inhabited by "people of the same class, the same income, the same age group, witnessing the same television programs, eating the same tasteless pre-fabricated foods, from the same freezers, conforming in every outward and inward respect to a common mould."[20] Sociologist William Whyte was likewise critical of suburbia. In *The Organization Man* (1956), Whyte described suburbia as the quintessential manifestation of a conformist society, an aberration of American values which promoted mindless conservatism and uncritical consensus, shaping individuals who were almost interchangeable as they fought to climb the corporate ladder. However, Whyte also argued that the suburbs fostered a "communal way of life" which had analogies with the frontier or the early colonial settlements – which was the concrete testimony of America's new social mobility, where middle classes had found "the ideal way station" in an endless upward trajectory towards ever higher income and ever higher status and comfort.[21]

More recently, James H. Kunstler's *The Geography of Nowhere* and Duany and associates' *Suburban Nation* have tallied up the huge economic, social, and spiritual costs that America has been paying for its car-crazed lifestyle. These scholars have especially focused on the depletion of resources commanded by the suburban fantasy to "update Eden," the loss of community intrinsic to the suburban ideal, and the alienation that younger generations in particular suffer in the contrived suburban space. Kunstler has argued that if on the one hand the suburbs improved the whole way of life of many Americans, over time they exacerbated inequality by segmenting America and dissolving its social diversity. Duany and associates have argued that suburbs, by destroying the traditional concept of the neighborhood, have eroded such vital social values as equality, citizenship and personal safety. Economically and environmentally "unsustainable," the suburbs have altered in-family relationships because they have isolated and placed undue burdens on at-home mothers, children, teens and the elderly and proven ultimately "not functional."[22]

This suburban loss of community has been a recurring focus in the novels of Philip Roth, a first-person witness of the massive postwar urban transformations in the greater New York metropolitan region, and particularly in Newark, where he was born and raised. Roth's highly autobiographical fiction bears witness to how the multi-class, multi-ethnic, multi-racial tangle of "competing minorities" became after World War II "a black urban core surrounded by a white suburban periphery."[23] Roth's fiction has analyzed the white, and especially Jewish, class segmentation occurring in Newark in the 1940s and 1950s, when ethnicities first grew further and further apart and then separated themselves through the white flight in the latter part of the 1950s and 1960s. In the 1959 novella *Goodbye Columbus*, his first study of Jewish assimilation into the American melting pot, Roth captures the growing social distance between Neil Klugman, a working-class Newark resident and Newark community college student, and upper-middle class suburbanite Brenda Patimkin, who grew up in the elite subdivision of Short Hills and is a student at the prestigious Radcliffe College. In the novella, their summer romance turns into a textbook case of suburban alienation. As Neil travels to Short Hills to visit

Brenda, he draws a mental map of the new city/suburb dualism and of the sharp line dividing two incompatible ways of living:

> Once I'd driven out of Newark, past Irvington and the packed-in tangle of railroad crossings, switchmen shacks, lumberyards, Dairy Queens, and the used car lots, the night grew cooler. It was, in fact, as though the hundred and eighty feet that the suburbs rose in altitude above Newark brought one closer to heaven, for the sun itself became bigger, lower, and rounder, and soon I was driving past long lawns which seemed to be twirling water on themselves, and past houses where no one sat on stoops, where lights were on but no windows open, for those inside, refusing to share the very texture of life with those of us outside, regulated with a dial the amounts of moisture that were allowed access to their skins.[24]

By characterizing suburban life as removed not only physically but above all spiritually from the world outside, Roth engages in a critique of the suburbs which touches upon the very foundations of their myth: the suburbs are no retreat in nature – their residents in fact defy nature, by living behind closed windows and relying on artificial climate control. They also reject, rather than embrace, community, as no one partakes of communal life in the simplest of its street forms – sitting on stoops. What is left is their lush prosperity, the visible marker of their difference that the Patimkins have chosen to embrace: the American way of consumption, the prime mover of America's suburban dream, which was best embodied in the temples of affluence rapidly emerging alongside the suburban subdivisions – shopping malls.

The Malling of America

In 1953 the *New York Times Magazine* observed: "there is a widely held belief that American households are ready to do more buying than they presently do [...] They would do it more readily but for the difficulty of getting to the downtowns where the full range of goods is available." The solution proposed: "bringing the market to the people instead of people to the market."[25] The article came out at a time when the new subdivisions that had brought urban whites to the suburbs hardly provided any facilities for the new residents. At least until the mid-1950s, most suburbanites struggled to find adequate shopping options: the retail strips which had appeared along the highways since the end of the war had created enormous traffic congestion and were soon found to be inadequate for such large numbers of new consumers; returning to urban downtowns to shop was viewed as inconvenient; and the existing suburban town centers proved inadequate to support the consumption desired by the influx of new residents. As retailers came to realize that suburban residents, with their young families, new homes, and vast consumer appetites, offered a lucrative market that was ready to be conquered, the physical arrangement of American commercial life was reconfigured as new "regional shopping centers" emerged to create a new community marketplace for suburban residents.[26] Suburban land was cheap and widely available and the most profitable consumers had now conveniently clustered in the new communities housing tens of thousands of families (at the end of the 1950s, Levittown alone had 82,000 residents). Suburbanites earned more than other Americans, with average incomes of $7,114, compared to $5,940 for city dwellers and $3,228 for those living on farms.[27]

Shopping malls were conceived as fully-blown islands of consumption: typically rising at a highway intersection and surrounded by huge parking lots, their architectures turned inwards to fully absorb visitors into the experience of purchasing. In his *The Malling of America*, a memoir of the changing suburban landscape in postwar America, William Kowinski has argued that shopping malls were the catalyst of that change:

> Television, suburbia, the Highway, the Baby Boom, and the Bomb had all prepared the way for the mall – had even conspired somehow to create it. It was an intuition more physical than intellectual at first; just the way the mall sat on the landscape, the way it looked and felt inside – the way it *glowed.* I felt that somehow, for good or ill or quite possibly both, *this* was *it,* the embodiment of it all [...] The mall seemed to be the fruition of so many of the prophecies, promises, dire warnings, and false starts that I could remember [...] The mall was where all the postwar changes were tied together. It was the culmination of all the American dreams, both decent and demented; the fulfillment, the model of the postwar paradise.[28]

Although the concept dated back to the 1920s, the suburban shopping center, generally known as the "shopping mall," was officially codified in the postwar years as "a group of commercial establishments planned, developed and operated under a single ownership as a single unit."[29] Following widespread suburbanization, the first large size centers, called "regional malls," began to emerge in the mid-1950s, providing dozens of stores in climate-controlled, landscaped, fully-enclosed pedestrian environments offering a combination of stores, restaurants and services.[30] Although malls were almost exclusively reachable by car, they predicated a rigorously pedestrian experience, as automobiles were relegated to specially-designed parking lots that marked the separation of the mall from the surrounding suburban landscape.

The first fully enclosed mall, and the prototype of the mall as we know it today, was the Southdale Center in Minneapolis, designed by Viennese architect and shopping mall pioneer Victor Gruen in 1956. Gruen envisioned the shopping mall as a place for retail and respite: Southdale incorporated gardens and trees inside a two-story, climate controlled shopping wonderland. By 1957, 940 shopping centers had been built. The number more than doubled by 1960 and doubled again in the next three years, so that by 1963 there were some 4,000 regional shopping centers in the United States.[31]

Regional shopping centers were intended to provide not only shopping convenience but also a civic function, as they quickly developed into an equivalent to the town center where social, civic, and seasonal activities took place.[32] Away from urban downtowns, malls became resilient and adaptable forms which artificially re-created the lost sense of centeredness within the suburban sprawl, and in fact gave whole new meanings to the word "center."[33] Developers viewed the malls they were building as fully-fledged centers capable of creating old-style community with new-style unity and efficiency. In order to achieve that goal they laid out plans for commercial spaces that "idealized – almost romanticized – the physical plan of the traditional downtowns shopping street, with stores lining both sides of an open-air pedestrian walkway that was landscaped and equipped with benches."[34] Victor Gruen argued that these new "shopping towns" – as he called them – sought to overcome the "anarchy and ugliness" characteristic of many American cities. As the central sites of consumption, they offered the full range of retail and services that previously had existed downtown: shopping malls combined every possible shopping need in one stop-and-shop destination where consumers could find clothing and shoes, furniture, hardware, appliances, food, drugs, books, toys and records, garden supplies, and medical supplies. Shopping malls also came to include services such as restaurants, a post office, cleaning services, bank and financial services, barbershops, travel agencies, real estate offices, even religious services. Recreational facilities ranged from movie theaters and bowling alleys to ice-skating rinks and playgrounds. Besides, malls scheduled a full range of cultural and educational activities to legitimize their ambition as civic centers, which included exhibitions, concerts, plays, dances and classes for teenagers, campaign appearances by political candidates, and community outreach for local charities.

In *A Consumers' Republic* Lizabeth Cohen has argued that the shifting marketplaces of postwar America produced at least three major effects on community life. First of all, they forced a rationalization of consumption, which went hand-in-hand with the rationalization of domesticity that the suburban subdivisions were concurrently promoting, and which resulted in an increasing market segmentation of American consumers. Moreover, shopping malls dictated a privatization of public space: unlike downtown shopping districts standing amidst the city's core, malls were fully privatized, corporate spaces, privileging property rights of private owners over citizens' traditional rights of free speech. Third, they provided what Cohen has defined as a "feminization of public space" which on the one hand enhanced women's claim on the suburban landscape, but at the same time "circumscribed the power they wielded there." Rationalized consumption and carefully restricted access to a selected citizenship, owning automobiles or living along the carefully-planned bus routes that were designed to serve desired non-driving customers, made shopping malls feel particularly comfortable and safe for women, for whom the early shopping centers were specifically designed. At the same time, such "feminized" suburban spaces conspired, according to Cohen, "to limit the gains in domestic and public authority" of women, whose unprecedented access to consumption was thwarted by emerging discourses of limited female autonomy within the domestic sphere.[35]

Conflicting Family Narratives

Suburbanization was not a mere geographical population shift, but rather entailed a wide-ranging reconfiguration of American society and customs. Predicated upon a return to domesticity, marriage, child rearing and consumption, the white flight to the suburbs pivoted around the changing agency of the American family. In the 1950s, the social act of marriage and family raising became crucial in conveying that an individual's private sphere was healthy and prosperous. Like consumption, conformism, and the other holy facts of life in the 1950s, worship of the family was taught and reinforced through widespread media campaigns centering on popularized scholarship, magazines and television in particular.

By 1960, there were approximately one in three white Americans living in the suburbs. Because the U.S. population in 1960 was 89 percent white, this means that the same statistical ratio described an overall national trend, although excluded areas were by no means irrelevant.[36] The suburban family was traditional, nuclear and centered on parental authority. Division of labor between husband and wife was rigid: men earned wages, wives were homemakers; and although the myth of the woman-homemaker of the 1950s has been highly exaggerated,[37] only ten percent of suburban women held jobs outside the home in the 1950s. Within the institution of marriage, child-rearing acquired special emphasis, as 76 million children were born between 1945 and 1964.[38]

Books and media all contributed to fostering the paradigm of the nuclear family founded upon the woman-homemaker. *Modern Woman* magazine suggested that "only full-time mothers are right and healthy;" and the Christmas 1956 issue of *Life* magazine indicated that "of all the accomplishments of the American woman, the one she brings off with most spectacular success is having babies."[39] Although few families achieved the Fordist "minimum production goal" of six children suggested in the article, the average American woman in the late 1950s had 3.7 children over the course of her life.[40] The very popular *Common Sense Book of Baby and Child Care* by Dr. Benjamin Spock, published in 1946, drew its most unique points not so much from the idea that parents should have a permissive attitude with children, but rather from the fact that mothers should devote themselves to full-time child-rearing.[41]

In a decade that saw the national population growing by 18.5 per cent, child-rearing did become a national imperative. As the family became – to borrow from the 1958 bestseller *'Twixt Twelve and Twenty*, written by popular singer-turned-sociologist Pat Boone – a "happy home corporation," social roles began to be reformulated according to a vision of domestic democracy, where tasks and responsibilities were equally distributed between the husband, in Boone's description "the leader-president […] who can say 'it's going to be this way'" and the wife, the "executive vice-president."[42] Studies however showed that the democratic rhetoric of family was in fact exaggerated, as research indicated that not even 10% of husbands participated in essential chores such as laundry, ironing and cleaning.[43]

The metaphor of marriage as marker of personal health was widespread. Public discourse coalesced in this decade to create a guiding narrative of the role of women in society as nurturers – wives, mothers, homemakers – in a way as to divert attention from the fact that American women had only recently given up the much less feminine social role they were forced to take on during the war years. After the war, as genders came more and more to be defined as opposite of one another (women being described by scientific divulgation as irrational, emotional, gentle, obedient, cheerful, dependent; men, conversely, being described as rational, individualistic, unemotional, solid, aggressive), marriage was more and more seen as the "balancing measure" for such diverging opposites. A higher percentage of people were married and the median age of marriage was lower (just under twenty-three for men, and just over twenty for women) in the 1950s than at any time since the late 1800s: in 1955 it was estimated that 92 percent of all Americans were or had been married and marriage was regarded as a "natural state in adults."[44]

Single life, on the other hand, was frequently described with degrees that ranged from being undesirable to causing unhappiness and mental disorder. In 1956, *The Reader's Digest* railed against the "harrowing situation of single life," as marriage counselor and author Paul Landis wrote that "except for the sick, the badly crippled, the deformed, the emotionally warped and the mentally defective, almost everyone has an opportunity to marry."[45] *Modern Woman* magazine was no less explicit, as it suggested that "bachelors of more than thirty, unless deficient, should be encouraged to undergo psychotherapy" and advocated that "all spinsters be barred by law from having anything to do with the teaching of children on the ground of theoretical (usually real) emotional incompetence."[46]

Scholars have pointed out that prescriptive gender roles deprived individuals of choice: women and men were repeatedly urged to obey the dominant clichés, and if throughout the 1950s people seemed to try to live up to the roles imposed by society at large, by the early 1960s books like Betty Friedan's *The Feminine Mystique*, or Eve Merriam's articles in *The Nation* began exposing the damage that such narrow sexual roles were spreading in American society. Other cultural narratives have provided dissonant voices in the debate centering on family. If American literature has a long prewar tradition extolling the sanctity of family (in texts such as Eugene O'Neill's *Ah, Wilderness* of 1933, and Thornton Wilder's *The Skin of Our Teeth* of 1942), wartime and postwar narratives have often favored a darker outlook on the American institution of family. As hardboiled literature and film noir warned about the dark side of the American Dream, family was often a favorite context for debunking the myth of togetherness. James M. Cain's *Double Indemnity* (1943), which Billy Wilder turned into a film the following year with a screenplay by Raymond Chandler, is one the most notable cases: femme fatale Phyllis Nirdlinger rips her own family apart for the promise of financial security as she conspires to kill her own husband and collect his life insurance benefit. By 1945, films like *The Best Years of Our Lives* and *Since You Went Away* began suggesting that the war may have destroyed the sanctity of domestic bliss. Arthur Miller's *Death of a Salesman* (1948) followed the drama of a disintegrating middle-class family and Tennessee William's *A Streetcar Named Desire* (1947) discussed a rape taking place in the bosom of the domestic sanctuary. William's *Cat on a Hot Tin Roof* (1955) was yet another merciless look at family crisis, as the Pollitt family found itself involved in a complex web of self-deceit. Finally, Nicholas Ray's *Rebel Without a Cause* (1955) denounced the confusion of gender roles within the family as the core problem of America's middle class and Eugene O'Neill's A *Long Days Journey into Night* (1957) officiated over the dissolution of the home in full view of the audience, and theater questioned family as a possible agency for the raising of children and the fulfillment of the American Dream.[47]

Trouble in the Suburbs: *Rabbit, Run* and *Revolutionary Road*

Warren Susman has argued that 1950s American culture is best revealed if seen as caught in two competing visions of family: a dual collective representation in which "the traditional collective ideal persisted," but had now to deal with "the discovery of the horrors and hypocrisy of the modern world."[48] John Updike's 1960 novel *Rabbit, Run*, and Richard Yates's *Revolutionary Road*, published in 1961, are two of the most harrowing indictments of the dark side of the suburban idyll of the 1950s. Although focusing on different social typologies of suburban affluence and discontent, both novels present sharp, if demoralizing, vistas of the period and settings – its junk-oriented material culture, the pressures of the conformist consensus. They both highlight human failure, and distinctly connect that failure to the broken promises of the suburban dream.

Updike's *Rabbit Run* was the first in its author's masterpiece series chronicling the life and suffering of American everyman Rabbit Angstrom, whose restless life marked by professional underachievement, sexual discontent, and a broken marriage was immediately read as an allegory of a dysfunctional affluent society. Written and set in 1959, *Rabbit Run* is a moral tale about the downside of – and the difficulty of adapting to – the standards of American middle-class life and the protestant ethic. In the novel, Harry "Rabbit" Angstrom is 26, has a job selling a kitchen gadget called MagiPeel, and is married to his former high school sweetheart Janice. They have a two-year-old son, Nelson, and live in Mount Judge, a suburb of Brewer, Pennsylvania. Rabbit's life does not in the least match the excitement of his teenage years, when he was the school basketball star and was engaged in a "life of speed, grace, and precision" that compares poorly with the stultifying dullness and mediocrity of his present middle-class existence.[49] Far from the splendor transpiring through magazines and television, family and home life for Rabbit appear more and more like a prison. An "order-loving man," his home is a constant mess, physical and spiritual: Janice alienates herself from her new pregnancy by drinking too many old-fashioneds and spends hours lying half-unconscious in front of the television. Dissatisfied with his marriage, Rabbit comes to be convinced that his broken domestic idyll is the source of his existential dissatisfaction.

Upon several escapes from home and family, Rabbit becomes attached to a former prostitute (introduced to him by his erstwhile coach and role model Tothero), with whom he begins a three-month affair. Unable to master the complicated life he has built for himself, Rabbit flees repeatedly, from his lover as well as from his wife and from the social conventions imposed by his "legitimate" life, leaving the novel suspended in midair as it ends. Opposite his sexual prowess and escapades with Ruth stands Rabbit's other crucial figure of reference, Jack Eccles, the Episcopalian minister who tries in long conversations over golf games to persuade Rabbit to go home to his middle class respectability. Rabbit vacillates between his wife and his mistress, the middle-class consensus and his inner drive to recover his more authentic self. The external and codified morality, of which Jack Eccles is the chief instrument, demands that Rabbit return to Janice; but Rabbit's inner apprehension of what is "right" for him directs him to his lover Ruth.

Updike has said that the central theme of each of his novels is "meant to be a moral dilemma," and that his books are intended as "moral debates with the reader."[50] His novels frequently embody those moral dilemmas in the women between whom the protagonists must choose. To the world surrounding him, Rabbit appears insensitive to moral issues. At one point in the story Jack Eccles angrily takes him to task: "You don't care about right and wrong; you worship nothing but your own worst instincts."[51] But this objection is true only in terms of Eccles' Christian ethics and Rabbit realizes that much of what people like Eccles call "right" is in fact wrong. As Bernard Shopen has pointed out, "morally, the world of *Rabbit, Run* is one in which platitudes are piously pontificated and then winked at or invoked to excuse failure, mediocrity, or perversity."[52] It is the confrontation with this world that forces Rabbit to turn inward for guidance: caught between the demands of two different but equally unsatisfactory moralities – the one requiring adherence to those modes of behavior enjoined by religio-social codes, the other demanding a complete and honest response to an inner imperative – Rabbit's only possible response is to break away from it all. The short circuit leading to Rabbits' repeated elopements is symbolic of a world in which the external values of society no longer match the individual's inner desires and aspirations. Flight from reality appears as the only alternative available, but it is one whose moral implications can hardly be overlooked or easily dismissed.

Like *Rabbit Run*, Richard Yates' *Revolutionary Road* does not offer "any of the comforts of the standard best seller about struggle. No better tomorrow, no better house and better understanding of oneself."[53] Although several rungs above Rabbit in the social ladder, Frank Wheeler, the protagonist of *Revolutionary Road*, is just as frustrated as Rabbit, just as anxious to shape for himself a way out of middle-class ordinariness, and just as unable to find one. Like Rabbit, whose self-referential quest will ultimately drive his wife to near-madness and cause her to drown her newborn baby in the bathtub, Frank's inadequacy to shape a better life for himself and his wife will lead the latter to die during an abortion.

If for Rabbit, a working-class man, a major vital asset lies in his sexual prowess, for Frank and his wife, an upper-class couple fully immersed in a pseudo-intellectual appearance of cultured life, the main claim out of suburban drudgery is their proclaimed articulateness, replete with catch-words such as "individualism" and "identity:" although working a nine-to-five job, Frank would like to be a writer, an "intense, nicotine-stained, Jean-Paul Sartre sort of a man;" although a home-maker, his wife April is an untalented aspiring actress who struggles through small roles in her local theatre group.[54] The problem with the Wheelers is that they are stuck in the cul-de-sac of a suburban development called (ironically) Revolutionary Hills Estate, with their particular limitations which prevent them from taking their lives into their own hands and achieve the actual "revolution" that suburbia had only promised and never fulfilled. As far as the Wheelers are concerned, suburbia offers no redemption, but rather, in David Castronovo's words "makes them more inert and garrulous, lonelier and more self-deluding than they might be if they were challenged and disciplined by a big city."[55] When they try, in the second part of the novel, to escape their fate, they fail tragically, in the same way that Rabbit fails. As they conceive an articulate scheme to start a new life in a European city, Paris or Rome, their plan is thwarted by Frank's inability to go from abstract speech to concrete fact: he withdraws in the drudgery of his job, pretending he is going somewhere, as April, who finds herself deprived of an outlet for her "mad rebellion," sinks into despair and psychosis.

Disneyland and the Double Meaning of Freedom

The suburban American family quickly developed into a powerful weapon of Cold War rhetoric. On the one hand, suburban domesticity offered Americans the reassurance of a safe haven amidst the uncertainties of the outside world, especially in the international arena. On the other, American domesticity was heralded, at home and abroad, as the shining example that American superiority in the Cold War rested not on weapons, but rather on the secure, abundant family life of the modern suburban home.[56] At the juncture of suburbanization, domesticity and the nation's new consumerist ethos, Disneyland, inaugurated in July 1955, mobilized postwar America's leading ideological tropes by making a compelling case for ideas of America and Americanness within the Cold War's conflicting imaginaries.

Disneyland's conception and development drew from the amusement parks, at the time largely defunct, which mushroomed across American cities at the turn of the twentieth-century (New York's Coney Island was the most notable example), and updated that formula in ways that were consistent with the larger domestic transformations in the United States of the postwar years. Disneyland catered to the baby-booming middle class, relying on sophisticated design, state-of-the-art technology and Hollywood "imagineering" to create an autonomous space of family amusement which addressed issues of consumption, family, and national identity. Located in the Anaheim suburb of Los Angeles, Disneyland resembled many of the new suburban subdivisions of postwar America. In fact it was fully conversant with them. Circularly-shaped, it was conceived, like suburbs and shopping malls, as physically separated from the outside world; it offered, like suburbs and shopping malls, a fantasy pedestrian adventure which functioned as a counternarrative to America's automobile-dependent urban landscape. Walt Disney explicitly claimed he had conceived the park as an "antidote" to Southern California's automobile tyranny. Inward looking, and separated from the outside by a reduced-scale railway which looked like a toy train but in fact was a fully functioning "people mover," the park disguised its corporate nature by promoting the illusion of placing individuals back on the more humane dimension of a "public sphere."

The park's circular shape revolved around five "lands" emanating radially from a central hub, each land showcasing one of Disney's strategic narratives. Although adjacent to each other, each Land was conceived as a space of its own, aesthetically and ideologically separated from the others, with sophisticated staging devices used for placing public passageways and directing circulation in such a way as not to interrupt the narrative unity of each space. The first "theme park," Disneyland condensed a cultural map of parallel yet autonomous narratives (or themes) of America's past, present and future, emphasizing national celebration and patriotic rhetoric, which extolled America's manifest destiny.[57] Main Street U.S.A. celebrated America in the nineteenth century prior to the emergence of the metropolis, when small-town life was orderly and humane. Adventureland exalted the wealth and diversity of the continent's natural resources. Frontierland celebrated America's westward expansion during the nineteenth century. Tomorrowland presented a blueprint of America's future. Fantasyland materialized the fantasies of Disney's most popular cartoons and movies.

In a famous essay describing the park as "degenerate utopia," semiotician Louis Marin has pointed out that the mythical narratives of the park's five lands are powerful ideological tools that manage to confound guests about the relationship between reality and fantasy and in the process enforce "a fantasmatic projection of the history of the American nation."[58] This ideology addressed two quintessentially American middle-class concerns of the 1950s – the creation of a fantasy that would set itself against some of the ills of modern life and the delivery of a set of values which would prove instrumental in addressing specific postwar concerns – values which would define, in Emma Lambert's argument, "a coherent relationship between the park and the nation." According to Lambert, Disneyland was a specific product of the Cold War context within which it was conceived. As the Cold War pushed the country to negotiate "ideas of America and Americanness through all spheres of life," and consequently to define its own national self as opposed to that of an enemy, Disneyland proved instrumental in America's quest to define the essence of its nationhood by establishing a narrative based on the combination of the inheritance of the past and the promise of the future:

> By presenting and interpreting the American past in Adventureland and Frontierland, and the American Future in Tomorrowland, Disneyland entered into Cold War discourses of American identity and meaning of the nation's present. It became, therefore, a definition in progress of the meaning of nationhood, produced at a time when it was the supreme political importance to attempt to define oneself [...] in contrast to a perceived enemy.[59]

Connecting past and future with present at Disneyland was the idea of freedom, understood as both political freedom (i.e. democracy) and capitalist freedom (i.e. freedom to consume). Lambert has pointed out that such projections were fully convergent with Cold War rhetoric. In the 1950s the linking – often a short circuit in fact – of these two notions of freedom became common currency.

In the famous "kitchen debate" of 1959 between American Vice President Richard Nixon and Soviet premier Nikita Khrushchev, nuclear proliferation rhetoric moved to the domestic space and to the suburban home, as the two leaders tensely debated the merits of capitalism vs. socialism in front of a world-wide television audience at the inauguration of the American National Exhibition in Moscow. As the Nixon presented the wonders of American kitchens to his Soviet counterpart, he extolled the virtues of American freedoms as rooted in consumer choice: "We hope to show our diversity and our right to choose. We do not want our decisions to be made at the top by one government official that all houses should be the same [...] Let the people choose the kind of house, the kind of ideas they want." As a site of Cold War confrontation, the suburban home was the perfect embodiment America's double notion of freedom.[60]

Likewise, Disneyland was conceived under the same metaphor of "consumer choice" that placed Cold War American citizens' "bottom-up" choice at the extreme pole from communism's centralized "top-down" rule. A wonderland of brand names with a captive viewing audience of five million people a year, Disneyland operated, through cross-media interaction, advertising, marketing and promotion, as a paradigm of post-industrial capitalism. According to Lambert, "the close connection between capitalism and the political struggle against communism meant that the park functioned, through its omnipresent consumerism, as a political statement, a symbol of the success of the American system."[61]

Since its inauguration, Disneyland has come to symbolize "a set of values, based around capital, God and nation," conceived of as the most desirable of all lifestyles. Projected from day one in the trenches of Cold War propaganda, Disneyland became a must-see stop in the "grand tour" of America for heads of state and dignitaries visiting the country. In his 1959 official visit to the U.S., Nikita Khrushchev personally insisted on visiting Disneyland. As the trip to Anaheim was ultimately cancelled for alleged "security reasons," Khrushchev's child-like enthusiasms legitimized, in Lambert's words, "mass cultural forms within the elitist canon of 'suitable' public and state monuments," turning Disneyland into "a shorthand for the U.S.A. as a whole," the signifier of "multiple meaningful areas of American culture and politics, a kind of permanent 'World's Fair' dedicated to the American nation and American values as defined during the early Cold War."[62]

CHAPTER 4
Projecting America Through Television

> I think there is a misconception that sitcoms are made up of jokes: they're not.
> (Sioned William, TV and radio producer, 2005)
>
> We cannot defend freedom abroad by deserting it at home.
> (Ed Murrow, 1954)

By the end of World War II, radio was the most popular and most far-reaching medium of mass communication. In the 1930s, it had provided entertainment for Americans during the hardships of the Great Depression. By 1940, eighty-two percent of American homes had at least one receiver.[1] Greeting listeners with the signature opening "This is London," Ed Murrow's groundbreaking radio broadcasts brought the war in Europe into America's living rooms. But in the postwar years the radio days began to wane, as television, whose development had been put on hold by the war, resurfaced at the end of the conflict to gain unprecedented prominence.[2] The age of television did not merely imply the entry of yet another appliance in the (mostly suburban) home. As Alan Nadel has pointed out, and as I suggest in the title of this chapter, television turned out to be a medium that did not so much "represent" America – it was not merely a neutral observer of a changing nation – as it rather ended up "projecting" a new vision of normality to which the nation could aspire, as such aspirations proliferated, first and foremost, over America's airwaves. To recapitulate its history is, in many ways, to weave the central narrative of the American 1950s.

From Radio to Television

In 1945, seven television stations were broadcasting in the United States – three in New York, and one each in Philadelphia, Chicago, Los Angeles and Schenectady, NY (where General Electric was headquartered). Five years later the number of TV stations in the U.S. had reached 98, operating in 58 market areas, virtually all the major cities, and when the Federal Communications Commission (FCC) ended the freeze on new licenses in 1952, stations multiplied across the nation in both urban and rural areas.[3] The sale of television sets grew accordingly. If at the start of the war there were an estimated 10,000 sets across the country, half of them in New York, by 1948 the annual production of receivers exceeded 975,000 units, a fivefold increase over the combined production of the two previous years, which brought two-thirds of American households to own televisions as early as 1953.[4]

Initially, TV sets offered a standard 12-inch monitor – a very small box by today's standards. To compensate for the technical limitations, sets were at times sold with a magnifying lens placed in front of the screen to make the picture look larger. In spite of the infancy of the technology, Americans, who had been expecting a TV revolution since before the war, embraced the medium. Historians mark the season 1948–1949 as the cutoff moment when "television became an acceptable, attractive, and affordable national utility."[5]

It is around this time that popular radio shows began to migrate to the new medium. One notable example was *The Fred Allen Radio Show*, which was moved to television in 1949 as the new *Fred Allen Show* – a staple of American television in the 1950s. In spite of his immediate success in the new medium, Allen – a highly talented entertainment professional who wrote his own shows, rich with intelligent, literate, quirky humor – regretted the demise of radio entertainment, quipping that television was "a device that permits people who haven't anything to do to watch people who can't do anything."[6]

In spite of Allen's (and many others') misgivings, the rise of television was fast: Americans were switching to television in growing numbers as new stations became available across major cities. Television drove audience away not only from the radio: a 1951 *New York*

Times showed that, even in cities with just one TV station, movie theater attendance had dropped 20 to 40 percent. In New York City alone, fifty-five movie theaters closed between 1948–1951 and weekly attendance at movie theaters across the United States plummeted from roughly 90 million in 1946 to 40 million by 1960 – a period of steady demographic growth – leading film producer David Selznick to remark in 1958 that "television has killed the habit of motion picture attendance."[7]

Television not only replaced radio and film as the pre-eminent medium of entertainment, but also changed the nature of entertainment at a time when suburbanization was radically transforming the American way of life. Scholars have pointed out that television suburbanized the meaning of entertainment, which became focused on the private, the domestic, and the ideal of family togetherness within a single home space.[8] A popular *New Yorker* cartoon of 1951 quipped, not without urban cynicism, that "one nice thing about television is that you don't have to pick out where to look," implying that television might well provide an escape from the boredom of domestic life. Nevertheless, there is ample evidence in the narratives of the decade that television was in fact not so much an escape, but rather a device that repositioned its viewers as members of a "new suburban unit, which had left most of its extended families and friends behind in the city."[9]

Although several observers expressed reservations about the new medium, mainstream sociologists contended that television developed "family contact" and noted, as far back as 1949, that television was responsible for changes within the family as an institution, in that long-term TV owners were feeling more family solidarity and that television was helping close the gap between adults and children.[10] No other invention, historian J. Ronald Oakley has observed, "not even the motion pictures, automobiles, or radio, brought so much change to so many people in so short a time." Andrew Dunar has noted that for the first time Americans across the country were watching and listening to the same shows at the same time: like the homogenized suburbs, television made the United States a smaller place by hastening the decline of regionalism, diminishing differences in accent, attitudes, entertainment, cultural tastes, and preferences in food, clothing, and other consumer goods.[11]

The Golden Age of Television

In the late 1940s and early 1950s, television was a very different medium from the one that developed afterwards: in its so-called Golden Age, television catered for various tastes, with programs that covered, among other subjects, opera, fights, dramas, documentaries, variety shows, and the news. Most shows were broadcast live, as there was no technology available to tape those shows for later broadcast. The secret of television was its mix of immediacy, variety, and simplicity of message. In its infancy, television drew its programming ideas, styles, and conventions from other media: from radio, of course, but also from theatrical genres such as burlesque, vaudeville, drama, and film, as well as from the circus and the nightclub. TV absorbed these genres into a unique form of entertainment based on spontaneity and intimacy, using its ability to transport a stay-at-home audience to the site of events taking place elsewhere at the same moment. The unique power of the medium was, according to Stasheff Bretz, "its ability to bind public with private space."[12] Shows owed their success not only to the performers' talent, but also to what media historian Lynn Spigel has defined as having "a front row seat" at a Broadway show. Because of its live format, Golden-Age television was able to conjure up a sense of reality no other medium could, a sense of "presence," the idea of a "perfected view" of events which democratized leisure and made it accessible from the comfort of the home.

The early television genre that best synthesized this process was the comedy show, a genre derived from vaudeville, which privileged performance over plot and was attended by "all rungs on the social ladder."[13] It is no coincidence that in the late 1940s the most popular man on television was Milton Berle, the greatest of vaudevillians who quickly became "Mr. Television," the embodiment of the medium, "famous for running off the stage into the studio audience, making a mockery out of the 'aesthetic distance' so important to theatrical realism."[14] Berle began hosting the *Texaco Star Theater* in 1948 and became the first television superstar, dominating the airwaves for the eight-year run of his show. Relying on slapstick and humor that pushed the limits of fifties-era propriety, Berle made the comedy show into one of the most popular formats of early television. His success was matched by two other vaudeville veterans, Sid Caesar and Imogene Coca, who starred on the very popular *Tour Show of Shows*, a staple of Saturday-night television from 1950 to 1954, which benefited from the work of phenomenal writers such as Neil Simon and Mel Brooks.[15]

As the popular appeal of television grew, it became clear that its industry was rapidly changing into what Dennis Mazzocco has called "networks of power," which established the medium as a "potent political, economic, and social force" in the country.[16] This, in turn, led to substantial changes in programming, formats, and overall content. As the decade progressed, programming became homogenized and concentrated on a few successful genres; live television slowly disappeared as program recording became widely adopted, and the nature of television entertainment drastically changed. In the meantime the American people became "the audience," a term charged with the negative overtones of passivity and proneness to manipulation, mostly by the pervasiveness of advertising, which quickly emerged as the true core of the television business.

Revenue became an obsession for television stations. The three major networks – ABC, NBC and CBS – exploited the advertising machine in order to construct an oligopoly that would dominate the business of broadcasting in America well into the 1980s. Programming rapidly became a magnet to capture an audience, which would be sold to a corporate sponsor, and as broadcasters and advertisers were mutually exploiting each other for their own benefits, the television audience was rapidly reduced to a market of consumers.[17]

The television age also transformed the advertising business. If in 1950 television only accounted for roughly 3 percent of total advertising expenditures (most of the share still being held by newspapers, direct mail, radio, and magazines), by 1960 television advertising had reached nearly 14 percent of the total. Television executives soon began to spend more on producing commercials than on regular programming and historians have estimated that, by 1960, television budgets allotted about $2,000 per minute for programming, and $10,000 to $20,000 per minute for ads.[18]

The need to control and sell an audience spawned a flourishing industry of its own – that of audience analysis, market research, and above all the so-called "rating system," an instrument that was developed with the sole purpose of determining the value of advertising space. Media historian Denis McQuail has pointed out that "the media need[ed] their audience more than audiences need[ed] their media," to the point that not only TV programming, but even audience analysis itself came to be regarded as a tool "for the close control and management (call it manipulation) of media audiences."[19] By 1956, sponsors had come to control almost the totality of programming and pushed programming to become uniform in order to capture as wide an audience as possible.[20]

Portraits of an Affluent Nation: the Prize Show

Sponsor control was particularly savage on one of the most popular catch-all genres of 1950s television, the "prize show," also called "game show" or "quiz show." A carry-over from the radio era, quiz shows were projected to new heights of popularity by television, which churned them out by the dozen throughout the decade. Each show had its peculiar formula and all shows centered on turning an audience member into a television protagonist – and perhaps a richer person. *You Bet Your Life*, hosted by Groucho Marx, debuted on NBC-TV in 1950 and awarded minor money prizes ($ 100) to the person who happened to guess the secret word of the day. *Strike it Rich*, which opened on CBS in 1951, was known as "the quiz show with a heart," where the contestants were people in need of money or down on their luck who told tales of misery; even if players lost, host Warren Hull might ask viewers to call in and send money or merchandise on a "heart line." In *Queen for a Day*, another carry-over from radio and running on NBC-TV from 1955 to 1964, the winner was the most pathetic story, fostering, according to Miller and Nowak, "a false picture of American poverty" based on "the assumption that there were hardly any poor people in America, and those few were all being gradually taken care of ... on TV."[21] *Beat the Clock*, which ran first on CBS, and then on ABC, and *Dollar a Second*, running on DuMont Television (an early major player in the commercial television business, which operated from 1946 to 1956), were among the "humiliation shows," a crowded genre in which the contestants volunteered to do something contrived or foolish.

Towards the middle of the decade, broadcasters raised the stakes in the prize show business, as they began offering the lure of gigantic money prizes in shows such as *The Big Surprise* (also called *The $100,000 Big Surprise*), which ran on NBC between 1955 and 1957, or *The $64,000 Question*, which ran on CBS from 1955 to 1958. Of this new, high-stakes genre, the most popular show on American television in the 1950s was unquestionably NBC's *Twenty-One*, which ran from 1956 to 1958, bringing the genre first to its peak and then to its demise. The formula of *Twenty-One* – which was sponsored by Geritol, a vitamin maker – revolved around an attractive contestant answering obscure questions for a lot of cash. In 1957, Charles Van Doren, an assistant professor at Columbia University, became an overnight celebrity after winning $ 100,000. As a spin-off to his success in the show, Van Doren also received a job co-hosting the highly popular *Today* show on NBC. Rumors of foul play, which had circulated for some time in the industry, made the news in August 1958 when Herbert Stempel, a former star contestant in the show who had been dethroned by Van Doren, testified before a New York grand jury that the program was rigged. The ensuing scandal marked the end of the fixed TV giveaway programs and dealt a severe blow to the genre, if not to television altogether, and it would take forty-two years before CBS returned to the quiz show format.[22]

Robert Redford's docudrama *Quiz Show* (1994) revisits the events of the *Twenty-One* scandal, specifically focusing on the firm grasp that advertisers held over the television industry and on the latent ethnic bias in that industry and in American society in the 1950s. Redford's narrative centers around Herbert Stempel, the "know-all nerd," a Jewish working-class former GI, whose drab, ordinary existence in the Queens borough of New York City is suddenly projected to televised fame. Not good looking, shabbily dressed, prone to sweating, with a prominent bad tooth, he is not liked by the sponsors, who ask the network to replace him with a contestant who would better match the product that pays for the show (in real life, sponsors and producers always denied any such intrusions). Studio producers Dan Enright and Albert Freedman (people's real names are used throughout the film) oblige when they find Charles Van Doren, a young, handsome, Columbia professor and the offspring of the cream of the WASP intelligentsia. Although people like Van Doren are strangers to television (in a crucial scene, Charles is seen giving his father – the renowned literary critic – a television set as a birthday present: it is the late 1950s, and the elder Van Doren still does not have one), his aristocratic background is seen as an asset by the producers, who are confident he will boost the show's ratings. But because Van Doren is unlikely to beat Stempel at the game, he is persuaded by the network to compromise his intellectual integrity for the sake of celebrity and material gain and accepts being fed the answers before the show. Concurrently, the producers induce Stempel to take a dive, promising him a spot on another TV show, but further humiliate him when they order him to lose by failing a question so easy which turns his defeat into personal shame. Disgruntled by the network never making good on their promise, Stempel brings public charges, triggering investigations by a New York grand jury first, and then by a congressional subcommittee on legislative oversight.

The congressional investigation reveals that not only Van Doren, but also Stempel had been fed answers while on the show. The producers take the fall, clearing the sponsors and the network of any wrongdoing. In a bitter ending, everybody suffers from the truth revealed, except for television: Stempel loses his dignity in front of the audience, his family and community, who discover that his televised fame was the result of a scam; Van Doren loses not only his TV job, but also his professorship; Dick Goodwin, the congressional lawyer who investigated the scandal, sees his case vanish as the producers refuse to implicate the network and the sponsors, and realizes that his hope of "getting television" has turned out in "television [getting] us."

On an allegorical level, *Quiz Show* dramatizes a moment in television when innocence was lost and the medium revealed itself in all of its ambiguity: a site of representation and not a mirror of reality, television measures its truth not in the accuracy of the stories it portrays but in the extent of the success it harnesses. As producers Enright and Freedman argue in their final statements before the congressional subcommittee, no harm is done in deceiving a television audience:

> ENRIGHT: Well: the sponsor makes out, the network makes out, the contestants see money they probably would never see in a lifetime, and the public is entertained. So who gets hurt?

No one, probably, got hurt. Nevertheless, *Quiz Show* projects a sensitive area of mass communication in which the medium remains suspended in the unresolved ambiguity of what its representations imply and what they actually stand for.

Watching TV on TV: the Sitcom

Treading that very thin line between reality and representation became the crux, as well as the blessing, of the most popular of all TV subgenres in the 1950s, the situation comedy, or sitcom. Emerging at a time when, following new technical developments, recorded shows were beginning to take pre-eminence over live broadcasts, the half-hour sitcom took the live variety and anthology drama shows off air, by assimilating their aesthetics into a new format that had been specifically tailored for the new television medium. The sitcom merged the traditions of live entertainment with stories about wholesome American families, by taming, as Lynn Spigel has argued, "the unrefined elements of the theater, while still maintaining the aesthetics of presence so important in the early period of television," thus bringing together theatrical realism with the physical humor and immediate impact of vaudeville.[23]

At the core of the sitcom is a set of recurring characters engaged in an ongoing comedic storyline and sharing a common environment (often, a living room). Each week the audience encounters the same people in the same setting and each episode is generally finite: what happens in one given episode is closed off, explained and solved at the end of the half hour. Generally performed in front of live audiences, the genre emphasizes its nature as performance by the metadramatic inclusion of the studio audience's laughter, which punctuates the action as it develops.[24]

In a telling early rendition of the genre, the radio comedy *Easy Aces* made its television debut in December 1949 with an episode consisting of the two protagonists, a married couple, sitting in their living room, watching television. The story had no plot and was fully carried by the couple's witty commentary on the show they were watching. The show's appeal lay in its "ambiguous blend of fiction and reality," i.e. in creating the pretense of the home audience being at home with the Aces, sharing with them the simple act of watching television.[25] This created, according to Spigel "the fantasy of a social experience" which provided "a heightened instance of a more general set of cultural meanings and practices surrounding television's arrival in postwar America."[26] By luring the viewer with the promise of entering a world of "fictional friends," *Easy Aces* offered a sense of commonality and shared experience that was typical of this highly prolific genre, where viewers felt connected to a new electronic neighborhood which encouraged them to perceive spatial and social relationships in new ways and helped neutralize the strange new technology with stories about everyday situations that took place in familiar settings.

In merging "the wild spontaneity of vaudeville performance with the more genteel – and decidedly non-controversial – aspects of theatrical realism," two distinct and preexisting theatrical genres, the sitcom created an aesthetics attuned with television's overall aim of reaching a family audience, at the time when the television set became a central figure in the representation and in the re-shaping of family relationships in America. As the ideal sitcom was expected to highlight both theatricality and naturalism experienced in domestic life, sitcoms were ideally placed to bridge the gap between the new medium and the American family, in that they could convey "a sense of intimacy and authenticity by encouraging viewers to believe that the characters were real families who just happened to live their lives on television."[27]

Naturalism, a quintessentially theatrical genre, entered the family comedy to make it a virtual "theater of the everyday," showcasing reality in a heightened, exaggerated fashion. At the same time, the medium "had to be carefully controlled so that it harmonized with separate gender roles and social functions for individual family members."[28] This controversy was a central tension in popular discourses on television and the family in 1950s America. Women's magazines played an important role in defining television within the domestic space. In 1954, *Mc Call's* magazine coined the term "togetherness," a sociological idea postulated on the notion of the family members spending time doing things with one another. If under different social circumstances the members of a family might have used the little leisure time they had seeking individual pursuits, the notion of togetherness instead predicated the modern idea of a nuclear family. Magazines went to great lengths discussing how to rationally arrange family space in the home, in terms of proximity, distance, isolation, integration, and in ways that would overcome the physical divisions of the Victorian household and create the preconditions for togetherness.

It was "within the context of the spatial problem," explains Spigel, "that television was discussed." Questions such as "where should you put the television set?" took on great importance in the decade. The magazines tended to suggest that it be placed at the center of family life, as a replacement for the fireplace or, more typically, for what had been the piano in the Victorian home. Soon television "seemed to become a natural part of domestic space," taking upon itself the attribute of the family unifier, fitting very well with "the more general postwar hopes for a return to family values."[29] Magazine ads for home appliances – and especially television sets – graphically depicted the idea of the "family circle," in which family members were grouped around the TV set in semicircular patterns. And because most of these ads targeted the new suburban family, the idea of television as the great "suburban minstrel" became a dominant trope. Leerom Medovoi has observed that "the very apparatus of television seemed to require [...] the spaciousness of a suburban home," the only space in which bulky, space-demanding TV consoles allowed viewers to properly occupy the required field of vision.[30]

The ads suggested that television would serve as a catalyst for the return to a world of domestic love and affection – a claim in blatant contradiction with the realities of coming home. For many GIs, return from the war meant finding a world in which men had to face the new social tensions of the "organization society" and the "crisis in masculinity." Women as well had to come to terms with the tension between the public idea of the wife and homemaker and the harsher realities of more and more women entering the workforce, mostly in low paying jobs.[31] According to Spigel, "[t]he transition from wartime to postwar life thus resulted in a set of ideological and social contradictions concerning the construction of gender and the family unit," which advertising tried to soothe by presenting images of "domestic bliss and consumer prosperity."[32]

Within this context, the choice of actors became a special challenge for producers of sitcoms and other shows: both male and female roles had to respond to the new condition of postwar gender dynamics, as well as conform to the dual, often contradictory, model of bourgeois respectability and comedic abrasiveness, both of them necessary to draw the suburban viewers to the shows and keep them glued to the screen for the whole half-hour.

Among women, a new class of female comics emerged – performers like Lucille Ball, Joan Davis, and Gracie Allen, who did not upset middle-class codes of femininity and whose humor was deemed acceptable for television. By embedding the female comics' wild physical humor in domestic scenarios, television turned them into loving daughters, devoted teachers, and especially charming housewives – roles that were at the same time central and marginal and always consistent with suburban housing, the consumer product industry, and market research.[33] Mary Beth Haralovich has shown the extent to which women were central, in that they, as homemakers, were key subjects of consumption and responsible "for establishing the value of domestic architecture and consumer products for quality of life and the stability of the family."[34] They were marginal, on the other hand, in that they were placed inside the home and contained within their prescribed social role.

In the *Burns and Allen* show (1950–1958), one of the earliest televised sitcoms, Grace Allen's actions are constantly explained and glossed over by George Burns, whose role of the authoritative narrator provides a template for "containing" her female role. In *The Adventures of Ozzie and Harriet* (1952–1966), another highly successful sitcom of the period centered on celebrity (a musical family featuring mom, dad and two children), mom and the kids deferred to Ozzie, the respected patriarch. Female roles such as Margaret Anderson in *Father Knows Best* (1954–1962) and June Cleaver in *Leave it to Beaver* (1957–1963), two among the most successful of 1950s sitcoms, were particularly significant in this context, as they represented the promises of the economic and social processes that established their social subjectivity as homemakers.[35] *Father Knows Best* concentrated in drawing humor from parents raising children to adulthood in suburban America, and the press praised the Andersons as "a family that has surprising similarities to real people" – people who "managed to ride through almost any family situation without a violent injury to their dignity" and have been capable of raising children "who will probably turn into useful citizens."[36] *Leave it to Beaver*, which premiered three years later, showcased a suburban context highly reminiscent of *Father Knows Best*, and offered a special glimpse into the life of a white American middle-class boy and his parents' efforts at adapting to less hierarchical, more democratic approaches to child rearing.

Male sitcom roles were no less ambivalent. As warnings of an increasingly feminized American society were coming from several parts of the cultural spectrum in books such as Philip Wyle's *Generation of Vipers* (1947), male sitcom actors were chosen in a way that allowed them to fit the new role of the American male, caught in the changing dynamics of the postwar family. Although on many sitcoms the male dominance in the home was openly challenged, male figures mostly came across as softer, good-natured individuals, at times even laughable, and always emphasizing a very strong faith in marriage. In most sitcoms, men appeared as idiots, or sideshows at best, in a social representation where the feminine role was predominant. A *Time* reviewer claimed, in 1954, that "in television's stable of 35 home-life comedies, it is a rare show that treats Father as anyone more than the mouse of the house – a bumbling, well-meaning idiot who is putty in the hands of his wife and family."[37]

In another highly popular sitcom of the 1950s, *The Honeymooners* (1951–1955), the larger-than-life male star comedian, Jackie Gleason, surrounded his pursuit of male power with an aura of glamour and romance both on and off the air.[38] Nevertheless, although Gleason the star made an ostentatious display of dominating women, Ralph Kramden, his working-class alter-ego on the show, was unable to dominate even the woman to whom he was married, as he suffered from pathological jealousy and eternal anxiety. And while most sitcoms repressed images of the gender conflict, *The Honeymooners* brought to the surface and undermined the image of the dominant male, by both challenging and supporting his patriarchal authority. As the strategic medium of pop culture, television was made to appeal mostly to women, which the medium saw as ideal representatives of the "low-brow" culture it personified. Within this context, the trivialization of men came through as one strategy in the gender identification of television's targeted audience.

I Love Lucy

The unsurpassed champion of all sitcoms, and probably the greatest success on American television of all times, was *I Love Lucy,* which began during the 1951–1952 season and ran until 1959 for a total of 181 thirty-minute episodes. Its debut on CBS on October 15, 1951 was an immediate sensation. Four of its six prime-time seasons received the highest ratings of any series on American television and it never finished lower than third place. In the second series, Lucy's real-life pregnancy was worked into the show's script (although CBS did not allow for the word "pregnant" to be used on the show) and the episode in which Lucy gives birth to Little Ricky ("Lucy goes to the Hospital") was aired on January 19, 1953 to coincide with her real-life delivery. The episode drew forty-four million viewers (72 percent of all U.S. homes with a television set, roughly one of every four Americans), while Eisenhower's presidential inauguration the next day drew no more than twenty-nine million. When it ceased production as a weekly series in 1957, *I Love Lucy* was still the number one series in the country.

I Love Lucy centered around former B-movie actress Lucille Ball and her real-life husband and orchestra leader Desi Arnaz, who played Lucy and Ricky Ricardo on the show, a fictional young married couple living in a converted brownstone on the upper east side of Manhattan. Lucy was a frustrated housewife who longed to escape the confinement of her domestic role and participate in a larger public world, preferably to join Ricky (an orchestra leader on the show, just like Arnaz in real life) in show business. Ball and Arnaz were joined by former vaudeville comedians Vivian Vance and William Frawley, who played Ethel and Fred Mertz, the Ricardos' landlords. *The Encyclopedia of TV* thus summarizes *I Love Lucy*'s plot rationale:

> Conflicts inevitably arise when Lucy's fervent desire to be more than a housewife run up against Ricky's equally passionate belief that such ambitions in a woman are unseemly. This dynamic is established in the pilot episode – when Lucy disguises herself as a clown in order to sneak into Ricky's nightclub act – and continues throughout the entire series. In episode after episode Lucy rebels against the confinements of domestic life for women, the dull routines of cooking and housework, the petty humiliation of a wife's financial dependence, the straightjacket of demure femininity. Her acts of rebellion – taking a job, performing at the club, concocting a money-making scheme, or simply plotting to fool Ricky – are meant to expose the absurd restrictions placed on women in a male-dominated society. Yet her rebellion is forever thwarted. By entering the public sphere she inevitably makes a spectacular mess of things and is almost inevitably forced to retreat, to return to the status quo of domestic life that will begin the next episode.[39]

By staging the real-life protagonist couple's own family life in the funhouse mirror of a sitcom fantasy, *I Love Lucy* was one of several "family-play-family" sitcoms that aimed at stretching the boundary of visual representation into a whole new territory. In showcasing the intimate setting of one family playing itself on screen, sitcoms blurred the boundaries between real-life and screen-life, reality and its representation, and in so doing empowered the new medium with an extraordinary flair of authenticity. *I Love Lucy* suited the new medium perfectly, as it involved its audience in telling them how a television program could rescue a rocky marriage, and in the process bring forth an emotionally renewed and financially triumphant family.

I Love Lucy was one of many early sitcoms to blur the boundaries between real life and televised life for the explicit purpose of promoting the new television medium. Typically, family comedies included self-reflexive plots which revolved around the television set and its effects on the household. Spiegel has argued that television's first families were, above all else, families that owned television sets and thought quite a bit about the medium's place in their daily lives. Concurrently, many of these programs "acknowledged the theatrical artifice involved in representing a naturalistic picture of domesticity." As television strove to affirm itself as a natural element of the household, many early sitcom plots centered on characters watching television. In *The Burns and Allen Show*, the most reflexive of all sitcoms, George Burns and Gracie Allen "played themselves playing themselves as real-life performers who had a television show based on their lives as television stars." George, in particular, continually stepped out of his role in the family scene, reflecting on plot and representation. Spigel has described in detail one of the most self-reflexive episodes of the show:

> A 1952 episode took this to the extreme, basing its plot on a TV party that George and Gracie held for the producers of their show. While Gracie scuttled around the house "performing" her hostess chores, George sat with his network cronies, somehow miraculously watching himself on his own live television program. In the final scene, George turns to the home audience and smirks into the camera, calling attention to the plot's absurd premise.[40]

Like the *Burns and Allen Show*, *I Love Lucy* made ample use of this device, exploiting its plot line to this purpose. Between 1951 and 1955, there were at least twelve "TV" episodes on the show. In the classic "Lucy Does a TV Commercial," which aired in 1952, Lucy asks Ricky to let her appear on a TV special hosting his band as the show's pitch girl. Facing Ricky's stern refusal, she manages all the same to appear on the show after a good dose of deception and advertise a medicine called "Vitameatavegamin." Not knowing that it contains alcohol and it is meant to be taken once only a day, Lucy goes through several takes of the commercial, gets drunk, and spoils Ricky's show.

Suburban comedies such as *The Ruggles* or *Father Knows Best* frequently adopted self-refential elements in their narratives: as they "mirrored" family life by exposing the suburban household dealing with its everyday problems, they also reflected on television and their own conventionality. In an episode of *The Ruggles* entitled "Charlie's Lucky Day" (1950), in the middle of a tranquil, uneventful night at home, TV crews storm into the home, informing the protagonists that they are on the *Tender Delicious Raspberry Show* to receive a case of the sponsor's product and a check for $1,000. Although the Ruggles protest the invasion, the show goes on, to confirm that the Ruggles are indeed a television family. And as the final scene returns to the domestic doldrums of the show's opening, the artifice of naturalistic representation is revealed. By this point, however, the naturalistic picture of family life, as Spigel has observed, has a very different meaning, "since it seems only to highlight the artifice entailed in staging domesticity."[41] Rather than looking like a slice of life, this scene now seems blatantly theatrical, with the "actors" back in place as if nothing had happened.

As 1950s television expanded its fourth-wall audience viewpoint, it included constant interaction between the actors and the live audience – and, by proxy, with the audience at home – to highlight that the theatricality of self-display had become a significant part of social relations in postwar America. Often with the purpose of advertising consumer products, or filling in the audience about off-stage portions of the plot, the domestic space was often construed as "theatrical," with many industry publications insisting that "the family home may be most aptly described as a theater," where family and neighborly relations are staged and acted out. Players and spectators were "invited to visit the people in the theater next door," who welcomed viewers into "a simulated neighborhood where everyone was putting on a show, which was ultimately conducive to the display of sponsors' products."[42]

Television and the Red Scare

Current events were another area that rapidly drew the attention of broadcasters. Although technical and union issues delayed television's all-round presence in the news arena, the televising of the HUAC hearings during the early 1950s proved to be the ideal resonance chamber for both McCarthy and the medium: for the former, because TV gave national and dramatic voice to his red-baiting campaign; and for TV itself, because McCarthy gave it an immediate boost as a relevant medium.[43] Americans read less in general throughout the 1950s than previously and readily accepted television as a source of information on current events, although many criticized television's dubious trustworthiness: TV lacked the necessary independence for scrutinizing the truth, as many program sponsors found themselves in conflicts of interest when newscasts were involved; technical limitations in newscasting, with few newscrews and an ability to only cover predictable events, such as press conferences and political speeches, rather than breaking news, drastically curtailed the scope of the news; news analysis, which had been a longtime staple of radio news, was shunted aside by TV as "non-visual."[44]

A notable exception to the blandness of television news in 1950s was Edward R. Murrow's *See It Now*, which CBS transitioned from its radio predecessor *Hear it Now* in 1951. *See It Now* became so influential among newscasters that it remains to this day "the standard by which broadcast journalism is judged for its courage and commitment."[45] Following along the path paved by his wartime radio reporting, Murrow strongly emphasized the continuity between the old and the new medium, and brought his courage and commitment to television. Amid charges that it was threatening the audience/sponsor "balance" so central to television, Murrow took the tense political climate of the early part of the decade head-on, discussing nuclear proliferation, the frustration of the Korean War, and the consequences of the *Brown v. Board* decision[46] in the south of the country. Late in 1953, Murrow decided to take on the Red Scare, investigating a story centering on an Air Force Lieutenant, Milo Radulovich, who had been forced to resign from the U.S military based on two of his relatives' alleged radical leanings. Against the network's and the sponsor's (aluminum manufacturer Alcoa) attempts to sabotage the story (CBS refused to pay for newspaper advertising, crucial for its success, which Murrow and his producer Fred Friendly ended up paying out of their own pockets), Murrow brought the Radulovich story to the air with a promise to persevere in his campaign against anti-communist hysteria at home, which he voiced in his "tail" commentary to the program:

> Whatever happens in this whole area of the relationship between the individual and the state, we will do ourselves; it cannot be blamed upon [Soviet Premier] Malenkov, Mao Tse-tung or even our allies. It seems to us – that is, to Fred Friendly and myself – that it is a subject that should be argued about endlessly.[47]

Indeed Murrow went back to the subject, as he took senator Joseph McCarthy head-on in an episode that aired on March 9, 1954. The episode consisted of a compilation of recordings of McCarthy himself in action interrogating witnesses and making speeches, interrupted by only brief comments and a final piece by Murrow, who argued that the fault of the Red Scare lay not so much with McCarthy, but rather with the complacency of American society:

> As a nation we have come into our full inheritance at a tender age. We proclaim ourselves – as indeed we are – the defenders of freedom, what's left of it, but we cannot defend freedom abroad by deserting it at home. The actions of the junior Senator from Wisconsin have caused alarm and dismay amongst our allies abroad and given considerable comfort to our enemies, and whose fault is that? Not really his. He didn't create this situation of fear; he merely exploited it, and rather successfully. Cassius was right: "The fault, dear Brutus, is not in our stars but in ourselves ..." Good night, and good luck.[48]

The McCarthy programs set the stage for the televised hearings of the senator's dispute with the Army where, according to TV historian Erik Barnouw, "a whole nation watched him in murderous close-up – and recoiled."[49] The televised Army-McCarthy hearings would indeed strike the decisive blow to the senator's career.[50]

Some of the salient moments of *See it Now* are captured in George Clooney's *Good Night, and Good Luck*, a 2005 biopic written by Clooney and Grant Heslov. With skilful usage of black and white film stock and detailed re-creation of the 1950s ambiance, the film highlights a debate on media responsibility and celebrates the bygone days when television was committed to expose inequities and injustice. Barnouw has observed that "the Murrow documentaries helped to make television an indispensable medium," as few people "now dared to be without a television set, and few major advertisers dared to be unrepresented on the home screen."[51]

The Murrow documentaries also cemented the relationship between the U.S. political establishment and television: seeing it no longer as "foolish nuisance," many politicians soon came to realize television's potential. Richard Nixon's "checkers speech" of September 23, 1952, which actually predates the Murrow documentaries, is a famous example of early mastery of the TV medium for political advantage. Accused of accepting $18,000 in illegal campaign contributions (Nixon was running for the vice-presidency in Eisenhower's campaign against Adlai Stevenson), Nixon went on TV to rebut all charges with a speech that made television history. Denying all wrongdoing, Nixon claimed before the cameras that the only gift he ever received was a black and white little Cocker Spaniel, which his children had named Checkers. Then, he delivered his punch-line: "And you know, the kids, like all kids, loved the dog, and I just want to say this, right now, that regardless of what they say about it, we are going to keep it." By shifting the focus from illegal appropriation of funds to his sentimental coup-de-théatre portrayal of the wholesome American family playing in the yard brought an outpouring of public support which enabled Nixon not only to clear himself of the accusations but also brought final consent to the Eisenhower campaign.[52]

As the 1950s drew to a close, American television had reached full national coverage: there was now one TV set in most American homes and the three networks, ABC, NBC, and CBS had taken total control of the industry, whose core dynamic had by now been fully established – creating an audience to sell to a sponsor.

CHAPTER 5

Gray-Flannel-Suit Nation

> America constantly outdistances its interpreters.
> (David Riesman)

> I'm just a man in a gray flannel suit. I must keep my suit neatly pressed like anyone else, for I am a very respectable young man.
> (Sloan Wilson, *The Man in a Gray Flannel Suit*)

The reframing of American society after World War II – as it developed through the rise of television, the new affluence, the spreading of the suburbs as both geographic and cultural phenomenon – attracted from the outset the attention of commentators and opened a new season for sociology as both an academic discipline and a forum for public debate. The 1950s witnessed the emergence or, more precisely, the reshaping of the concept of mass society, according to values that are normally described as conformity and a middle-class ethos.[1] In the wake of more recent criticism, however, this book would like to take a more nuanced approach to the 1950s, one which should account for what sociologist Daniel Bell has defined, in his landmark book *The End of Ideology*, "the complex, richly striated social relations of the real world" in that decade.[2] Concurring that mass society in the American 1950s was a "striated" one, one that cannot be accounted for with the simplistic, stereotypical view of a conformist, etherized decade, this chapter will study how some of the leading cultural narratives of conformity in the decade were shaped.[3]

Conforming to the "Lonely Crowd"

In describing American society in the 1950s, breakthrough studies in the field of the social sciences are a necessary starting point. David Riesman's seminal book *The Lonely Crowd* (1948) opened up a whole new way of looking at postwar American society – and white adult males in particular – in an attempt to capture their changing and more elusive roles. A sociologist, lawyer, and educator, Riesman taught at the University of Chicago – which pioneered American urban sociology in the 1920s and 1930s – and at Harvard. Arguably one of the most influential publications of the twentieth century, *The Lonely Crowd* first introduced sociological concepts such as "the new middle class," "inner-directedness," and "other-directedness" to a wide audience.

Riesman's central argument was that, throughout the centuries, societies have developed three main human personality types, which he defined as "tradition-directed," "inner-directed," and "other-directed." Tradition-directed individuals – typical, Riesman argued, of agricultural societies – move along paths well defined by the preceding generations. A tradition-directed person conceives of himself not as an individual, but as part of a group – be it the family or the society at large. For him, self and group coincide, and values are respected as the result of long-established custom. The tradition-directed individual does not even contemplate the possibility of shaping his own destiny in terms of personal interest, as he is "not sufficiently psychologically separated from himself, his family or group to think in these terms."[4]

A later stage of social evolution, the inner-directed individual was the product of late nineteenth-century society, when capitalism and the protestant ethic pressured individuals to rely on themselves rather than on ancestors and family groups as a source of meaning and direction. Perfectly embodied in the venture capitalist of the Gilded Age, the inner-directed person favors rationality over superstition, as well as faith in one's own courage and potential. Inner-directed individuals, Riesman pointed out, are capable of achieving "a feeling of control over their lives, and see their children also as individuals with careers to make."[5] It was this historical phase that established "individualism" as a marker of Western civilization.

In yet another stage, as agrarian societies gave way to industrialized societies and material abundance and leisure expanded, people found themselves in a world both diffusely bureaucratized and "shrunken and agitated by the contact of races, nations and cultures," so that self-reliance and inner-directedness were "somewhat less necessary, if not altogether counterproductive."[6] Such change was the social force behind the emergence of the other-directed individual, whom Riesman believed to be the predominant postwar sociological type. The other-directed individual was the product of ever-expanding metropolises and the tertiary economy, whose requirements favored sensitivity to the immediate social setting rather than the echoes of past custom, as well as a higher attunement and tolerance to the feelings, wishes, and expectations of the people one encountered in the diverse situations of daily life.[7] Other-directedness is rooted in the transition from the "scarcity economy," that fueled "heavy capital accumulation" to the "abundance psychology" of modernity, characterized by "wasteful luxury consumption of leisure and of the surplus product."[8]

These three social types – the tradition-directed, the inner-directed, and the outer-directed individual – are, in Riesman's analysis, all present at the same time in advanced societies. However, Riesman believed that each epoch witnessed the prevalence of one type over the others. Population surges and technological explosion, notably during the Renaissance and in the nineteenth century, inspired the inner-directed quest for fame, power, truth, and beauty. In America, inner-directedness produced both the Gilded Age capitalist and the rugged frontiersman. Conversely, non-dynamic eras, in which technology was no longer the outcome of individual talent but rather a commodity for many, put the stress on conformity and acceptance. In post-World War II society, middle-class desires for domesticity, Cold War anxieties and consumer passivity drove society to conform: according to Riesman, this gave rise to other-directed individuals among the urban middle classes, thereby "affecting an increasing number of people in the metropolitan centers of the industrially advanced societies."[9] Writing at the dawn of the 1950s, Riesman appeared positive that the postwar era had spawned a direct shift in social attitudes, which he expected to further solidify in the rest of the decade:

> It seems appropriate to treat contemporary metropolitan America as our illustration of a society – so far, perhaps, the only illustration – in which other-direction is the dominant mode of insuring conformity. It would be premature, however, to say that it is already the dominant mode in America as a whole. But since the other-directed types are to be found among the young, in the larger cities, and among the upper income groups, we may assume that, unless present trends are reversed, the hegemony of other-direction lies not far off.[10]

Riesman's pioneering analysis of postwar America had far-reaching implications and was instrumental in shaping an understanding of 1950s culture as one primarily of conformity and diminishing individuality. Other-directedness, the term used by Riesman to define this tendency, was characteristic among the new middle class of bureaucrats and corporate employees – a social group sharing a tendency to rely on "[e]ducation, leisure, services," which went together "with an increased consumption of words and images from the new mass media of communication."[11] Riesman was among the first to understand that in a society where the second industrial revolution was focused on the middle class, leisure and the soft economy of media and communication prevailed.

Educating Other-Directedness: Dr. Benjamin Spock

As success and personal adaptation were no longer seen as a matter of individual achievement but rather of group conformity, more socialized behavior was required which encompassed an individual's whole existence – including childhood, which became in the 1950s a whole new arena of debate concerning behavioral changes. Childhood emerged as a delicate area of contention which affected both children and the adults responsible for their upbringing, involving discussions of whether to give up old standards of discipline in favor of more "permissive" child-rearing practices. Such a cultural shift, epitomized by the sudden postwar fame of Dr. Benjamin Spock – whose 1946 best-selling *The Common Sense Book of Baby and Child Care* revolutionized approaches to child-rearing by advocating an end to old-style, restrictive discipline, and called for the adoption of a new upbringing process centering on child needs and parental instincts – created a new framework where individuality came to be understood as a direct function of the surrounding peer group. As Spock warned, "children raised in loving families *want* to learn, *want* to conform, *want* to grow up."[12]

In his book, Spock prescribed a child-centered home in which mothers subordinated their interests not only for the sake of their husbands, but also for creating a loving environment for their children. Under the guise of a pedagogy aimed at developing independent, and positively-thinking individuals, Spock's vision pursued a conservative agenda, with an emphasis, Nancy Weiss has argued, "on getting along, avoiding confrontation, and pursuing a balanced life" that could "more easily lead to conformity."[13]

As with Spock, Riesman suggested that, in other-directed epochs, social conformity was taught from an early age, as parents exercised pressures on their children to seek their peers' approval rather than to find direction in inner morality: "under these new patterns [of child rearing] the peer-group becomes much more important to the child, while the parents make him feel guilty not so much about violation of inner standards as about failure to be popular or otherwise to manage his relations with [...] other children." The role of social and peer pressure on the individual became a decisive factor of social psychology. As the media reinforced the weight of such pressures, the range of "others" to which to compare one's behavior dramatically widened, and the number of those with whom one was acquainted came to include not only neighbors and friends, but also the virtual community of television. As other-directed individuals learned very early to "read" others as the main source of direction, the family ceased to be a closely-knit unit and source of meaning. Family became one of many agents of the wider social environment, one to which the other-directed individuals paid no special attention, since they were expected to feel "at home everywhere and nowhere, capable of a rapid and sometimes superficial intimacy with a response to everyone."[14]

"Oppressed but Cheerful:" Charles Wright Mills and the White Collar

Riesman was the most popular, but only one in a cohort of postwar public intellectuals who sensed a broad transformation in American society and institutions in the early years of the Cold War and whose writings focused on the rising middle class of bureaucrats and corporate employees of postwar America. Charles Wright Mills, a sociologist interested in the structures of power and class in the United States, mostly remembered for his 1956 book *The Power Elite,* and one of the most outspoken intellectuals of the time, expressed very keen concern as a staunch advocate of active political engagement and as a critic of non-committed academic research. In *White Collar* (1951), Mills contended that bureaucracies had overwhelmed and seriously compromised the individual city worker, robbing him of all independent thought and turning him into a sort of oppressed but "cheerful robot," alienated from the world because of his inability – or passive unwillingness – to affect or change it.[15] In the book, Mills argued that a significant transformation had taken place in American capitalism between the nineteenth and the mid-twentieth century, connected with a decided corporatization of labor which began in the wake of the Industrial Revolution and intensified in the first part of the twentieth century. If in the early part of the nineteenth century four-fifths of the population were self employed, that ratio fell to one in three by 1870, and further dwindled to one in five by 1940, when "[m]any of the remaining four-fifths of the people now work for the 2 or 3 percent of the population who own 40 or 50 percent of the private property in the United States."[16]

According to Mills, a new social class had arisen as a result of the concentration of capital in the hands of very few: a "white collar" workforce, which amounted to 750,000 individuals in 1870 and exceeded 12 million by 1940, for whom the benefits of class receded into the distance – a nation of employees "for whom private property has become out of range." Mills understood this process as responding to a shift in the nature of the skills demanded by capital in order to deal with an economy increasingly bent on abstraction – paper, money, and human resources – rather than on material production. In an economy where technology had "narrowed the stratum of workers needed for given volumes of output," thereby driving labor away from production, a new middle class of "masters of the commercial, professional, and technical relationships" had arisen that was well versed "at dealing with people transiently and impersonally."[17]

Mills believed that the problem of modern capitalism lay in the extraordinary increase of what he defined as "distributive occupations," i.e. jobs in the fields of trade, promotion, and advertising which drew more and more workers (up to one-fourth of the labor force) and whose middleman functions consisted in creating more new markets large enough to absorb the expanding production output.[18] Mills contended that capital and production were concentrated in the hands of very few big business conglomerates which, in turn, generated a form of "big government" intended to coordinate an ever more complex marketplace. In this process Mills saw the origin of bureaucracies which, in spite of their relationship with business or government, functioned as centers where "many men and women [...] plan, co-ordinate, and administer new routines for others," within a context of increasing specialization and ramification of corporate units.[19]

Crucially, in this new bureaucratic white-collar class, Mills saw the emergence of what can be defined as a "new proletariat:" as the skills employed by white-collar workers in distributing, co-ordinating, and promoting were "similar in form and required mentality" to those of the wage workers and were rooted, like wage labor, on owner-employee relationships, the new middle class looked to Mills more like an updated version of the working class than like an expansion of the moneyed and privileged industrial elite. At a time when suburbanization was opening avenues of homeownership for the average American, Mills insisted that white collars, precisely like wage workers, had "no serious expectations of propertied independence," hence little hope to reach the other side of the social divide. This represented a crucial shift in understanding the just-as-crucial concept of the new middle class: whereas the old, nineteenth-century middle class was one that could aspire to "property," the new white-collar middle class did not share such privileges. Amid the public hype celebrating America's new economic status, Mills argued that white collars did not form one coherent horizontal class, since there was no "central, positive *function* that can define them [as class]."[20]

Mills' diagnosis of 1950s American capitalism was ultimately gloomy: "the occupational structure of the United States," he maintained, was being "slowly reshaped as a gigantic corporate group," and was depending not only on "the pulling of autonomous markets and the pushing of technology," but also on "an 'allocation of personnel' from central points of control."[21] In other words, individual autonomy and self-direction had to be severely compromised to fit into the intricate interdependence demanded by the big industrial conglomerates.[22] This threefold subordination was rendered all the more hopeless as Mills claimed that consciousness and agency in the occupational change was only the prerogative of those in charge of controlling such a transition.[23] Commenting on Mills' work, David Riesman did not overlook *White Collar*'s "drab mood," in remarking that it lacked hope and presented readers with "a verdict on modern industrial society not many steps from Orwell's *1984*." According to Riesman, Mills failed to acknowledge the white collar class as possessing any "ethnic, religious, or other cultural dye," thereby implicitly denying the new middle class the very possibility of action and an active role in their work.[24] Mills shared Riesman's scepticism toward the postwar other-directed middle class, seeing a society mired in alienation and brought to the abyss of hopelessness. The Marxist edge on his analysis of America's new affluence struck an eerie note amidst the generalized boom-era enthusiasm.

The Culture of the Organization

Published in 1956, William H. Whyte's *The Organization Man* soon became another milestone in the sociological effort to define the transformations of post-World War II American society. A committed analyst of urban life, Whyte had been an author for *Fortune* magazine on topics of corporate culture and the suburban middle class. By drawing on extensive interviews with executives of large corporations such as General Electric and Ford, *The Organization Man* focused on how America's postwar urban transformations were closely connected to the reshaping of the country's middle class. A bestseller, Whyte's book decisively pointed out the continuity between economic growth and suburbanization, arguing that such growth was specifically centered around the creation of a new suburban middle class which was less rooted, more eager to conform and readier to consume than its predecessors.

Somewhat resembling Riesman's other-directed individual, Whyte's "organization man" described those members of the American middle class "who have left home, spiritually as well as physically, to take the vows of organization life." For the purpose of his analysis and for illustrating the pervasiveness of what he called a new "social ethic," Whyte focused on the new middle-class suburbs, which he called "packaged villages that have become the dormitory of the new generation of organization men." In Whyte's description, the American suburbs catered to a specific sub-class of individuals: people who identified themselves with the corporate world and shared the problems of collective work – thus functioning as the quintessential embodiments of the new society. It was these new individuals who were developing a veritable "social ideology," based on an unstoppable, mechanized process of production (the "treadmill"), which was subjecting the individual to the vilification of constant competition to succeed ("the rat-race"), as well as the overall realization of one's inability to control one's own personal direction.[25]

The men of the organization, according to Whyte, shared and redefined, although in a problematic way, the concept that sociologist Max Weber had described in the earlier part of the century as the "protestant ethic," a cornerstone of American culture which was rooted in the "pursuit of individual salvation through hard work, thrift and competitive struggle." In describing what he named the new "social ethic," Whyte argued that the three pillars of the traditional protestant ethic were crumbling. The first pillar, thrift, was undermined as the organization man handed that very precept over to the "financial and personnel departments of his organization:" as thrift is incompatible with consumerism, the man of the organization "not only has to persuade people to buy more but persuade them out of any guilt feelings they might have for following his advice." In a similar vein, the pillar of "hard work" was ultimately seen as compromised, as consumerism called for improved life conditions, which in turn implied increased possibilities for leisure. Split between leisure and "the Puritan insistence on hard, self-denying work," which is as much a requirement of capitalism as leisure is its by-product, Whyte saw the organization man as taking on the collectivized way of work based on team and committee – the extreme opposite of the far-off rugged individualism of the industrial entrepreneur of the American Gilded Age and the third pillar of the protestant ethic. Within this context, "the man of the organization resorts to the discourse of individualism as a strategy for coming to terms with the newly-emerged collectiveness," in an attempt to keep at bay the very idea of being trapped in a collective society "as pervading as any ever dreamed of."[26]

Although employing a different vocabulary, Whyte was substantially in agreement with Riesman in arguing that American individualism was nothing more than an ideological layering which disguised a transformation of American society towards the reduction of the individual to a pawn in a structure of production that emphasized collective work (the "team") and the logic of the corporation. Whyte did not mince words and admonished that harbingers of socialism, demonized in Cold War rhetoric, were creeping through America's new collectivized order: the organization man redefined social ethic in such a way as to make "morally legitimate the pressures of society against the individual."[27] In so doing, he endorsed a sense and an idea of belonging which transferred the act of creativity to the "group."

Unlike Mills and, to a lesser extent, Riesman, Whyte sounded nevertheless quite optimistic about the fate of postwar American society. He considered America as intrinsically dynamic, regardless of its several faults, the main one lying not in the "organization" itself, but rather in "our worship of it."[28] In an article that appeared one year prior to *The Organization Man*, Whyte had been so upbeat about the 1950s as to argue that one of the outcomes of the new organization culture was the "displacement of the old class criterion."[29] In that article, he claimed that the 1950s had brought along a new understanding of class, in which individuals come together in a horizontal grouping, rather than according to Marx's classic vertical vision – a new order that Whyte saw instrumental in alleviating difference. If Whyte's optimistic view is a world apart from Mills' much more dire vision of the class pyramid in the age of corporate capitalism, it joined other voices ushering in the "classless prosperity" of the age.

One of these voices was Russell Lynes' article "High-brow, Low-brow, Middle-brow," which appeared in *Life* magazine in 1949 and helped popularize this idea of obsolescence of class. Presenting a striking two-page chart depicting the cultural tastes of the different "brows" in ten categories ranging from furniture to entertainment, Lynes claimed that social classes were obsolete: people now chose their pleasures and consumer goods strictly on the basis of individual taste.[30] And although Packard had drawn a rather bleak portrait of "taste" in postwar American society in *The Hidden Persuaders*, when he argued that taste lay totally at the mercy of the unscrupulous "depth men" of Madison Avenue, Whyte claimed that values were coming together in the "second great melting pot" of the American suburbs.[31] Along with conformity to total corporate control, the organization society seemed to have brought the ultimate American Dream to fruition – the achievement of that highly-mythicized "classless society" in which, as the Bureau of Labor Statistics was concurrently claiming, "the distinction between economic levels in the ownership of tangibles is diminishing, [thus] breaking down the barriers of community and class."[32]

Narratives of Other-Directedness:
The Man in the Gray Flannel Suit and *High Noon*

Literature and film in the 1950s claimed a less optimistic vision of organization life and of the consumption society. One novel and one film in particular confronted the problematic role of American males *vis-à-vis* the demands of suburban consumerism and other-directed individuality.

A best seller of the decade, Sloan Wilson's *The Man in the Gray Flannel Suit* (1955) studied its protagonist Tom Rath's conflictual adaptation to corporate conformity and consumerist ambitions, both of which threatened older norms of masculine hegemony and inner-direction. The book was published in the wake of Riesman and Mills' prognoses on the dangers of conformity in American life, particularly as the modern corporation became bigger as well as an increasingly important force in American life. It responded to a debate that emerged in America focusing on the question of whether, despite the significant and dramatic increase in the standard of living, the new white-collar society was turning into something of a trap and whether the greater material benefits it promised and delivered were being exchanged for freedom and individuality.

In the novel, Tom Rath is fighting – one full decade after the end of the war in which he served as a "citizen soldier" – the personal demons that have plagued him since his return. Over the years, his interior discomfort has disconnected him further and further from a fast-changing world where new concerns with consumption and prosperity have replaced old values such as integrity and decency, which Tom continues to hang on to. Holding a corporate job, he refuses to play by the rules of the "rat-race." At home, he feels a strong commitment as provider but resents his wife's material concerns. In 1950s America, Tom is the odd man out, a remnant of a bygone past.

Tom's corporate life revolves around his new job as public relations specialist for a media conglomerate (he is a ghost writer to the company's president) – a job that his wife, Betsy, has pushed him to seek in her desire for upward mobility. This desire Tom does not share: he would prefer his "absolutely safe spot" with his previous employer, the only motivation driving him to interview for a new post being to please his ambitious wife with a higher family income, as he explains to her early in the novel:

> "I heard about a new job today," Tom said. "Public United Broadcasting Corporation."
> "How much does it pay?"
> "Probably a good deal more than I'm getting now."
> There was an instant of silence before she said, "are you going to try for it?"
> "I might."

Betsy finished her drink and poured herself another. "I've never thought of you as a public-relations man," she said soberly. "Would you like it?"
"I'd like the money."

Family life for Tom is in no way easier, as Betsy pressures him to overcome his limited ambition and he struggles between worries about his children's obsession with violence and death and his unresolved wartime past, which prevents him from fully embracing the other-directed ethos of postwar civilian life.[33] Housing arrangements are another area of concern. Betsy hates their suburban home because it smells of "defeat." In a suburb populated by individuals described by William Whyte as the "new transients," life is no more than a stopover towards the next rung on the social ladder:

> Almost all the houses were occupied by couples with young children, and few people considered Greentree Avenue a permanent stop – the place was just a crossroads where families waited until they could afford to move on to something better.[34]

On Greentree Avenue, community life revolved around dreams and concerns for material betterment: "budgets were frankly discussed," public celebration of "increases in salary was common," and "the biggest parties of all were moving out parties, given by those who finally were able to buy a bigger house." *The Man in the Gray Flannel Suit* made it obvious that domesticity was no respite from the stress of civilian readjustment, never the "happy place" that public rhetoric was so profusely advertising: "On Greentree Avenue contentment was an object of contempt," and Betsy is the perfect embodiment of that malaise.[35]

Betsy's discontent revolves around her anger at her husband, whom she perceives as sitting too comfortably in his middle-class humdrum: "You plan to live the rest of our lives *here*?" she asks Tom, whom she resents for no longer being the man who had left her to go to war. She accuses him of being "spoiled" and "licked:"

> In spite of all you did in the war, you're not willing to go out and fight for what you want. You came back from the war, and you took an easy job, and we both bellyached all the time because you didn't get more money. And what's more, you're a coward. You're afraid to risk a god-damn thing!

Betsy would like a more civilized life, with less television, more family contact, and, above all, more affluence: "no more hotdogs and hamburgers for dinner," but "stews and casseroles, and roasts and things."[36]

For his part, Tom is plagued by his inner-directed drive for traditional values – honesty, decency, thrift – at a time when the world around him rather prizes other-directed performance and consumption. The eponymous film version of the novel, directed by Nunnally Johnson in 1956, adds an interesting dialogue in this context. In one of the film's early scenes, after he is alerted by his friend Bill Hawthorne to the spot opening up in public relations, Tom is attracted by the potential salary increase the new job would offer, although he is unsure about his professional qualifications for the new post, and candidly admits "I don't know anything about PR." "Who does?" his friend rebuts. "But you have a clean shirt. You bathe every day. That's all there is to it." Tom is ill at ease in a world whose sole requirement seems to be "to get along" and conform. One evening, as Tom reveals to Betsy the ethos of organization culture, his restlessness and cynicism in face of this new America come into full view:

> There is a standard operating procedure for this sort of thing [...] It's a little like reading fortunes. You make a lot of highly qualified contradictory statements and keep your eyes on [your boss'] face to see which ones please him. That way you can feel your way along, and if you're clever, you can always end up by telling him exactly what he wants to hear.[37]

In spite of its critique of 1950s conformity, *The Man in the Gray Flannel Suit* appears unable to resolve itself or choose among viable alternatives. The burden of the past weighs heavily on the postwar social readjustment of American males. As such, they appear out of place in a world fully focused on getting ahead. The organization society adds further complications, as the demands of the workplace appear at times incompatible with those of outer-directed social conformity. The novel (and the movie) amply articulate such ambivalence: if suburban life is geared towards allowing families to spend more time together, its material comforts demand higher income expectations, which only more work and less family togetherness can deliver.

Faced with yet another chance for professional advancement in the second part of the novel, a new position that would keep him even more away form home, Tom resolves to put family first, as he reminds Hopkins, his boss: "I have to be home with my family this evening. Remember those nine-to-five fellows you were talking about? I'm afraid I'm one of them." Responding to Tom, Hopkins presents his reluctant version of the protestant ethic:

> Big successful businesses just aren't built by men like you, nine to five and home and family. You live on them but you never build one. Big successful businesses are built by men like me, who give everything they've got to it, and live it, body and soul, lift it up regardless of anybody or anything else. Without men like me there wouldn't be any big successful businesses. *(Pause)* My mistake was in being one of those men.

While the novel seems to pursue two parallel, and conflicting, agendas, "very quick to criticize the conformist ethos of contemporary business, and its 'organization' underbelly – but also quick to diagram how inadvertently easy success in that material and vocational world can be, once one has attuned oneself properly to the social surroundings," the film version tries to bridge that ambivalence in presenting Hopkins as a repentant tycoon, the personification of inner-directedness who values financial accomplishment over domestic fulfillment but has come to bitterly suffer from that outcome.[38] As a *Hollywood Reporter* review of the film has argued, *The Man in the Gray Flannel Suit* opts for "moral decency" over "success," and this resolution endorses Tom's choice of his family over his career, an ideological mediation which allows the film to transform Tom Rath from a problematic leftover of inner-directed culture in postwar society to the presentation of the exemplary middle-class domesticated male breadwinner, whose (w)Rath is sublimated into a more benign version of postwar conformity.

A very popular area of mass culture in the 1950s, Western narratives also participated in the decade's debate over the merits of social conformity, within the framework of their containment-related agenda.[39] A favorite genre both on television and in movie theaters, the Western appealed to most segments of the audience. Centering on the frontiersman, the paradigmatic champion of inner-directedness, Western narratives also proved instrumental in critiquing the other-directed mood of the age. The ideological implications of this approach to the genre were fully articulated in Stanley Kramer's production of *High Noon* (1952), directed by Fred Zinnemann and written by blacklisted screenwriter Carl Foreman. In *High Noon*, the frontier acts as a proxy for a discussion on the status of the American male in a changing society.

In the film, ageing Hollywood star Gary Cooper plays Will Kane, marshal of Hadleyville, who is about to retire to please his young wife. His plan to retreat into the privacy of married life is suddenly aborted as Frank Miller, an outlaw Kane had formerly brought to justice, returns to the town in order to seek revenge against him. Concerned that his own life will never be safe while Miller is alive, and that his lifelong law-keeping effort will be wasted if Miller regains control over the community, Kane chooses to face the impending danger and tries to raise a citizen posse to help him take on the enemy. His former deputies refuse to help, choosing to conform to the general sentiment: there is prospect of new business coming to town and gunfight in the streets of Hadleyville would make it seem "just like another wide open town," stalling economic growth. Kane has no choice but to take on Miller alone and, aided by his "converted" wife who has embraced a gun against her non-violent Quaker beliefs, kills Miller in the film's central gunfight scene and saves the people of Hadleywille. At the end, Kane contemptuously drops his badge in the dust at the mayor's feet, to protest the community's refusal to back him up, and rides out of town.

The film has been generally interpreted as an allegory of Hollywood's surrender to McCarthyism, in which Miller's return to town functions as a metaphorical way of identifying McCarthyism with a returning totalitarianism fed by social complacency, this time made worse by the country's economic upturn and people's consequent unwillingness to challenge the status quo. Its formal structure, based on a narrative device by which each minute in the story, punctuated by recurring shots of the town clock, corresponds to one minute in real life, leading up to the central gunfight at noon, adds urgency to the drama and subliminally suggests to the viewers that the "return" is impending and the danger is actual and current, and not just fictional speculation. In his classic study of the Western genre, Richard Slotkin has elaborated on the film's guiding metaphor, suggesting that "the same people who in an earlier and less prosperous time had risen up to defeat the enemy have now grown too comfortable or complacent to risk their lives and fortunes for the public good."[40] In a similar vein, others have seen the film as an allegory of blacklisting, among them John Wayne, who strongly disliked the film, which he defined as "the most un-American thing I have ever seen in my whole life."[41] Particularly revolting to Wayne was the sequence in which Kane rips off his badge and throws it on the ground: "That was like belittling a Medal of Honor," Wayne commented in an interview.[42]

The film's direct assault on McCarthyism was not only suggested by its screenwriter's radical leanings, but openly confirmed by Foreman, which makes the choice of Gary Cooper to play the film's hero, Will Kane, something of an irony.[43] A conservative Hollywood veteran who had been a founder of the Motion Pictures Association of America and had appeared in front of the HUAC as a friendly witness, Cooper was known in Hollywood for turning down "quite a few scripts because I thought were tinged with communist ideas."[44] This has led some commentators to challenge the movie's actual ideological positioning. Likewise, I would like to suggest that the issues of conformity addressed in the film make it both a warning of totalitarian danger and a discussion of a society losing its inner-directed drive. By framing its positive hero at the polar opposite of a complacent society which refuses to take action against obvious danger for fear of jeopardizing its material well being, the film appears even more concerned with critiquing postwar other-directedness. Because Kane acts, as Slotkin has well argued, on the ideological premise that "the defense of civilization is more important than the procedures of democracy," *High Noon* exposes the dangers of social conformity and predicts that it might lead to loss of freedom.[45] A cultural text that raises the question "of how strongly the private sense of right and wrong – and of personal honor – can resist the tyranny of the majority," as well as an indictment of the dangers of other-directedness, *High Noon* extols the virtues of rugged frontier individualism versus the vices of a conformist society.[46] Kane reluctantly serves justice alone, yet is prepared to do so for his own and the common good.

Crisis in Masculinity

Riesman's intimations of an other-directed individuality, Whyte's critique of the "organization man," Wilson's "gray flannel suits," and the other texts discussed so far in this chapter all seem to converge into a powerful critique of Fordist masculinity, by reflecting on the way in which the imaginary of the new suburban white collar was being shaped by pressing Cold War demands. A 1954 humor piece in *Life* magazine entitled "The New American Domesticated Male" used a series of cartoons to show the other-directed American male's incipient fascination with domesticity; and a 1958 series of articles in *Look* magazine entitled "The Decline of the American Male" pointed to economic and demographic data indicative of women's "domination" of men.[47]

In his study of masculinity in the 1950s, cultural historian James Gilbert has argued that the postwar years were "unusual (although not unique) for their relentless and self-conscious preoccupation with masculinity," generated by an emerging conflict between an assumed norm of masculinity in Western societies and new forms of masculinity based upon notions of domestic and workplace companionship and cooperation which were developing in those years.[48] In the 1950s men grew anxious and insecure about their role and expectations within the culture. Although the myth that subordinated women in the social hierarchy granted men power, both economic and social, their submission to the organization society placed them in a role of subservience: at work, they were expected to display loyalty and dependence, not unlike the role expected of wives in the domestic realm. Within the domestic realm, new expectations of males to participate in household chores and in the children's upbringing also shaped a new imaginary of male roles as subordinate, or at least analog, to those of women. Consequently, "men, like women, chose to hem themselves into a narrow social space" which, if not a genuinely stable world, gave them "the illusion of stability."[49]

Gilbert has argued that although causes of masculine crisis have been typically located in increasing participation and leadership by women in social spheres previously dominated by men (such as education, specific employment domains, religion) and in an overall "feminization of culture" (centring on the adoption of women's values and tastes in the arts, media mass culture, and consumption), intimations of a presumed masculine decline criss-crossed discourses of male hegemony and masculinity triumphant. Male uncertainty was quite evident in men's ambiguity toward their sexual roles: although biologist Alfred Kinsey had found in his groundbreaking study *Sexual Behavior in the Human Male*, published in 1948 and generally known as the *Kinsey Report*, that diverse sexual orientations were common in more than one third of the American population, homosexuality remained a social stigma in the 1950s, which resulted in varying degrees of violence towards homosexuals and in laws that condoned that violence by labeling homosexuality a crime.[50]

From Riveter to Nurturer: Women in the 1950s

Within the changing social landscape of the 1950s, the role of women was just as problematic as that of men.[51] Many sociologists saw the transformations in women's roles in the decade as directly related, and in opposition to, the major changes that took place after World War I: in the Roaring Twenties, after decades of feminist struggle, women gained social and economic independence by entering professions, working outside of the home, participating in cultural and political life and receiving university degrees. In 1920 the Nineteenth Amendment was added to the U.S. Constitution, granting women the right to vote.

That atmosphere of growing opportunities for women had suddenly come to a halt in the 1930s, when the depression reversed most of those advances: as men found it suddenly difficult to fulfill their role as sole breadwinners, women had to take on low-paying jobs to help their families make ends meet. During the Great Depression, women went back to work because of need, and not because of choice. With the beginning of World War II, things changed once again, as an unprecedented number of women moved into the workplace to replace men at every level, from manufacturing to management. The predicament of working women during the war years has been the subject of extensive scholarship, much of which has focused on legions of "Rosie the Riveters" entering the workforce to support the war effort. Still a matter of temporary expediency, women's work during the war years – no matter how widespread – did not alter social perceptions of female subordination to male authority: in a famous line in Michael Curtiz's *Casablanca* (1942), Ingrid Bergman whispers to Humphrey Bogart "You'll have to do the thinking for both of us."[52]

Wartime employment for women was characterized by deep ambivalence: although women's work had become a necessity dictated by the war effort, many wartime commentators expressed alarm that employment of women outside the home would generate marital friction. The U.S. government was particularly torn on the issue: on the one hand, it repeatedly told women that victory could not be achieved without their entry into the labor force; on the other, it stood earnestly by its belief that "now, as in peacetime, a mother's primary duty is to her home and children."[53] Women's wartime work was planned as temporary from the beginning. Moreover, Maureen Honey has argued that wartime working women were specifically "drawn from homes in which wives did not need to work and therefore would leave the labor market at the war's end" – an attitude that left women in the perpetual limbo of unachieved ambitions while official orthodoxy described women as "gladly" willing to "quit riveting and [return] home at the war's end."[54]

In the postwar years, attitudes towards working women remained just as ambivalent. If on the one hand public rhetoric extolled the role of women as homemakers, on the other more women joined the workforce in the 1950s than ever before. Public rhetoric depicted working women mostly as negligent mothers and a menace to their husbands' careers and to family stability. Books such as Farnham and Lundberg's *Modern Women: The Lost Sex* (1947) convincingly spread the notion according to which working women would provoke a disgraceful confusion of gender roles, by which males would become feminized and children would grow up in such disarray that they may end up being homosexual. No such confusion, however, took place when it came to defining careers for working women, as typical female jobs included occupations such as clerks or "demonstrators," and women's wages lagged significantly behind men's. In the postwar years, media, schools, and therapists began disseminating the notion that happiness was dictated by an individual's "proper functioning," with movies and popular psychology relentlessly emphasizing, as Stephanie Coontz has shown, "the dreadful things that happened when women became more interested in careers than marriage or men resisted domestic conformity."[55] Promoted by books, magazines and television shows, this "mock-Victorian vision of life" of mom the homemaker and dad the breadwinner, unwaveringly standing by their traditional roles, was transformed into a prescriptive set of rules to which relations between sexes should conform. This was a predetermined social vision which most Americans chose to follow without questioning its core assumptions and which relied on a sexual bias in which women and men had characteristics so different as to appear almost members of separate species.[56]

A woman's guiding principle was that of the nurturer: she was wife, mother, and homemaker. Her self-fulfillment came from childbearing and serving other people. Men were the breadwinners, programmed to work out of the home and concentrate on their own success. If, on the one hand, women were described as irrational, emotional, gentle, obedient, cheerful, dependent, men were, conversely, represented as rational, individualistic, unemotional, solid, and aggressive. In *Modern Women: The Lost Sex*, Farnham and Lundberg argued that modern women were unhappy and uncertain precisely because they had neglected their womanly roles, i.e. their natural state.

Also in the realm of sexuality, women were endowed with very specific roles: lovemaking had to be heterosexual, between married people, and it was the woman's responsibility to preserve her chastity until marriage. Sexuality was man-centered: in 1957, Hannah Lees claimed in the *Reader's Digest* that "what every husband needs [is] simply, good sex, uncomplicated by the worry of satisfying the woman." A woman's sexual satisfaction was regarded as sheer frivolity, because she was expected, in Lees' sharp turn of phrase, to make "love a substitute for desire," or to sublimate sexual desire into desire for motherhood.[57] *Modern Woman* magazine claimed that in order to be fully satisfactory to a woman, the sexual act had to depend on the "desire to be a mother."[58] And whenever female sexuality became the subject of media discussion, it was mostly within the context of questioning the quality of female pleasure, with lengthy debates on the difference between acceptable orgasm (vaginal orgasm) vs. unacceptable orgasm (clitoral orgasm).[59]

In the same way that society expected women to curb their libido, it also expected them to tone down their brains. Education for women was essentially regarded as a waste of time; and those women going to college were strongly encouraged to focus on homemaking classes above anything else. In *Educating our Daughters*, one of the books at the forefront of the debate against education for women, Lynn White, Jr., president of Mills College, a women's college in the San Francisco area, declared that higher learning was harmful to women, or at best irrelevant, and reported "rumors that the divorce rate of home economics majors is greatly below that of college women as a whole."[60] Campaigns of this type produced visible results: in the 1950s women made up a far smaller percentage of college students than in the 1920s.[61]

Defining Womanhood on Daytime Television

In the insulated world of the home, television contributed to reinforcing the established definition of womanhood. Lynn Spigel has analyzed the way in which television in the 1950s intervened in shaping gender roles in American society and the way it drew on those roles to establish its round-the-clock presence in the American household. As the postwar suburban home became a site of female labor, television adapted its programming to accompany women's daytime domestic routines. Spiegel has suggested that 1950s television positioned itself within a general pattern of everyday life where work and leisure merged: constantly addressing them as housewives, television approached women with "a notion of spectatorship that was inextricably intertwined with their useful labor at home."[62]

In its infancy, television worked hard to identify how much disruption it could bring into a housewife's work schedule. Before 1950, advertisers were reluctant to buy daytime commercial slots assuming that, unlike radio, the more disruptive nature of television would work against its overall affirmation as medium of mass culture. In the early 1950s, stations tried to address the household vs. TV conflict by producing shows advertised to be pleasurable "as much for listening as for watching."[63] As women's magazines began promoting daytime television viewership, they specifically addressed the gap between the home's postwar identification as place of labor and television's inherent leisurely nature. These ads suggested that "television viewing could be conducted in a state of distraction" and that "the housewife could accomplish her chores in a state of 'utopian forgetfulness,' as she moved freely between her work and the act of watching television."[64]

On several shows, hosts explicitly urged housewives not to stop doing what they were doing. The first format to fully cater to the difficult, inattentive daytime audience was the soap opera, a perfect fit for women's viewing pattern: with minimal action and very low visual interest, the "soap" allowed housewives to listen in while working in another room. Another popular daytime format was the segmented variety show (NBC's *Today*, which premiered in January 1952 with host David Garroway was a prime example of this format), which allowed entry and exit into the text according to its discrete narrative units, derived in form and style from the popular press, in particular women's magazines and the women's pages.

In spite of the broadcasters' efforts, female integration into the unified "family circle" of television spectatorship remained problematic, as women's participation in the dynamics of the unified family was at all times contested by the competing demands of her domestic labor.[65] As women labored to "[shape] their moods and demeanor to their conceptions of proper wifely behavior," they also struggled to accept the division of labor upon which suburban life was predicated as well as the "feminine mystique" that was shaping their social roles.[66]

The Feminine Mystique

By mid-decade, a malaise was creeping through the ranks of American society: magazines were frequently representing women as suffering from neuroses and depression, often as a consequence of divorce, abortion or alcoholism.[67] When writer and feminist activist Betty Friedan published the results of research she had conducted at the turn of the decade, "hundreds of thousands, if not millions, of women in the United States" were awakened to possibilities beyond housekeeping and child rearing.[68] Published in 1963, *The Feminine Mystique* was a cultural breakthrough. It played a pivotal role in the rebirth of feminism in the U.S. and is widely regarded as one of the most influential non-fiction works of the twentieth century, a crucial exploration of the rationale behind, and the consequences of, the rhetoric of femininity in the American 1950s.[69]

Originating from a questionnaire that the author sent in 1957 to former college friends (Betty Friedan had attended Smith College, an elite women's college in Massachusetts), *The Feminine Mystique* discussed the general unease with women's lives as it emerged from the responses to the questionnaire. Friedan coined a phrase to describe this sense of unease – a phrase now ingrained in twentieth-century American intellectual history – "the problem that has no name." This problem, Friedan argued, affected many of the women who were apparently fully immersed in America's middle-class consensus: affluent, with large and apparently healthy families, living in spacious, comfortable homes. Friedan described the problem as a "buried, unspoken [...] sense of dissatisfaction" deriving from a so-called "feminine mystique," a constructed beliefs system that required women to find identity and meaning in their lives through wifehood and motherhood. Friedan came to believe that this generalized depression stemmed from images of femininity generated in the newly-idealized suburban lifestyle, "those pretty pictures of the American suburban housewife," and quickly passed on to all women. However glamorous this kind of life was made to appear, Friedan contended, this fabricated image of femininity ultimately brought women to ask themselves "the silent question – 'Is this all?'"[70]

According to Friedan, the roots of the problem lay in a society that imposed a specific image for women to follow and that publicized education and professional achievement for women as undesirable, while at the same time celebrating women's "natural" role as nurturers and companions. Women, wrote Friedan,

> learned that truly feminine women do not want careers, higher education, political rights – the independence and the opportunities that the old-fashioned feminists fought for [...] A thousand expert voices applauded their femininity, their adjustment, their new maturity. All they had to do was devote their lives from earliest girlhood to finding a husband and bearing children.[71]

This postwar feminine model became such an unquestioned norm that everything about women revolved around the expectation and reinforcement of that role: "interior decorators were designing kitchens with mosaic murals and original paintings, for kitchens were once again the center of women's lives. Home sewing became a million-dollar industry. Many women no longer left their homes, except to shop, chauffeur their children, or attend a social engagement with their husbands." For women with responsibilities of wifehood and motherhood, work outside the home was no longer an option: "Girls were growing up in America without ever having jobs outside the home. In the late 1950s, a sociological phenomenon was suddenly remarked: a third of American women now worked, but most were no longer young and very few were pursuing careers."[72]

A constellation of domestic must-do chores defined a woman's daily routine and her typical day was fragmented "as she rushes from dishwasher to washing machine to telephone to dryer to station wagon to supermarket, and delivers Johnny to the Little League field, takes Janey to dancing class, gets the lawnmower fixed and meets the 6:45."[73] A notion of "unfemininity" developed as a counterimage, depicting all those activities that did not conform to the generalized norm as socially and culturally unacceptable: using brain power at college, or even using life-saving medicines with potential "de-feminizing side-effects," began to be questioned as appropriate behavior for the healthy American woman. If something was wrong with a woman, this never lay with the norm regulating her behavior, but rather with the woman herself. If a woman had a problem, "she knew that something must be wrong with her marriage, or with herself" and talking about it was virtually impossible, because "even the psychoanalysts had no name for it."[74]

The problem, argued Friedan, was so widespread that, by the end of the 1950s, it came to erode that very same myth of American familial bliss, as "a number of psychiatrists stated that, in their experience, unmarried women patients were happier than married ones."[75] As the suburban home had turned into a "comfortable concentration camp" which fostered "passivity, softness, boredom" for children and unsatisfying sex and false promises of abundance for their mothers, Friedan proposed "A New Life Plan for Women," calling on women to pierce the feminine mystique by combining marriage and family with "a commitment to profession and politics."[76]

Discussions of society in the American 1950s seemed to concur on a general trend towards conformity to the status quo, a national tendency to regroup and create a common front against pervading Cold War-era anxieties of national and individual vulnerability. Men's roles appeared to be particularly at stake in the social drive to conform, as both academic and popular sociology (including fiction and film) seemed to suggest: inquiries into the changing nature of American society appeared to constantly identify a crisis of masculinity, be it in the arena of the nation's new "team work" agenda or in the domestic sphere of new marital and familial roles. Likewise, women found themselves under significant stress within the strict requirements of middle-class conformity. As a vast and widely-read literature emerged around social and cultural conformity (and especially suburban life and mass culture), fundamental elements in those narratives were fears of a masculine decline, the specters of female alienation, and the viability of the solutions proposed to uphold the middle class consensus. In the next three chapters, I will look at crucial voices that took exception to that consensus.

CHAPTER 6
Beats, Rebels and the Other 1950s

> The wheel has come full circle, and now America has become the protector of Western civilization, at least in a military and economic sense. Obviously, this overwhelming change involves a new image of America. Politically, there is a recognition that the kind of democracy which exists in America has an intrinsic and positive value [...] If [however] a reaffirmation and rediscovery of America is under way, can the tradition of critical non-conformism [...] be maintained as strongly as ever?
> (*Partisan Review*, "Our Country and Our Culture," 1952)

> We've stopped trying to teach [youths] how to live. Instead, we're asking *them* how they think *we* should live.
> (*Cosmopolitan*, 1956)

Emerging Identitarian Discourses

When Viking Press finally decided to publish Jack Kerouac's novel *The Beat Generation* in September 1957, not before renaming it *On the Road*, they chose to market the book as a *Bildungsroman*, a novel about American youths' unceasing quest for identity outside the confines of the 1950s middle-class consensus. To make this point, the copy on the original dust jacket evoked a postwar group "roaming America in a wild, desperate search for *identity* and purpose, [that] became known as 'The Beat Generation.'"[1] The novel's immediate success was proof that Kerouac had identified an emerging powerful social force of individuals seeking respite from materialism and generalized conformity and who felt that America had come to exert a restraining force on the individual freedom of its citizens.[2]

In the book publisher's view, the affirmation of beat culture in the second half of the 1950s was framed within the dilemma of identity in postwar America, a concern that – as I will discuss in this chapter – lay at the root of larger Cold War discourses of nation, gender, and race. In a historical era marked by prevailing indications of social conformity, parallel discourses of identity, setting themselves precisely in opposition to those notions, emerged forcefully.[3] While recent interpretations of 1950s culture have begun to give heed to this powerful area of "difference," more traditional and nostalgia-laden accounts of the 1950s have typically tended to ignore such concerns.[4]

In *Rebels*, Leerom Medovoi has contended that "identity" first became a word freighted with political meaning precisely during the early years of the Cold War, when it came to signify "the achievement of a self-made and self-governing personality," which was "equally vital to individual persons as they approached adulthood and to collectivities as they developed into sovereign nations or peoples."[5] A trope for "adulthood," identity became, in the early Cold War years, an operative term in sociological research when Erik Homburger Erikson, a Viennese-American clinical psychoanalyst out of the Freudian tradition, began formulating the concept of ego identity and suggested that the problem of identity was characteristic of the modern world.[6] Drawing on Erikson's highly influential *Childhood and Society* (published in 1950) and its affirmation of the subject's triumphant self-transformation as it detaches itself agonistically from the coerced expectations of such entities as society, government or family, Medovoi has analyzed the paradoxical question of how postwar America – a purported era of social conformity – spawned a heightened sense of self, based on race, gender, class, and age, which was unknown until that moment in American and Western culture. This new sensibility, Medovoi has contended, presided over the emergence of a full-blown "politics of identity" which would mark deep transformations in late twentieth-century American society.

Erikson's book was the first to define the word "identity" as the normative psychic achievement of selfhood, both at the level of individual selfhood and of such elements as nationality, racial grouping, and even sexual orientation. Medovoi has argued that these two elements of identity discourse rapidly permeated U.S. postwar culture in no small part by relating the two "key terms" on which they were predicated: individual identity and group identity. As discourses of national sovereignty began to emerge in parallel with new discourses of individual identity, notions of sovereignty began to be applied to the emerging social agency of self in a historical period that coincided with the beginning of the Cold War and the decolonization process within which the Cold War played itself out.[7]

In particular, Medovoi has contended that the postwar emergence in the U.S. of non-normative identitarian narratives (especially in literature and film) which he has defined as "rebel narratives," was not in contrast with the decade's purported conformist mood, but rather instrumental to it. Within the Cold War context of a "three worlds imaginary," where "first world" and "second world" (the United States and the Soviet Union) engaged in a protracted confrontation for hegemony over a decolonizing and self-affirming "third world," identity narratives served to confirm America's claim to its monopoly over a more "benign" discourse of freedom, which lay in stark contrast with Soviet totalitarianism.[8]

Postwar American culture specifically singled out the emergent sociological category of youth as the hegemonic agent for the representation of identitarian discourses in postwar America. In this chapter, I will seek out the leading narratives of this developing agency of youth which emerged as a defining containment tool for Cold War America.

Rebellious Youth: Identity in Postwar Suburbia

Erikson's theory of politicized identity focused on post-colonial emerging nationalism, seen as an analogy of the human life-cycle: the achievement of national identity by formerly colonized nations through a phase of decolonization mirrored the way in which individuals went from an identity-deprived childhood to adult selfhood via an "adolescent" phase of identity formation. As Medovoi has pointed out, Erikson's analogy was particularly significant in the Cold War era, which not only shaped discourses of nation formation through the metaphor of a transition from infantile dependence to adult self-determination, but which was also an age in which both areas of identity formation – individual and group/national – became crucial factors of change: not only did nations come of age, but also new social formations began to emerge in the early Cold War years, by processes of "uncoerced 'self-recognition'" which became "a prelude and a precondition to achieving social recognition."[9]

The key emerging identity in 1950s American culture was the teenager; these children of the postwar baby boom (which in fact began during the war years) were, by the mid-1950s, growing into adolescents, early consumers, and problematic citizens.[10] As youth became, in W. T. Lhamon's words, "the most seething area of fifties culture," early critics began defining adolescents as members of either an apathetic or delinquent generation of "college boys" vs. "corner boys."[11] Although "the magnitude and staying power of youth culture was of course not evident at first," there was, according to James Gilbert, "increasing recognition that teenagers had a major impact on the shaping of American popular culture."[12]

In the postwar world, youths began to affirm specific styles and behaviors which set them off from previous adolescents: for the first time in history, youths acquired social and cultural identities that no longer allowed their assimilation with either children or adults, as they associated themselves with changing forms of speech, fashions, music, and mores.[13] Postwar adolescents equivocally trod the line separating childhood and adulthood in a quest for self-identification, which led them to establish a culture of their own which incorporated, all at the same time, hijinks, premature adulthood and antisocial delinquency.[14]

As a social category, the "teenager" was a brand-new postwar fabrication and coterminous with the introduction of the concept of "identity." The word itself made its very first appearance at the close of World War II, in a 1945 *New York Times Magazine* article by Elliott Cohen entitled "Teen-Age Bill of Rights." Unlike earlier notions of adolescence as a stage of sexual, moral and intellectual immaturity requiring subordination to the elders, Cohen's article empowered the teenager as the member of an identitarian group endowed with a set of psychopolitical rights (the "rights of the teenager") which defined him/her within "a specific arena of sovereignty."[15] Obviously responding to "an apparent crisis in the historic relations of age inherited by the wartime years," the idea of the teenager as an autonomous social category emerged at a time when adult supervision of adolescents had become impracticable as a consequence of the war.[16] As fathers were fighting abroad and mothers had to replace their husbands in the factories, adolescents were left on their own to establish which path in life to pursue. Moreover, as more adolescents joined the workforce alongside their mothers, teenagers suddenly acquired financial independence, which turned them for the first time in history into autonomous consumers. The "Teen-Age Bill of Rights," and related books that were published at approximately the same time, petitioned readers to honor youth as the embodiment of emergent identity and to respect the efforts that adolescents made toward independence.[17]

Teenagers developed comprehensive institutions that reflected their new, if uncertain, status. They drove cars, married early, approached sexual relations in young age. They looked and acted differently and often seemed remarkably hostile or even criminally inclined, appearing to adults like outright "juvenile delinquents."[18] It is around these complex areas of transformation that adult society had to respond and attempt to make adjustments in order to accommodate and contain what many saw as "premature adulthood." One highly sensitive area of premature adulthood was that of changing sexual attitudes. *The Kinsey Report* had shown that conventional ethics of sexuality in the country had little place in the actual behavior of American males and females – a behavior that Kinsey's research demonstrated to be less constrained than many had expected.[19] To confirm generalized concerns, sociologist Pitirim Sorokin published in 1956 a study entitled *The American Sex Revolution*, which argued that American culture had become dangerously "sexualized" and encouraged parents to take action before this revolution could claim physical and mental damage among the nation's youths. Sorokin indicted consumer culture as the main culprit and advised parents to protect their children from rock 'n' roll, dancing, and certain radio shows and films.[20]

Most discomfiting for adults was the fact that youth culture appeared more and more incomprehensible to the rest of society. Youths carved out a space of their own by developing a semiotics that set them distinctly apart from adults. Postwar teenagers began gathering around the virtual space of specific languages, jazz for some, the language of rock 'n' roll for most – in other words, the languages of Norman Mailer's "White Negro," the hipster who refuses to integrate in society at large.[21] On July 23, 1957, *Look* magazine published a researched "primer for parents" entitled "How American Teenagers Live," which tried to help bridge the growing generation gap in America by addressing three central issue areas: "why they go steady," "why they go wild," and "why they don't listen." The research devoted special attention to teenage lingo as marker of cultural difference. By enlisting experts to decode teenage newspeak in words such as "Banana," "Blast," "Bread," "Cattle Wagon," "Dad," "Drag Main," "Hit the Flik," "Ronchie," "Shad," and "Shook up," the magazine tried to make sense of a generation that had enveloped itself in a set of codes, revolving not only around language, but which were in fact deployed within a seamless web of culture. This culture involved souped-up cars, teen magazines, music, dance, the social order of gangs, new dating customs, drive-in theaters, haircuts, and clothes.

Much of this new behavior emerged from high schools, which, after World War II, had become, in Gilbert's words, "the universal mold of teenage culture." By the early 1960s, over 90 percent of working-class students attended high school, compared to only 50 percent before World War II. The high-school population also broadened in terms of race: by the early 1960s the percentages of blacks and whites completing high school were nearly equal. Awash in peer culture, some of which was socially approved and much which was not, the high school became an arena of clashing values and customs, where teenagers emerged as part of two distinct cultures: eager consumers on the one hand, potential criminals on the other. A dual vision of youth emerged in the 1950s, which simultaneously celebrated them as full-fledged participants in the country's economic boom and chastised them as threatening rebels and delinquents.[22]

Celebrating Youths as Consumers

Lizabeth Cohen has contended that although adolescents had been labeled to signify a developmental stage since the nineteenth century, "it was not until the majority of teens were graduating from high school in the 1940s that the teenage period of life – from ages 13 to 18 – took on the attributes of the mass cultural experience."[23] According to Cohen, behind the rapid growth of a separate youth culture lay burgeoning consumer independence, a trend that started during the war years (when adolescents were carried, alongside women, into the workforce), suddenly transforming teenagers into independent earners and consumers of distinct goods and services. Often credited with establishing the notion of a teenage consumer market was Chicago-born advertising pioneer Eugene Gilbert, who attributed to himself the "salient discovery [that] within the past decade the teenagers have become a separate and distinct group in our society with control over $9.5 billion of income (almost all of it discretionary) and influence over much more."[24] To parallel that trend, magazines like *Seventeen*, which debuted in 1944 and prided itself on catering to "the needs, the wants and the whims" of teenagers, helped define this new, growing market for advertisers. Teen magazines became a direct communication channel between advertisers and this new class of consumers who, Eugene Gilbert estimated, controlled a significant average personal budget of $3.03 a week for discretionary spending.[25]

Teenagers came to define a unique consumer experience, centering around buying certain kinds of things – records, clothes, makeup, movies, and fast food – in certain kinds of places – shopping centers, drive-in theaters, and car-hop restaurants. Teenagers thus set themselves aside from other consumers and assembled as a market group of their own to be serviced.[26] The discovery of a teenage market coincided with, in fact preceded, a new trend in marketing known as "market segmentation," the idea that each product should be targeted at a specific group of consumers and which became the guiding law of advertising beginning in the late 1950s.[27]

One area of consumption in which adolescents were creating a specific culture of their own was automobiles, whose use and appearance they transformed into new fetishes of social interaction.[28] While it would take another good decade before car ownership extended significantly to the youth market, a new cult of the automobile (which imitated and caricatured adulthood) emerged among America's youth amid a larger range of new social patterns that were specifically connected with an automobile culture: the "joy ride," the drive-in theater business (by 1958 there were more than 4,000 drive-in theatres in America), and above all the rise of "hot-rod" culture.[29] Hot-rodding was centered on the fetishization of the automobile as a sex object, whose care and customization gave owners, in the words of automobile historian John Heitmann, "a distinctive individuality and, if desired, entrance into a subculture of fellow enthusiasts."[30] Automobile subculture was well captured by Henry Gregor Felsen's low-brow novel *Hot Rod* (1950), the story of Bud, a 17-year-old orphaned highschooler whose life meaning revolves around driving the family vehicle that his parents have left him:

> No matter what his mood or his feeling, his trouble or his joy, it made everything right and good to be guiding this car, the car he had built, that belonged to him, that owed everything it was to him. Not a day passed without Bud's taking time for a spin. It was more than a ride; it was more than the speeding; more than killing time. In some ways these daily lessons on the road were his hours of meditation, of true expression, the balm for his soul and the boasts of his spirit. In these flying hours he had sought himself out, molded himself into what he was, and found his creed.[31]

As youth culture largely became the main culture of the 1950s and, in the words of W.T. Lhamon, "the atmosphere of American life," it became one of the pillars of the decade's economic boom.[32] By the end of the decade, even manufacturers of mainstream merchandise like RCA and Pepsi-Cola saw their future profits, even survival, linked to how well they managed to insert their product into the fantasy world of the teenage market segment, and were ready to embrace the concerns of that crucial new customer base.[33]

Chastising Youths as Rebels

The teenager as consumer was the bright side of youth's other dark persona: the "rebel," with its potential to upset the Cold War conformity consensus. By the mid-1950s, a growing fear that a whole generation had turned sour overlaid society's initial bewilderment and curiosity towards youths' new identitarian quest. To many, the frenzied dances, music, and ritualized family rebellions forewarned of a larger and very serious social problem. The media concurred, spreading anxiety about postwar American youths: juvenile delinquency had bounded upward after 1940, clearly as a result of lesser adult supervision during the war years, but had not stopped after families were reunited in the postwar years.[34] By the early 1950s, the American media reported with concern a storm of youth criminality rumbling across the nation. The arrest and trial of four boys in Brooklyn in 1954 for the murder of a vagrant led to the widespread impression that vicious and bored youths had turned to murder and mayhem for amusement.

James Gilbert has shown that intimations of spreading juvenile delinquency were more the product of ad-hoc media campaigns than the result of actual variations in crime rates: as public fears of growing juvenile delinquency peaked from 1953 to about 1956 and diminished thereafter, actual delinquency rates among American youths did not decline after 1956.[35] Following the media scares, senate hearings were held in an effort to pinpoint and shield against the problem. The culprit was found in the fact that the mass media stood between parent and child, and that, consequently, parents could no longer impress their value systems onto their offspring. Children, it turned out, were influenced as much by a new peer culture spread by comic books, radio, movies, and television as by their elders. In a widely debated book, *Seduction of the Innocent* (1954), psychologist Fredric Wertham persuaded a significant element of the American public that comic books and films incited delinquent behavior, and that a breakdown of generational communication and control provoked youthful misbehavior. High schools became the obvious area of concern, as they were seen as the nurturing ground of peer culture. Particularly worrisome were the large urban comprehensive schools, which were seen as fostering "the interchange of youth cultures" and increasing "the possibilities of cross-fertilization between middle-class and working-class and blacks," as well as providing fertile ground for the clash of class and ethnic subcultures.[36]

The most sensitive problem area, however, was felt to lie within domestic walls, where postwar fears of juvenile delinquency were linked to the broader anxiety that parents and children had been divided by the new peer culture spread, as Wertham had warned, by mass culture. As children were growing more and more estranged from their parents, many upholders of tradition were bemoaning a growing separation between parental aspirations and children's behavior: as the American family itself now exercised less influence in the cultural formation of youngsters, the cultural codes of the latter diverged to such an extent as to have become irreconcilable with those of the adults. Within this full-fledged parent-adolescent confrontation, parents sought to regain authority by controlling teenage behavior with repressive measures, such as banning jeans and other fashionable items of clothing in schools, or banning motor races in communities with high numbers of hot-rods.[37]

If anything, restrictive parenting produced the opposite effect of fostering youthful detachment and self-affirmation. Gilbert has argued that by the mid-1950s "the styles and behavior of young people were less frequently denounced than they were emulated."[38] And as terms such as "teenager" and "rebel" began to orbit around an emerging Fordist consumer youth market, they gave rise to rebel metanarratives that further contributed to the affirmation of a distinct and autonomous youth subculture in America. Beat literature, captivating young readers' attention beginning in the middle of the decade, marks the obvious literary explosion of such metanarratives, although issues of social nonconformity were first explored in texts such as J.D. Salinger's *The Catcher in the Rye* or in some of Hollywood's purported denunciations of youthful rebellion, notably *The Wild One* (1953), *Rebel Without a Cause* (1955), and *Blackboard Jungle* (1955). As I discuss in the last chapter, rock 'n' roll culture became the site where these two contrasting yet complementary views of youth in the 1950s found their ideal convergence, as teenage consumerism met youthful rebellion on levels that touched new and unthought-of notions of racial blending and dialogue.

Interestingly enough, as the 1950s progressed, youth culture became not only emulated and celebrated, but it turned into a powerful weapon of Cold War rhetoric. Medovoi has shown that, through the context of the liberal theory exposed by Erikson, American culture was able to internalize youthful rebellion: as a transitional stage between childhood and adulthood, youth came to signify a free-space of self determination which became instrumental to the Cold War confrontation over the arena of third-world decolonization.[39] Rebel metanarratives emerged as obvious examples of a celebratory rhetoric of America's benign democracy, paragons of a country capable to internalize adolescent rebellion within its own liberal system in the same way that it would guarantee self-determination to any third-world country willing to adopt its political template. The remainder of this chapter will discuss some of the leading rebellion narratives of 1950s American culture.

Portraits of Angered Youths: Rebellion Literature

Criticism of 1950s literature tends to group the wide galaxy of writers falling under the "beat generation" umbrella as prime examples of the decade's rebellion narratives. Typically associated with the beats in recent interpretations are other writers of the period who cast themselves, or their characters, as outsiders of sorts – books like J.D. Salinger's *The Catcher in the Rye* (1951), which David Castronovo ranks on a par with Jack Kerouac's *On the Road* (1956) and Allen Ginsberg's *Howl* (1956) as celebrations of instability, impulsiveness and immaturity.[40] Or books such as Nelson Algren's *The Man with the Golden Arm* (1949) and Norman Mailer's *Advertisements for Myself* (1959), whose anger and resentment towards America and its culture makes them epitomes of rebellion and resistance to postwar conformity.

Salinger and the beats are crucial for their superior outlining of the traits of youth as the new postwar other. Their antagonistic literary styles and their narratives of the inability or explicit refusal to conform situate them as representing voices of discontent and dissent to the imperatives of Cold War conformity. Salinger rails against the hypocrisy (or "phoniness") of an affluent society that has lost all sense of authenticity and compassion; Kerouac rebels against societal expectations of young adults settling down and accepting middle-class mores of marriage, parenthood and corporate work; Ginsberg elaborates a quasi-philosophical critique of American civilization and its discontents:

> America, I've given you all and now I'm nothing [...]
> America when will we end the human war? Go fuck yourself with your atomic bomb.
> I don't feel good don't bother me.[41]

Likewise, Algren's *The Man with the Golden Arm* and Mailer's *Advertisements for Myself* are testimonies of rebellious existences that refuse any allegiance to the comforts of middle class affluence, by depicting lives that deny middle-class expectations and champion drugs, brutality, and contempt of authority. And whereas Algren's novel (which was also made into a movie in 1955 directed by Otto Preminger) straddles the delicate line between adaptation and exclusion in its depiction of a returning war veteran who strays into drug addiction and finds himself unable to stir from his existence back into normalcy, Mailer's rage at the decade's consensus is self-begotten, and results in pompous, rhetoric-laden tirades against liberalism, the establishment, and their rigid orthodoxies.

"Standing on the Edge:" Salinger's Misfit Hero

A very controversial book from the moment of its first publication in 1951, *The Catcher in the Rye* hit right at the core of postwar America's new social climate. At a time when the emergence of youth as a new social category was a source of anxiety for many, the novel touched on the delicate cord of the disruptive potential of teenagers. Its insistent use of expletives, as well as its presentation of an adolescent hero who drinks, smokes, engages a prostitute and insists that the adult world is a masquerade, the empire of "phoniness" where nobody is given a chance to be his or her true self, was met with uneasiness across the nation.

The Catcher in the Rye is the story of Holden, an urban upper middle-class boy who, caught at the delicate point of adolescent crisis, finds himself alone and misguided while undergoing traditional rites of initiation into manhood and ends up choosing an adulterated life in the "real" world, rather than an escape from it. He does so because, despite his frustrations with the hypocrisy of his peers (which he repeatedly denounces as "phony") and of adults, he still believes he has a mission to carry out – a utopian dream of collective salvation that he expresses in the famous passage bearing the novel's title:

> I keep picturing all these little kids playing some game in this big field of rye and all. Thousands of little kids, and nobody's around – nobody big, I mean – except me. And I'm standing on the edge of some crazy cliff. What I have to do, I have to catch everybody if they start to go over the cliff – I mean if they're running and they don't look where they're going. I have to come out from somewhere and catch them. That's all I'd do all day. I'd just be the catcher in the rye and all.[42]

Holden often shares with the reader his awareness of living in a decadent society ("you can't ever find a place that's nice and peaceful, because there isn't any," he quips after finding obscenities on the walls of his little sister Phoebe's school), whose symptoms are the very stuff of his teenage life: he has been through the death of his younger brother Allie, who represented for him all that was good in the world; he has seen his other brother "prostitut[e] himself" to his career; and school has presented him with another sizeable dose of inauthenticity. As Christopher Brookeman has pointed out, while the official image of the prep school presents it as an idealized family standing *in loco parentis*, Holden's commentaries on the value of the system of Pencey Prep lead him to conclude "that the whole official vision of the school as a cooperative caring family is a mask for an actual ideology of intense competitive struggle." In the novel, school is shaped within the decade's framework of socialization and the role of the peer group as analyzed by David Riesman in *The Lonely Crowd*.[43]

In the tradition, which he in fact pioneers, of post-World War II existential dissatisfaction and societal rebellion, Holden chooses to become the spokesperson for a widespread anxiety over threats to authenticity. Like others in that tradition, Holden chooses his own dysfunctional path of life outside the folds of the affluent society. Yet – which is less common within the tradition – he does so within a utopian vision of communal salvation, rather than the all-out violent juvenile rebellion that will be typified in the canonic "misfit" texts later in the decade. Nevertheless, Holden's scathing comments about the flaws he perceives in the dominant ideologies of his society and the limitations they impose upon him as an individual take him, according to Sarah Graham, to an even higher level of rebellion and make him "a much more challenging, even subversive, figure than the stereotypical teenage rebel."[44]

What makes Holden particularly threatening to the status quo – and the obvious cause of much of the criticism poured out over the book in the last half century – is the way in which he exposes the demise of a social type, what Riesman called the inner-directed individual, one who is no longer welcome within the Cold War consensus. Holden cracks up and breaks down under the pressures of a society in which social leisure and communication have become full-time occupations and where the culture of the adolescent has been invaded by the needs of the peer group. It is precisely Holden's unwillingness to share in the consensus that renders *The Catcher in the Rye* a dangerous book, one that, as recently as in the year 2000, ranked at number thirteen in the American Library Association's list of the "100 Most Frequently Challenged Books" – a euphemism indicating repeated attempts to remove it from public or school libraries.[45] Salinger went as far as inscribing the waning of the inner-directed individual into his conscious parody, at the beginning of the novel, of classic inner-directed culture as embodied in the realistic novel of the nineteenth century:

> If you really want to hear about it, the first thing you'll probably want to know is when I was born, and what my lousy childhood was like, and how my parents

were occupied and all before they had me, and all that David Copperfield kind of crap, but I don't feel like going into it.[46]

As Medovoi has argued, like rock 'n' roll and the beat writers, *Catcher* was in no way meant to be an anti-American text: in fact, it placed rebellion at the heart of Americanness. Emerging at the dawn of the Cold War, it became instrumental in demonstrating America's "emancipatory character, whether in relation to the Soviet Union, the new nations of the third world, or even its own suburbs."[47] According to Medovoi, *Catcher* allowed for a wide array of political positions, encompassing at one end of the spectrum rather conservative critiques of America's naïve democratic tendencies as embodied in Holden, all the way to leftist-liberal appreciations for the boy's egalitarian spirit at the other end. *Catcher* could, in other worlds, accommodate "the entire scope of the imaginary Cold War consensus."[48] When Leslie Fiedler commented that literature was being "cannibalized by America's rapidly growing youth culture," he was not only commenting on *Catcher*'s unexpected popular success, but was in fact voicing the liberal intellectual's anxiety over the advance of mass culture which was jeopardizing their own elite status as proprietors of culture in general, the same fears that in a bitter polemic of 1959, "The Salinger Industry," George Steiner voiced from across the Atlantic on the need to distinguish between genuine and commercial literature (of which *Catcher* was obviously the threatening prototype).[49]

"Spectral Nations!" The American Century According to Ginsberg

Condemnation was also dispensed to the exploits of the beat writers who, according to Castronovo, shared with Salinger a desire to make "the energies and moods of youth their master theme," thus writing books "that assaulted the reading public with an entirely new version of what it was to be young, besieged by messages from the heart and libido."[50] The beat generation came under fire from both fronts, conservative and liberal, and on all counts – aesthetic, moral, social. Lionel Trilling, who had been Ginsberg's teacher at Columbia, dismissed *Howl* as all rhetoric and rant with no music or poetic beauty; Louis Simpson refused to include Ginsberg in his anthology *New Poets of England and America* – a book that would define the college canon of American poetry for many years; and Norman Podhoretz scolded the beats in an essay as "Know-Nothing Bohemians," his scorn spearheaded at Kerouac's alleged lack of narrative distance and choice of subliterary levels of speech.[51]

"Beat" is a slippery definition. In an article published in the journal *Friction* in 1982, Ginsberg attempted to capture the several meanings of the term, which he said originated from a remark by Jack Kerouac, who "un-named" his own generation in comparison to the earlier, so-called "lost generation" of writers.[52] If the previous was a "lost generation," Kerouac had argued, his own was "nothing but a beat generation." The label was officially launched by John Clellon Holmes in an essay for the *New York Times Magazine* in 1952 entitled "This is the Beat Generation," which came out a few month's after Holmes published *Go*, a *roman à clef* about the beat circle in late 1940s New York. "Beat," explained Ginsberg, came from street usage, from the language of hipsterism, and carried connotations of feeling "emptied out, exhausted, and at the same time wide-open and receptive to vision," or else, "finished," as well as "connected to words like beatitude and beatific – the necessary beatness or darkness that precedes the opening up to light [and] religious illumination."[53]

When the word came to define "no less than a whole literary movement," beat referred, according to Ginsberg, to "a group of friends who had worked together on poetry, prose, and cultural conscience from the mid forties to [the] late fifties" in New York – a group consisting of Kerouac, Neal Cassady (Kerouac's prototype hero in *On The Road*), William Burroughs, Herbert Huncke, John Clellon Holmes, Ginsberg himself, and which would later grow to include Carl Solomon (to whom *Howl* was dedicated), Philip Lamantia, Gregory Corso, and Lawrence Ferlinghetti. Not just an existential condition or a literary movement, beat generation also came to refer, according to Ginsberg, "to the broader influence of literary and artistic activities of poets, filmmakers, painters, writers, and novelists" who "refreshed the long-lived bohemian cultural tradition in America," in a movement that ended up shaking progressive American culture to its roots, by ushering in "essential effects" that would deeply affect American culture in the decades to come.[54]

When *Howl* was published in 1956 by San Francisco's City Lights bookstore, it was underground, outlawed literature, and because of that it created a new sense of identity for those who read it as "members of a new generation that had come of age in the wake of World War II and the atomic bomb."[55] Over the years it became "the great poetic testament of youth from the 1950s," signaling a cut-off point for American culture as a whole: from an artistic point of view, it marked the definitive rebuttal of avant-garde, modernist aesthetics from an art form that celebrated, rather than eschewed, personality. From a cultural point of view, it marked the start of the free-speech and non-conformist revolution that would sweep across America in the following decade.[56]

An avid reader of modernist poetry, and of T.S. Eliot in particular, during his Columbia education in the 1940s, Ginsberg went to great lengths to dispel his anxiety over his predecessors and disavow any legacy from modernism – a break clearly perceivable in the poem's overall philosophy of composition. *Howl* bears no trace of Eliot's "extinction of personality."[57] Rather, in the wake of Walt Whitman's "One's-Self I sing, a simple, separate person," Ginsberg celebrates himself in the first person and creates a striking public persona and overall personal mythology. But whereas Eliot's *Waste Land* was capable of controlling the urban hell it represented via a coherent spiritual vision which is subsumed in its cultural acquisition of mythology (as signaled in the poem's explicit acknowledgement of Jesse Weston's and James Frazer's scholarship on pre-Christian rituals as archival source), Ginsberg's portrayal of the current decline of civilization carried no coherent unifying vision. Rather, Ginsberg espoused Whitman's avowal of contradiction as expressed in the famous assertion in *Song of Myself*: "Do I contradict Myself? / Very well then I contradict myself, / (I am large, I contain Multitudes)."[58]

Ginsberg wrote *Howl* in San Francisco, where he had relocated from New York, presumably with the specific intention, according to Jonah Raskin, to "wake Americans from what seemed like a narcotized slumber." "God damn the false optimism of my generation," Ginsberg wrote in his journal while musing on what he believed to be the misplaced boosterism of the so-called "American Century." He intended the poem to provide a different representation of America, one that would be faithful to his "bottom-up vision of society," highlighting "wealth and power from the point of view of the down-and-out people in the streets.'"[59]

Like much of beat literature, *Howl* is highly autobiographic. It condenses the universe of Allen Ginsberg during his New York years in the 1940s, his bohemian existence, his closeted homosexuality, his expulsion from Columbia, his internment in a psychiatric institution, as well as the new intellectual circle that had gathered around him since his arrival on the West Coast. Each line of the poem, no matter how hermetic, suggests some kind of autobiographical reference. In the long Whitmanian listing at the beginning of the poem, all dependent on the opening clause "I saw the best minds of my generation," each line bears the trace of lived experience. "Who were expelled from the academies for crazy & publishing obscene odes on the windows of the skull," for instance, refers to the episode that led to Ginsberg's banning from Columbia University when, one day in March 1945, he traced two drawings, one of a phallus and testicles, the other of a skull and crossbones, on his dormitory window. Each drawing was glossed with one daring phrase: "Fuck the Jews" (Ginsberg was Jewish himself) and "Butler has no balls" (referring to Nicholas Murray Butler, the president of Columbia). Ginsberg was readmitted to Columbia in the following year and eventually graduated in 1948.[60]

In spite of Ginsberg's gift for creating stories and situations, and the ultimate traceability of the individual episodes, *Howl* remains a poem that resists meaning. Although I do not subscribe to Castronovo's view that "the dynamic of the poem is totally without any reason or logic," I certainly agree with his assessment that *Howl* opens out the themes of Ginsberg's generation, turning frustration "into more than a dry social problem" because in *Howl* all seems "urgent in a new way."[61] Ginsberg himself appears to have been vague, or at least ambivalent, about the poem's meaning. Over the years, he gave several inconsistent interpretations of it, saying at different times that *Howl* was "an acknowledgment of the basic reality of homosexual joy," "an homage to art," a literal "coming out of the closet," a poem "about my mother," and even "an emotional time bomb that would continue exploding [the] military-industrial-nationalistic complex."[62]

If meaning in *Howl* is elusive, the undisputed strength of the poem lies rather in its form, the "open poetic line – long, free, colloquial, packed with images and phrases that tumble out," the "illogical connection, the bardic shout, and the bizarre juxtaposition," all contributing to highlight the beats' ultimate celebration of "First Thought, Best Thought" spontaneity and the rejection of everything mannered and mannerly.[63] Ginsberg's radical approach to metrics is the outcome of the stratification of all his poetic influences, from William Blake to William Carlos Williams, from Whitman to Garcia Lorca and Eliot. His free rhythms and widely varying lengths of line reflect his attempt to remain faithful to the natural flow of the mind in a state of intense imaginative excitation. The poem's slang and explicit sexual language (in the mid-1950s, "sex-talk" was considered pornography and subject to criminal prosecution) expanded the vocabulary of American poetry, at a time when the uncommitted, sadomasochistic homosexuality the poem proclaims was alien to the standards of acceptability of American society.

As Raskin has pointed out, *Howl* expresses the extremes of American feeling and the extremes of the American character. In the poem, Ginsberg moves "from futility to ecstasy, paranoia to inner peace, and from a sense of terror to a sense of holiness," well capturing the feeling of despair that many Americans experienced in the wake of World War II. Ginsberg also records the American sense of renewal and rebirth: his America is both hell and paradise, and *Howl* presents a full inventory of all those possibilities, the "quintessential poem of the mid-twentieth century [...] a scream that woke the country, shocked it, and reminded it of its dreams, possibilities and joys."[64]

Hipsters, Beats, and Kerouac's Contradiction

The multifaceted ethos of the beats was a recurring concern in Norman Mailer's *Advertisements for Myself* (1959), a collection of daring, albeit often long-winded, essays whose centerpiece was arguably an article entitled "The White Negro," originally published in *Dissent* magazine in 1957. A reflection on the existential condition of the "hipster," "The White Negro" singled out the prototype of postwar rebellion that the word "beat" subsumed. Reflecting on the "conformity and depression" of the 1950s, Mailer saw the only hope in the "isolated courage of isolated people"[65] who attempted to escape Cold War-era conformity. Vaguely reminiscent of – but also sharply removed from – Sartre's original version of existentialism, "hipsterism" called for a reaction to the "stench of fear [that] has come out of every pore of American life." Mailer thus defined the hipster:

> It is on this bleak scene that a phenomenon has appeared: the American existentialist – the hipster, the man who knows that if our collective condition is to live with instant death by atomic war, relatively quick death by the State as *l'univers concentrationnaire*, or with a slow death by conformity with every creative and rebellious instinct stifled (at what damage to the mind and the heart and the liver and the nerves no research foundation for cancer will discover in a hurry), if the fate of twentieth century man is to live with death from adolescence to premature senescence, why then the only life-giving answer is to accept the terms of death, to live with death as immediate danger, to divorce oneself from society, to exist without roots, to set out on that uncharted journey into the rebellious imperatives of the self.[66]

Trapped "in the totalitarian tissues of American society," the only defense for the individual was, according to Mailer, to imitate "the Negro [...] who has been living on the margin between totalitarianism and democracy for two centuries."[67] As social outcasts, Mailer reasoned, African-Americans offered alternative versions of the meaning of life. By "absorb[ing] the existentialist synapses of the Negro," the hipster would achieve a new identification as a "White Negro," whose necessary "barbarism" was "preferable to totalitarianism." Existing at the other extreme of adult maturity, which was shaped by logic and rationality, the "White Negro" claimed a space for "individual growth" allowing individuals to feel their existence, spontaneously and without ideological mediation. In Mailer's argument, black culture offered inroads to that spontaneity, through its emphasis on unfettered sexuality and rebel music, jazz in particular, "the music of orgasm, food orgasm or bad." Mailer's questionable – and by today's standards highly offensive – vision of blackness celebrated African-Americans' lack of repression, the latter a prerogative, in his view, of white culture. Practiced in the art of survival, African-Americans lived with hopelessness by focusing on the present, on the joys and pleasures that could be snatched by living here and now, feeling and expressing emotion, especially sexual desire, rather than deferring gratification to plan for a future that might not come.[68]

Although reminiscent of white stereotypes on "blackness" and "black aesthetics" (including the inherently racist position that African-American culture is best expressed through non linguistic arts, such as dance and music), "The White Negro" remains a testimony of an urge to escape the narrow confines of 1950s mainstream culture into larger spaces. Mailer advocated an existential dimension where senses, emotions, spontaneity and primitive instincts prevail over the forces that constrain the individual into nonbeing – in Mailer's words, the liberation "of the self from the Super-Ego of society," and the opening of "limits of the possible for oneself, for oneself alone because that is one's need." Liberating the mind, opening the limits, creating wider spaces for the senses: these are the imperatives of a new culture of rebellion that the beat generation has expressed with the fullest force.

If Mailer's essay is the manifesto of a new sensibility, Jack Kerouac's 1956 *On the Road* can be seen as its fictional exegesis. No work of literature is more incisive in capturing the ethos of the beat hero and *On the Road*, critics have argued, is to the 1950s what Ernest Hemingway's *The Sun also Rises* had been to the 1920s – a *roman à clef* revealing the full depth of an artistic generation.[69] The novel's crucial breakthrough lies not only in epitomizing the cultural and artistic ideology of the beat generation (of which immediacy and spontaneity are the most controversial aspect), but also in its challenging the idea of the 1950s as a decade of conformism and accommodation to the demands of society. According to Martin Halliwell, *On the Road* should be inscribed into a wider context of "resurgence of individual freedom" that marked the second half of the decade.[70]

The novel, "not structured like a novel, but more like an extended jazz riff" inspired by late 1940s bebop, narrates the trip across America of Sal Paradise. In an attempt to disengage from the by then "stultified" experience of northeastern middle-class life, Sal takes Dean Moriarty – a man "all impulse, all possibility, all irresponsibility" – as a companion and role-model. During their trips, the two men experience everything from drugs to free sex to alcohol, leading Sal, in an ending that triggered copious critical response, to finally head back home after having realized that there is "no more land" ahead of him.[71]

In a wide-ranging essay on Jack Kerouac's "contradictions," prefacing an Italian edition of Kerouac's collected works, Mario Corona has underlined the "painful paradox" of a novel that – although exerting a long-lasting, profound influence and sense of identification among its readers – persistently vacillated between the effort to testify the spirit of a new artistic generation and an inescapable compromise with the publishing industry and the reading public. Such compromise appeared all the more difficult to achieve and conceive of for a novel whose language was self-referential and was aimed, by reason of its own stylistic and ideological nature, at a closed group of readers and fellow artists. Likewise, the objective nature of Kerouac's gaze restricted his vision to the group of people immediately around him. Like *Howl*, *On the Road* offered no wide-ranging engagement with the world outside, but rather an insistence on portraying one's own world and community of peers in its own specific language. Kerouac intended all of this as part of "a purification therapy from the poisons of mass society, the most insidious of which was the flattening out of standards, also in the cultural field."[72]

On the Road signaled a bold attempt to shape an unconventional form of literary language, based on the reproduction of ordinary speech by ordinary people, a tradition that has a long history in American literature, beginning with Mark Twain. Yet it was not Kerouac's linguistic experiments that drew a vast readership to the book, but rather its success derived from the real-time portrayal of an anthropological transformation in American society. As youth emerged as a distinct sociological category in postwar America, Kerouac was quick to capture the early signals of malaise among lower-middle-class white males. This malaise triggered, in turn, the distancing from the Cold War consensus and the affirmation of models of survival at the margins of society as a consequence of the rejection of its imperatives of production and consumption.[73] A novel firmly rooted in "the consciousness of youth," *On the Road* expanded Mailer's vision of the hipster, not only by adopting the terms of the specific street lingo of hipsterism, but also in terms of the overall aesthetics that the hip lingo subsumes.[74]

Writing after Ginsberg's principle "First Thought, Best Thought," Kerouac insisted on the need to capture the flow of consciousness without mediation, in the dada and surrealist tradition, as well as in the tradition of bebop and of action painting, whose aesthetics of unmediated expression were closely akin to that of the beats.[75] Kerouac's "scroll" of paper, which he adopted to avoid interrupting the flow of writing, was an attempt to preserve the spontaneity of artistic creation and, in this respect, reached back both to Romantic aesthetics as well as to Joyce's idea that free associations best help the subconscious emerge. Mirroring Kerouac's composition technique, *On the Road* resulted in a vertigo of experience, all movement and variety, where every episode was swallowed up by the next, each significant moment erased by the next significant moment in a continuum of pure, unmediated existence, putting the pleasure of the here and now at the center of its endeavor.

Resisting the demands of adult conformity, *On the Road* sought ways out of a spiritually impoverished America not only for the beats it self-referentially addressed, but for the nation at large. Medovoi has argued that the beat generation's most significant achievement was its ability to establish its own special authority to "name" a generation of young Americans and in that naming process lay most of their claim to inflect the normative principle of identity. Works like *Howl* and *On the Road* laid a special claim to the naming process: by "retroactively call[ing] into being that which they name[d]" these beat texts managed to provide "a rhetorically persuasive historical roadmap to the development of that generational identity" and established, through their popular success, an authoritative path to identitarian values above and beyond those connected with America's consumer or militaristic culture.[76] Published after most of the decade's rebellion narratives, Ginsberg's and Kerouac's texts came to subsume their predecessors by enlisting them under that powerful title, beat, which became the synecdoche of 1950s identity narratives.

Rebellion Triptych: *The Wild One*, *Rebel Without a Cause*, *Blackboard Jungle*

Hollywood exhibited great ambivalence in portraying youth during the early Cold War years, with films whose messages ranged from pedagogies of white youths' apparent "normality," to alarming renderings of America as having suddenly become a country in the throes of an unruly generation of delinquents. Films such as Kazan's *Splendor in the Grass* (1961) and Curtiz's *King Creole* (1958) promoted the edifying message that the only alternative to conformity was the psychiatric ward or outright death. Conversely, such films as Benedek's *The Wild One* (1953) and Ray's *Rebel Without a Cause* (1955), although allegedly denouncing youth rebellion, ended up delivering a celebration of the rebel misfit through the sexualized male bodies of their star protagonists, Marlon Brando and James Dean. Emerging through these films as youth icons of the era, Brando and Dean imbued the rebel youth with glamour and appeal so as to concurrently heighten and defuse their social chastisement. Brando's athletically-shaped body and Dean's fragile, neurotic, feminized self, narcissistically exhibited in the sensuality of the flesh, ritualized a teen figure that was impossible to inscribe within accepted norms of postwar adult masculinity.

Laszlo Benedek's *The Wild One* raised scandal upon its release at the end of 1953. It was the first in a crop of biker-gang genre movies appearing during the 1950s to draw a younger market to the movie theatre through mostly low-budget productions that preached to kids, warning of the many dangers that lay in store off the beaten track of normality, while simultaneously seducing them with the nerves of steel that their rebel-heroes exhibited. *The Wild One* was based on a real-life incident that happened in California in the late 1940s, when a biker gang disrupted a motorcycle race and ransacked the small town of Hollister over a two day period – a story that was then popularized in a 1951 *Harper's Magazine* article entitled "The Cyclists' Raid." The film is exemplary of 1950s Hollywood's genius for stretching the boundaries of acceptable narratives: framed within the rhetoric of liberal moralizing, the film successfully absorbed its viewers in its nonconformist protagonists and ambiguously celebrated the rebel as youthful hero.

The film opens with a low-angle, long still shot of an empty one-lane country road, as captions roll with a warning to adults to closely police teenage behavior: "This is a shocking story. It could never take place in most American towns – but it did in this one. It is a public challenge not to let it happen again." Brando's off-screen voice sets the tone of the narrative: "It begins here for me on this road. How it all happened, I don't know. But it could never happen again. Maybe I could have stopped it early. But once the trouble was on its way, I was just going with it." Gradually, as tiny blurs on the horizon approach and the rumble in the background rises to full-blown motorcycle noise, forty black leather-jacketed cyclists threateningly roar towards the camera and the audience. The motorcycle gang rides in a tightly-knit squadron formation, led by Johnny Strabler (Brando), who wears, like the others, a black-leather jacket, round dark shades, white T-shirt, aviator's cap, skin-tight jeans, and black gloves and boots.

Brando and his gang are portrayed as representing a social type clearly inspired by the Hell's Angels, a group of nonconformist white motorcyclists which formed in San Bernardino, California, in the late 1940s and frequently made the news for unruly behavior. The macho, leather-clad bikers terrorize the local "squares" and coalesce around a jargon that pits them against the stereotypes and preconceptions of 1950s society. For Johnny, the slouch, the leather, and the bike symbolize mobility, the lack of commitment to anything other than intensity of feeling in the present, resistance to legal authority, and an ambivalence in relation to women, seen as sites of pleasure, fun and fantasy but also as a threat of containment in middle-class domesticity.[77]

The Black Rebel Motorcycle Club, Johnny's gang, is an outlaw, outsider group of working-class Americans whose rebellion is recreational, fundamentally a leisure activity, defined within the boundaries of the working-class cycle of work and non-work. Rejecting the comfort and apparent security of middle-class America, Johnny and his associates place mobility and rebellion above the specific nature of the rebellion. Although most critics have viewed the film as thematizing the relationship between youth mobility and social disruption, law and the breakdown of order, David Baker has made the point that the film omits to clarify the real context and consequence of the incidents incurred by the rebellious bikers and thus makes it difficult for the viewer to pass judgment and take definite sides.[78]

What triggers a moral confrontation in *The Wild One* is Johnny's motivation for acting. He is not seeking social justice, but is rather pushed by a romantic sense of authenticity, a sense of integrity within his own referential self which triggers his wish to defend his own difference and reject all "fake" attitudes. The problem with Johnny's rebellion is that it appears unfocused, lacking a center. It is a self-referential response to his own sense of inadequacy and lack of a proper place, not a structural rebellion aimed at challenging the status quo. In one famous line, Johnny is asked by one of the town girls: "Hey, Johnny, what are you rebelling against?" Tapping out a jazzy beat on the top of the jukebox, as though to formulate a thought that he does not possess, Johnny raises his eyebrow and drawls an amorphous: "What have you got?"

Unlike Johnny Strabler's inner-directed rebellion in *The Wild One*, rebellion in Nicholas Ray's *Rebel Without a Cause* (1955) unfolds within a middle-class leisure space which is already highly delimited and which functions through a recognition and respect for those limits. *Rebel* is a family drama centering on the incidence of troubled teenagers among middle-class American families in the 1950s, set against the decade's widening generation gap and growing confusion of gender roles. The film draws its premise from the clinical work of psychiatrist Robert Lidner, whose *Rebel Without a Cause: The Hypnoanalysis of a Criminal Psychopath*, published in 1944, centered on the psychological consequences of deprivation and abuse by tyrannical fathers on their teenage sons.[79] Drawing from Lidner, Ray's film studies juvenile rebellion as the response to dysfunctional family relations which may result in psychosis, the ultimate mental illness.

Narrated from the perspective of the youth protagonists, and focusing – unlike *The Wild One* – on the affluent suburban middle class, the film gains the edge of an unprecedented social critique. *Rebel* is about middle-class America and its teenage protagonists are not the outlaw delinquents leering out of *The Wild One*, but rather members of a widening affluent class where parents are at odds with the demands of domestic democracy and their teenage children's anger and discontent alienates them from the conformist society of the 1950s.

Set in Los Angeles, the prototypical sprawling city, *Rebel* focuses on the inadequacy of middle-class affluence to provide suitable responses to teenagers' expectations of guidance and leadership. The film centers around Jim Stark (James Dean), whose family has been forced to seek a fresh start in a new neighborhood because of Jim's unsocial and violent behavior at his previous school. Jim's conflicting social adaptation resurfaces on his first day at the new school when he challenges Buzz, the leader of the local gang, to gain acceptance into the new peer group and to stake his claim over Judy (Natalie Wood), Buzz's girlfriend. Jim's claim for new social territory results in Buzz's tragic death during the "chickie run" – a souped-up car race testing the contestants' bravery – in which the two boys engage. Feeling at least indirectly responsible for Buzz's death, Jim returns home and seeks his father's advice on whether to give himself up to the police (as his authentic conscience would have him), or not compromise himself (as his domineering mother orders). A weak parental figure, at odds with the new challenges of liberal education, Jim's father is unable to respond to his son's quest for adult guidance. Wearing a housewife's apron in the film's central confrontation scene, symbolic of his loss of authority within the suburban family unit, he is no longer the role model for his identity-seeking son to look up to, and hence is rejected: "I don't ever want to become like that," proclaims Jim, gesturing towards his father.

Having become estranged, each for different reasons, from their own families, Jim, Judy and their companion Plato, a social alien who sees Jim as a substitute for his own absent father figure, seek refuge in an abandoned mansion, a liminal space where they replicate middle-class visions of family togetherness. Contrary to the rebellion driving each of them to reject middle-class values and seek identity in their peer group, Jim, Judy and Plato enact fantasies whose horizons and substance are entirely defined by the middle-class American Dream against which they are rebelling: Jim and Judy play newlyweds while Plato plays a real estate agent; Jim and Judy play surrogate parents to Plato; Jim and Judy profess the depth of their newfound love for one another.[80] When Plato shoots one of the gang members and runs away, Jim re-enacts his own family drama: fantasizing fatherhood, he strives to overcome his own father's weakness as a parent and persuades Plato to do the right thing and give up his ammunition, as the police raid his hiding place. However when one shot is fired, accidentally killing Plato, Jim finds out that his substitute parenthood is no less a failure than his father's.

In this travesty of adulthood, conformism works as a disguise under which teenagers mask their dissatisfaction and discontent with society at large, since they do not seem to hold the secret to a valuable alternative social model. They are, in fact, "rebels without a cause," alienated youths who perceive the adult society surrounding them as a waste land, but have no viable solution through which to overcome middle-class conformity. Desperately seeking a new identity, all they are able to do is get away and isolate themselves, escaping adult hypocrisy by re-enacting their own version of that same hypocrisy. In *Rebel*, not only is juvenile rebellion hollow, but youthful rage results in yet another version of the middle class consensus: as one of the characters in the film complains that "with the kids, nobody acts sincere," *Rebel* seems to close the circle on youth's quest for identity in a place where identity boils down to an almost self-assured validation of confusion and alienation, a primal rage against that which cannot be articulated, conceptualized, or in any way overcome.

Based on Evan Hunter's 1954 eponymous best-selling novel, *Blackboard Jungle* shifts the discussion of juvenile rebellion away from youth delinquency and middle-class family to the sensitive arena of schooling and to the inherent dangers of the ethnic melting pot in the urban jungle of the socially excluded. Broadly understood as the locus of youth's subjection to adult pedagogical training, as well as the central drama of adolescence, school functions in *Blackboard Jungle* as a mirror reflecting the limitations and dangers of the middle class consensus. Holding together "adult concern and youthful pleasure in the figure of the juvenile delinquent," *Blackboard Jungle* presents an inner-city school in the Bronx plagued with troubling antisocial behavior, as well as by an imaginary multiracial alliance of inner-city youths rebelling first and foremost against (white) adult society.[81]

In *Blackboard Jungle* Glenn Ford plays the role of English literature teacher Richard Dadier, who is new to a difficult urban high school. From his first day of work, Dadier is confronted with the students' disobedience, hostility, and rough physical violence, leading to the attempted rape of one of Dadier's female colleagues and to the attempted murder of Dadier himself. The film's principal delinquents, African-American Gregory Miller (Sydney Poitier) and "white trash" American Artie West, depict forms of rebellion that are removed both from Stark's middle-class discontent in *Rebel* and from Strabler's working-class authenticity in *Wild One*. The rebels in *Blackboard Jungle* push the boundary of juvenile unrest to the socially excluded: lacking access to both leisure and social mobility, the students of inner-city North Manual High School pose an even harsher challenge to the Cold War rhetoric of juvenile rebellion as democratic space.

The film articulates two competing ideologies regarding the delinquency problem: the conservative approach, embodied by the school principal, who views North Manual as a garbage can of the educational system and suggests that nothing can be done about it other than contain it as best as one can; and liberal ideology, embodied by Richard Dadier, who views education as a positive investment in youth and the sole instrument available for drawing excluded minorities into the middle-class consensus. Dadier fails with West, because he stands too far outside that consensus and is ultimately unreachable. But he is more successful with Miller, whose delinquency is more the result of racial attitudes towards him than actual alienation: as an African-American, Miller is presumed to be a delinquent because of circumstantial (and ultimately false) evidence. Miller turns out to be a skilled and resourceful individual, whose final alliance with Dadier simply confirms his adherence to a middle-class consensus of which he is already a part.

By pushing the envelope of identity discourse into the less-trodden territory of racial and ethnic exclusion from the middle class,

Blackboard Jungle appears to function as a linking narrative between 1950s identitarian discourses of rebellion and delinquency and the coterminous early developments in the arena of racial integration. On this ground, however, the film and the novel on which the film is based come – as often happens – to divergent conclusions. Whereas the original Evan Hunter text stopped at a methodical, and largely pessimistic, analysis of ethnic and racial exclusion in inner-city ghettoes, Preminger's film, which was released within months of the *Brown v. Board* Supreme Court decision, appears more proactive in promoting an uplifting vision of racial justice. Collapsing juvenile delinquency and racial otherness into a singular narrative of social deviance, the film pursues, to a heightened extent if compared to both *The Wild One* and *Rebel*, its Cold War agenda within the geopolitical model of the "three worlds imaginary."

By weaving a cautionary tale of social delinquency as a social problem to be solved, and by extension of America's need to offer all its citizens equal access to its liberal consensus, *Blackboard Jungle* opens, more than most rebel narratives, a window on the drama of racial exclusion in American society and the dangers it poses to the stability of that consensus. In this respect, the adoption of Bill Haley and the Comets' "Rock Around the Clock" – the anthem of the rock 'n' roll revolution – as its theme song, signaled the film's two-pronged reach. On the one hand the song provided the film with a "musical ambiance" that set teenagers as distinct from the adults who ruled their homes, their schools, and their nation; on the other it announced that that, by mid-1955, American youths were ripe to overthrow many of the country's firmly-held tenets of racial division, as the rise of the civil rights movement in the mid-1950s and the concurrent emergence of rock 'n' roll culture signaled powerful dissonant voices in the narrative of middle-class consensus. The remaining chapters will examine these two decisive developments of the second half of the decade.

CHAPTER 7
Reshaping Race in America

> I am an invisible man [...] I am a man of substance, flesh and bone, fiber and liquids – and I might even be said to possess a mind. I am invisible, understand, simply because people refuse to see me.
> (Ralph Ellison, *Invisible Man*)

> We preach freedom around the world, and we mean it, and we cherish our freedom here at home, but are we to say to the world, and much more importantly, to each other that this is the land of the free except for the Negroes; that we have no second-class citizens except Negroes; that we have no class or caste system, no ghettoes, no master race except with respect to Negroes?
> (President John F. Kennedy, 11 June 1963)

The "Negro Problem"

Besides youth, the other crucial emerging identity group in 1950s America was the rising civil rights movement. Amid a society that was strongly focused on the economic ascendance of its white majority and historically mired in racial intolerance, if not outright hatred, early Cold War America became the breeding ground for the hopes of its black citizens that the words in the preamble of the 1949 United Nations Charter, proclaiming "universal respect for, and observance of, human rights and fundamental freedoms for all without distinction to race, language, or religion" would be applied to them as well as to colonized peoples in Africa and throughout the world.[1] As racial discrimination became an international embarrassment for Cold War America, since it stood in sharp contrast with the "benign democracy" announced in its containment rhetoric, the Truman and Eisenhower administrations found themselves as uneasy mediators between southern intransigence and calls for racial justice coming from other sectors of the country.[2]

For at least the first half of the twentieth century, the United States had been a brutally racist country. The Ku Klux Klan, preaching white supremacy in the South, had risen in the early 1920s as a response to early attempts by African-Americans to react to an all-white system of power relying on the "separate but equal" doctrine upheld by the Supreme Court in the 1890s which had given "legal validity to the system of segregation called 'Jim Crow.'"[3] By the mid-twentieth century, little had changed: although a large number of African-Americans had fought in and contributed to victory in World War II and had harbored hopes of a more equal participation in society upon their return home, white Americans (who accounted for just under ninety percent of the U.S. population) were still unprepared to offer them equality. The army they had fought in had been a segregated one and at war's end the country remained a deeply divided one, where African-Americans had become once again "the Negro problem."

Segregation of African-Americans was rampant and particularly vicious in the agrarian states of the South, where the Fourteenth Amendment (ratified in 1868 to ensure equal protection for the newly-freed slaves) was systematically denied by "a system of brutality, cruelty, economic disadvantage, humiliation, sexual subjugation, and, of course, the utter theft of legal rights."[4] Segregation was no less visible in the industrialized cities of the North, East and the West, into which impoverished African-Americans from the rural South had been pouring before, during and after World War II in what is known as the Great Migration.[5] Race riots had erupted in Harlem, Detroit, and in Los Angeles (the so-called "Zoot Suit Riots") in 1943.[6] Between 1945 and 1954 there had been nine race riots in Chicago alone and several more in the other industrial cities of the North, where African-American distress was particularly high as a consequence of the difficult social adjustment following the Great Migration.

At the end of World War II, some minimal steps towards better integration had indeed been taken. In 1944 the National Association for the Advancement of Colored People (NAACP) won a long legal battle to ban the white-only vote at the primaries. In the wake of a President's Committee on Civil Rights report addressing racism in postwar America and entitled *To Secure These Rights* (1947), Truman desegregated the U.S. army and the federal workforce in 1948. Graduate and professional schools in the South were desegregated following two Supreme Court decisions of 1950.[7] As the Great Migration continued after the war, average wages for black workers increased fourfold in the 1950s compared to the 1940s, leading some – even from within the black community – to boast of "the progressive improvement of race relations and the economic rise of the Negro in the United States" as a flattering example of "democracy in action."[8] Liberal intellectuals applied themselves to keeping up the false appearance of improving race relations in the U.S. Max Lerner's influential *America as a Civilization: Life and Thought in the United States Today* (1957) was typical of a widespread attitude to declare the solution of the "Negro problem" by emphasizing the few steps taken to end segregation. Several other desultory examples of African-American emancipation were widely publicized in the 1950s, based on the false assumption that the case of individual African-Americans who had in fact become successful was the norm for African-American society at large – people such as Ralph Bunche, the first African-American Nobel Prize recipient in 1950, or Jackie Robinson, first African-American major league baseball player in 1947, or Althea Gibson, first African-American on the world tennis tour in 1950. By the same token, great emphasis was placed on the first three African-Americans elected to the U.S. Congress in the 1950s, the 200 black professors teaching at white universities, or the election of black councilmen in fifteen U.S. cities. As it turned out, that was a very optimistic way of seeing things.

Those achievements were the exception, not the norm, and some scholars suggest that the greatest source of tension in the decade was not so much oppression itself as "the glowing rhetoric which promised the racial underclasses ever more equality, ever more freedom and uplift" – a rhetoric whose overall effect was to frustrate, rather than spur, actual change.[9] Increased wages still kept an average black American's salary at almost a half that of the average white man. As the 1950s wore on, the average income for black families in relation to white families fell, on a national scale, from 57 percent to 43 percent: throughout the 1950s, African-Americans were in fact getting poorer if compared to whites. Ben Wattenberg, a conservative commentator, wrote in *This USA* (1960): "regardless of level of education, on an income standard the Negro today can still be counted as that 'three-fifths of a person' that the unamended Constitution declared him to be."[10]

The changing urban landscape of 1950s America did nothing to improve racial integration. In fact, it made the racial issue worse. As discussed earlier, the white flight to the suburbs and the continuing flow of southern blacks into the twelve large metropolitan areas of the North were part of the same circular pattern: as whites moved to the suburbs, African-Americans moved into the inner cities; and since African-Americans were moving into the cities, whites were fleeing those very same cities. As the white flight deprived cities of their more affluent fiscal base, cities had to cut services for their (mostly black) citizens, thus becoming even less appealing to those who could afford to move out, thus spawning even more "white flight." Moreover, as a new housing ideal was created for white Americans (suburban, clean, spacious), cities in contrast became dirty, dilapidated, rotting away in chunks. All of this made for even more segregation: "at decade's end, America was literally more racially segregated in residential terms than it had never been before."[11]

For those black Americans who had managed to join the mobile, white upper classes, things were hardly easier. In a famous incident, William and Daisy Meyers, a black couple, moved to the all-white suburb of Levittown in 1957, to be welcomed by burning crosses and loudspeakers playing "Ol' Man River." It took the intervention of the New York Attorney General, who indicted eight Levittowners for conspiring against the black family, before the Meyers could be finally accepted into the community. Several other incidents of this kind were reported during the decade, the underlying idea being that a black family moving into a white neighborhood was not regarded as a fulfillment of the same status ambitions that whites relished; rather, their move often was treated "as a destructive, malicious act," since it carried with it the economic threat of bringing down property values, the only valuable asset for a middle-class family.[12]

By mid-decade, the civil rights movement began shedding the apathy of the silent white majority, with figures such as the reverend

Martin Luther King, Jr., who helped promote the civil rights cause among white moderates with a message of non-violence and black integration. His sober, dignified, non-antagonistic appearance reflected an intent to reach to black Americans as well as whites in search for a new middle ground. As African-American awareness grew in the 1950s and organized black groups began to diversify (besides the NAACP, other more militant groups came to the forefront of political action, among which CORE, the Congress on Racial Equality, and the SCLC, Southern Christian Leadership Conference), by the end of the decade white youths were beginning to question racial attitudes in America. The birth in 1960 of the SNCC (Student Non-Violent Coordinating Committee) brought this new, more militant approach to public attention and, with it, the beginning of the great season for civil rights in America in the first half of the 1960s.

Although the early 1960s are typically regarded as the core of the struggle for civil rights in the U.S., the 1950s were a crucial decade in which the system of racial segregation in America began to bend, in exemplary legal test cases which challenged the status quo before the U.S. Supreme Court and the Federal government. Those cases tested the purported right of the southern states to uphold a separate legal system whereby race relations would be governed under a different jurisdiction from the rest of the nation and whether the central government had a right to interfere with the states in matters of individual rights.

The Quest for African-American Identity: Early Civil Rights Landmarks

The cases litigated by the NAACP before the Supreme Court beginning in the mid-1950s became the springboard of the civil rights movement. The first was the *Brown v. Board of Education of Topeka, Kansas* suit of 1954 (followed by a second ruling in 1955), in which an African-American family fought school segregation and won the right to enroll their six-year-old daughter in a white school. Although it took years, even decades, before school desegregation extended to the whole country (the rulings' vague mandate that states end school segregation "with all deliberate speed" gave segregationists ample opportunity to resist change), *Brown v. Board* became a landmark in civil rights history, establishing a foundation to support aspirations to equality for African-Americans. By declaring unconstitutional the "separate but equal" formula, *Brown v. Board* legally empowered African-American communities across the nation to bring the whole system of racial segregation to general attention, placing it urgently at the top of the country's political agenda.[13]

The South resisted de-segregation with legal and illegal delays, often with violence. When Virginia Senator Harry F. Byrd called for "massive resistance" to school desegregation, a slew of brutal episodes of "private justice" spread across the southern states.[14] The most sensational of all was the lynching of Emmett Till in Money, Mississippi, in September 1955. A 14-year-old boy from Chicago, Till was in the South visiting relatives during that summer. Not aware of the many unwritten codes of racial separation in that part of the country, he broke one of segregation's unwritten rules: he talked to a white woman. He was beaten, mutilated, and shot through the head. The whole nation saw Till's open casket funeral photographs in *Jet* magazine, which exposed the huge gap between racial relations in the North and South of the United States. When two white men were arrested and accused of the murder, the U.S. Justice Department refused to step in to ensure a fair trial, claiming that it was Mississippi's responsibility to protect those under its jurisdiction. The Till trial, according to David Halberstam "the first great media event of the civil rights movement," was held in a segregated court of law and marred by extreme, at times illegal, defensive stalling tactics, which led to a "not guilty" verdict pronounced by a white-only jury.[15]

In another well-known episode of 1955, Rosa Parks, a civil rights activist, was arrested for refusing to give up her bus seat to a white passenger in Montgomery, Alabama. Like many other cities across the South, Montgomery enforced racial segregation on public buses, where the front seats were reserved for white passengers and the back seats for blacks; moreover, blacks were required to give up their seats to white passengers when the white section was full. Rosa Parks' arrest triggered a massive boycott of the bus system by the whole black population of Montgomery, lasting eleven months. Bringing together Montgomery's black community in full-fledged political activism, the boycott was led by still unknown 26-year-old Baptist minister Martin Luther King, Jr.: preaching love and non-violent resistance, King guided the community through the stand-off, until the Supreme Court ruled on November 13, 1956 that the segregation on buses was unconstitutional.

In the following years, more test cases for black integration were brought to southern courts: in 1956, Autherine Lucy was suspended from the all-white University of Alabama, as hostile white mobs protested her arrival on campus. Fighting back to win her right to return to campus, she was eventually expelled on the grounds that she was a "danger" to the university. President Eisenhower, who believed that "the hearts of men" could not be changed "with laws and decisions," refused to step in.[16] He did, however, intervene the following year, 1957, in Little Rock, Arkansas, when governor Orval Faubus mobilized the National Guard to prevent nine teenage black students from being admitted into Little Rock Central High School as the school year began. Eisenhower took action this time: he federalized the Arkansas National Guard, taking it out of the hands of governor Faubus, and sent elements of the 101st Airborne Division to Arkansas in order to protect the black students and enforce the Federal court order. In retaliation, Faubus shut down Little Rock high schools for the whole 1958–1959 school year: the civil rights movement was only in its infancy and visible, long-lasting breakthroughs were still several years away.

Beyond Invisibility: R.W. Ellison's *Invisible Man*

The trials of African-American existence in postwar American society at large are well captured in Ralph Ellison's literary image of the black American as an Invisible Man, an individual whose humanity is essentially betrayed in several different ways: in the South, through poverty, segregation and disenfranchisement; in the North, through life in the ghetto and social prejudice. Published in 1952, and one of the masterpieces of twentieth-century American literature, *Invisible Man* explores the paths open to black Americans after World War II: rural poverty, segregation in college, northern city ways, and the contradictions of political militancy. The book's opening states the case for the invisibility of African-Americans as a function of white society's refusal to see them:

> I am an invisible man [...] I am a man of substance, flesh and bone, fiber and liquids – and I might even be said to possess a mind. I am invisible, understand, simply because people refuse to see me. Like the bodiless heads you see sometimes in circus sideshows, it is as though I have been surrounded by mirrors of hard, distorting glass. When they approach me they see only my surroundings, themselves, or figments of their imagination – indeed, everything and anything except me.[17]

When *Invisible Man* was published, lynchings of African-Americans in the United States were not uncommon, and "miscegenation" was a crime in thirty American states, including the entire South.[18] Although Ellison's novel appeared on the cultural scene at a time when organized black protest against the status quo of racial inequality was expanding across the nation, *Invisible Man* did not attempt to document a plight. Ellison himself was "most irritated by those critics who overstress[ed] the book's narrowly racial or political aspects, those who prefer[red] to see it not as a novel at all but as a sociological case study, as a document of protest, or as an untransformed report of his personal or political reminiscences."[19] In the words of fellow Noble Prize recipient Saul Bellow, Ralph Ellison was, "[u]nlike the majority of his Negro contemporaries [...] not limited in his interests to the race problem. He was an artist."[20] Ellison created a literary place where race was reflected and distorted and where the canons of African-American social realism (and in particular those of the leading African-American writer at the time, Richard Wright, whose stance Ellison openly challenged) were dismissed. *Invisible Man* did not epitomize the sufferings of the black race: in writing "the book" during the seven-year span from 1945 to its publication year, Ellison brought onto the scene a new kind of black persona: if Richard

Wright's characters were angry, uneducated, and inarticulate – the outcome of a society that oppressed them – Ellison's Invisible Man was educated and articulate, self-aware and sophisticated.

In *Invisible Man* Ellison chose to emphasize the way in which African-Americans had created their own traditions, rituals and a history that formed a cohesive and complex culture on which a full sense of identity rested. He chose to represent such a tradition through the lens of literary modernism and its mythicizing strategies of representation, which by "mixing memory and desire" granted the Black Arts an "insurgency context" in which Ellison shaped his own work. An enthusiastic reader of T.S. Eliot's *The Waste Land* and a school-trained jazz musician (he studied trumpet at Tuskegee Institute in Oklahoma, his home state), Ellison gave voice to what he later defined as a "whole unrecorded history" of black America – in the words of Henry Louis Gates "an encyclopedia of black culture," delving "deeper than anyone before him, into the fullest range of African-American culture."[21]

The book's modernist paradigm allows its historical dimension to be diffused within the articulation of a developing human consciousness: Ellison, whose life (1913–1994) spanned most of the twentieth century, believed that fiction was the ideal instrument for the concurrent making of self and history, in a continuum that allowed for the changing of human consciousness and experience to be understood and represented. Structured according to the modernist belief that, in art, form and time should work "contrapuntally," *Invisible Man* consists of a prologue and an epilogue, in between which Ellison interposes twenty-five chapters of chronological narrative.[22] The first-person voice and the novel's modernist structure frame the narrative – a retrospective, chronological retelling of the major moments in the narrator's life, made relevant in the light of both the book's leading trope of invisibility and the ambiguous deathbed pronouncement of the narrator's grandfather, also presented in the prologue:

> He was an odd old guy, my grandfather, and I am told I take after him. It was he who caused the trouble. On his deathbed he called my father to him and said, "Son, after I'm gone I want you to keep up the good fight. I never told you, but our life is a war and I have been a traitor all my born days, a spy in the enemy's country ever since I give up my gun back in the Reconstruction. Live with your head in the lion's mouth. I want you to overcome 'em with yeses, undermine

'em with grins, agree 'em to death and destruction, let 'em swoller you till they vomit or bust wide open." They thought the old man had gone out of his mind. He had been the meekest of men. The younger children were rushed from the room, the shades drawn and the flame of the lamp turned so low that it sputtered on the wick like the old man's breathing. "Learn it to the younguns," he whispered fiercely; then he died.[23]

In a narrative interspersed with tropes of light and darkness, whiteness and blackness, the twenty-five chapters following the prologue tell a story of approximately a ten- or fifteen-year time-span, organized around five discrete stages, with each successive stage rendered more specifically in the narrative. Narrated in a highly realistic style, and paying great attention to detail, the events of each of these stages turn out to be highly calamitous, to the point of appearing fantastic or magical, thus overtly defying the realistic narrative form chosen for the representation. The epilogue contains a final avowal to leave the hideaway and re-enter the world: "Perhaps that's my greatest social crime, I've overstayed my hibernation, since there's a possibility that even an invisible man has a socially responsible role to play." The narrator concludes with a question to the reader, almost an invitation: "Who knows but that, on the lower frequencies, I speak for you?" As such, *Invisible Man* is a profound literary meditation on American citizenship and identity, seeking both to capture with precision the experience of African-Americans in the United States and, by implication, to suggest that in such an experience the emblem of citizenship's dangerous downside can be discovered.[24]

As Andrew Hoberek has argued, *Invisible Man* also represents a crucial documentary of changing American society in the 1950s, as it participates in the period's recurrent reification of threatened individuality that links it to postwar fiction and to works of social criticism like *The Lonely Crowd* and *The Organization Man*: "in this respect, the grandfather's individualism [...] anticipates not only the behavior of particular characters but the narrative project of *Invisible Man* as a whole." This a project aimed at generating "a sense of embattled individuality" in a world that is, as Ellison notes in the book's epilogue, characterized by a "passion toward conformity," in which "[n]one of us seems to know who he is or where he's going."[25] This aspect of the novel was also central to early praise by critics such as Robert Penn

Warren, who lauded Ellison for having transcended the confines of the debate on race and widened its scope into the larger context of the modern struggle for individual identity.[26] This point was re-iterated by many appreciations of *Invisible Man* and summed up in Tony Tanner's argument that *Invisible Man*, "so far from being limited to an expression of an anguish and injustice experienced particularly by Negroes, is quite simply the most profound novel about American identity written since the war."[27]

In the 1960s, on the other hand, intellectuals such as Irving Howe and the members of the Black Arts movement took issue with *Invisible Man* for the very same reason that white intellectuals such as Penn Warren and Tanner were lauding it, i.e. because it appeared to run from the political imperative that racism placed on each and every black artist in America. Accounts of the novel from the perspective of the African-American canon have been concerned with refuting the claims of such criticism and with demonstrating the novel's foundational engagement with questions of race.[28]

More recent re-appraisals of the wider canon of American literature of the 1950s have appeared interested in reconciling modernist and political readings of *Invisible Man* and in questioning what is there in this novel that still speaks to us fifty years later. David Castronovo has found that Ellison's modernism is a perfect fit for his political agenda: "Claiming to riff like a jazz musician [...] Ellison describes the phase of modernism he is in: a sort of Black American stream-of-consciousness punctuated with strong symbols representing moments of awareness for his protagonist."[29] In conjugating tropes of modernist sensibility with America's "original sin," its never resolved problem with race, Ellison's first novel (as well as his subsequent essays in *Shadow And Act* and *Going to the Territory*) has been crucial in transforming America's thinking about race and its own identity. "Ellison's book – Castronovo has concluded – stands as a protest against ideologies; in style and intellectual substance it blasts the conventions of its time and ours." At the end of the novel, the Invisible Man is an autonomous man – "living in hiding, it is true, but exhilarated by his own insights and by the escape from what was in store for men in gray flannel suits or members of the Brotherhood or Harlem Separatists."[30]

CHAPTER 8

The Age of Rock 'n' Roll

> People started realizing that if you can play the guitar and sing your ass off, you could be badder than Superman. And that was a strong feeling for a black man in the '50s.
> *(Cadillac Records*, Sony Music Film)

> Some people tap their feet, some people snap their fingers, and some people sway back and forth. I just sorta do 'em all together, I guess.
> (Elvis Presley, 1956 interview)

The Seventh Stream

The struggle for recognition of black identity in America begun by the civil rights movement in the mid-1950s was one in a cluster of forces emerging in postwar United States under the rubric of emancipatory movements for the affirmation of individual and group rights.[1] These movements paralleled the emergence of unrest around the world under the sensitive agenda of third-world decolonization. In the U.S., the early breakthroughs of the civil rights movement coincided with the widespread emergence in society of adolescents as autonomous consumers as well as critical voices of the middle-class consensus: the beat generation specifically developed a language of difference which looked at the African-American condition as a template for white youths' existential status beyond the narrow confines of middle-class culture. The widespread acceptance of beat culture in the latter part of the decade and especially the great commercial success of Kerouac's *On the Road* among young readers indicated that, as the 1950s wore on, American youths were yearning for a cultural space external to the middle-class consensus. Besides beat culture (widely defined), the rock 'n' roll revolution, which spread across America around the middle of the decade, was the other cultural indicator of ongoing transformations in America's youth culture.

Suddenly emerging in the mid-1950s as the "seventh stream" of the American music industry, rock 'n' roll was predicated upon a new conversation happening within certain layers of American society between white and black youth cultures and revolved around the blending of specific white and black pop music traditions into a new language that, for the first time in American culture, was the domain of neither whites nor blacks, but was in fact a space of cross-fertilization shared by whites and blacks alike and which came to define a new musical culture for the emerging baby-boom generation.[2] Most striking of all was the fact that such revolution was initiated and sustained in the U.S. South, which had been the cradle of both white and black American popular music traditions, the blues on the one hand, country music on the other, while at the same time it had functioned as the geopolitical space of highest resistance to racial dialogue, let alone integration.

Memphis, 1953: "I don't sound like nobody"

In the summer of 1953, an eighteen-year-old truck driver from Memphis, Tennessee, named Elvis Aaron Presley, walked into the Memphis Recording Service at 706 Union Avenue, a small storefront recording facility, to make a personal record and "surprise [his] mother."[3] The studio, which charged $ 3.98 plus tax for vanity recordings of this kind, also functioned as the headquarters of the fledgling Sun label – one of hundreds of small independent record companies specializing in country and blues which had mushroomed all across post-World War II America in the wake of recent technological developments that had made it possible for small entrepreneurs with limited capital resources to enter the sound recording business. Started in 1950 by Sam Phillips, Sun Records was in the business of recording "Negro artists in the South who wanted to make a record [and] just had no place to go."[4] Strategically placed in Memphis – the city at the crossroads of the U.S. South and a key stop on the Great Migration route from the Mississippi Delta to the industrial cities of the North, especially Chicago – Sun had in fact been among the first labels to record the soon-to-be-giants of postwar blues, Riley "Blues Boy" (B.B.) King, Junior Parker, and Howlin' Wolf, among others.[5]

A very ambitious young music entrepreneur, Phillips made no secret of being on the lookout for the next big thing in American music. At a time when American pop had become bland, predictable and increasingly unable to converse with the emerging juvenile market, Phillips was one of many small music impresarios in the country to understand that a large, yet untapped market of young, white, and mostly teenage consumers no longer shared the musical tastes of their elders and were ready for new sounds that would define their emerging social identity.[6] People like Phillips also knew that deeply-ingrained racial suspicion in the country, especially in the South, was preventing teenagers from appreciating the extraordinary Negro talent he and others like him were discovering and putting on record at an unprecedented pace in those years. To help bridge that gap, Phillips also began recording young white artists whose sounds fell outside the fold of mainstream hillbilly and pop, having become persuaded that the next new thing in American music lay in the blending of the black and white musical traditions, a persuasion well summarized in his apocryphal statement "If I could find a white man who had the Negro sound and the Negro feel, I could make a billion dollars."[7]

Presley was white, but he and his family did not share in the country's growing postwar affluence. He had grown up in modest working-class neighborhoods in Tupelo, Mississippi, where he had been born, and then in Memphis, where his family had moved after his father had been incarcerated for forging a four dollar check. Like many white southerners, he came from a deeply religious family. And like many white southerners, he was as conversant with the hillbilly (i.e. country) and the white gospel music traditions – a world "that was his as a given" – as he was with black music, black gospel first of all, which he heard upon brief Sunday incursions into the neighborhood African-American churches, and Mississippi blues, the music of "the real low-down Mississippi singers [like] Big Bill Broonzy and

Big Boy Crudup," which most southern whites frowned upon as the "Devil's music."[8] Moments before recording his gift record at Sun studio, Presley exchanged small talk with Marion Keiser, Phillips' partner and trusted right hand, inquiring if anyone around the studio needed a singer. Interviewed by Elvis biographer Peter Guralnik, Marion thus accounts for that conversation:

> He said, "If you know anyone that need a singer ...."
> And I said, "What kind of singer are you?"
> He said, "I sing all kinds."
> I said, "Who do you sound like?"
> "I don't sound like nobody."[9]

Then Presley went on to record his two-sided acetate, which included renderings of two pop standards, "My Happiness" and "That's When Your Heartaches Begin."

It was not until the next summer that Phillips decided to give the now 19-year-old truck driver a proper audition. During one of the sessions Elvis broke into an impromptu rendition of "That's Alright Ma," a 1946 hit record by Arthur "Big Boy" Crudup, a bluesman whose music Presley had probably heard on the local radio stations. Sam Phillips was awed by the white kid mimicking the black singer's scat note-for-note, "but also adding a rhythm that came out of country music with a heavy accent on the first and third beats in the style of the Carter Family records of the 1930s and 1940s."[10] The song was recorded in a long night session in which Presley, guitarist Scotty Moore and bassist Bill Black sought to lay down on tape Phillips' vision of the new musical style. The single was released on July 19, 1954. With crucial promotion from popular local DJ Dewey Phillips at WHBQ in Memphis, "That's Alright Ma," became a sudden regional hit, one that awed and confounded listeners who, although unable to decide whether the new singer was white or black, still rushed to buy the record. The rock 'n' roll revolution had begun.

This now canonical narrative of rock 'n' roll's inception includes several of the crucial elements that brought about that new wave in popular music in mid-1950s America. Among these were the white/black division in American society as reflected in the rigid separation of music markets by the mainstream recording industry; the meteoric rise of independent record labels in post-World War II America and their contribution to the affirmation of alternative musical styles; the role played by radio in the 1950s in shattering the white/black musical divide and in the formation of new musical tastes; the extraordinary cross-fertilization between black and white cultures as a central element in the formation of American music in the twentieth century; the inception of a new star system in which young black and white performers alike held prominent roles. Implicitly, it also addresses the core question – what exactly is rock 'n' roll? – which the rest of this chapter will try to untangle.

What is Rock 'n' Roll?

The U.S. South has been the breeding ground of the American popular music tradition in the twentieth century, as black and white musics developed there along unwritten rules of complete segregation of consumer markets and constant cross-fertilization. Scholars have repeatedly pointed out the way in which white "hillbilly" music was shaped by a combination of Anglo-Saxon and African-American elements of style (the white folk tradition on the one hand, the syncopated rhythms, raw vocal emotionalism, and work-chant "call and response" typical of black music on the other).[11] Likewise, scholars have also pointed out that the blues was in fact shaped by the combination of African, Caribbean as well as European musical elements (such as the reliance on mixed pentatonic and diatonic scales as well as the first-fourth-fifth-degree chord progression).[12] Despite evident cross-fertilization, the music industry that emerged at the beginning of the twentieth century kept white and black musics rigorously separated. Exercising total control over production and distribution, the industry operated according to a rigid post-Fordist model of market segmentation. At the heart of this practice was the popularity chart system, established by the trade magazine *Billboard* in 1934 to track sales of sheet music (at the time, the predominant property in the industry) and the extent of its exposure through radio plugs. Strategically positioned within the distribution chain of music properties, the chart system's circular logic (record sales and airplay influence ranking, which in turn influences sales and airplay) was designed to secure control of the business in the hands of a very few, very large companies and to preserve the separation of musical styles and of their audiences.[13]

Until the 1950s, American popular music revolved around three major, and highly segregated, markets, who were separately targeted for the sale of the industry's main properties – records, sheet music, jukebox play and airplay. One was a market for working class, rural whites, centering on hillbilly music (officially renamed "Country and Western" in 1949), a stream that emerged in the rural South in the late 1920s through founding figures such as the Carter Family, Jimmie Rodgers and, in the postwar period, with Hank Williams and Johnny Cash. Another was a market for African-Americans, revolving around rural blues and gospel music, as well as around an up-tempo, electric, guitar and horn-intensive energetic evolution of the blues, emerging in urban centers after World War II as a result of the Great Migration and officially dubbed "Rhythm and Blues" in 1948. The third, largest and most profitable of all, was the "pop" market, centering on the very popular, catchy sounds produced in the New York City district known as Tin Pan Alley and consisting of the large majority of music consumers across the country.

The emergence of rock 'n' roll in mid-1950s America brought a forcible challenge to this monolithic industry by bending its two central tenets: the separation of musical styles and the separation of consumer markets by race and class. Responding to young white consumers' demands for sounds that would more closely represent their identitarian quest for more authentic expression and rejection of middle-class values, rock 'n' roll emerged out of a complex process of convergence of the white and black musical streams at a historical moment when the predominance of the major labels began to be challenged by small regional record companies.[14] The emergence of rock 'n' roll is as much the story of the changing, enabling conditions of music production and consumption that made possible the newly-minted dialog between white and black music in America as it is the story of that dialog itself.

I will first look at the changing conditions of production. After the war, new and more affordable technologies for producing and listening to recorded music became available. Anywhere from four to six hundred record labels appeared in the country in the years immediately following the war, most of them specializing in black music. Los Angeles had the largest number of successful independent rhythm and blues (R&B) labels, such as Aladdin, Pearl, Modern, and Ebb. Across the country similar record companies were established from humble beginnings in the same period: King in Cincinnati, Peacock in Houston, Chess in Chicago, Savoy in Newark, and Atlantic in New York. The format standards of commercial records also changed in the immediate postwar years.

By the late 1940s, the industry-standard 78-rpm phonograph was replaced by new formats that were cheaper to make and offered greater fidelity of sound. Columbia developed the 33 1/3 long-playing record, soon known simply as the "LP," which the company targeted at its major market stream, classical music. RCA then introduced smaller 45 rpm records, which were ideal for single songs and appealed mostly to young consumers. Now capable of manufacturing records with smaller capital investments, the new independent labels filled a market gap created during the war, when shortages of shellac (the chemical used for the production of 78 rpm records) as well as their own cultural biases had led major recording companies to neglect the working class music streams (blues and country) in the 1940s and concentrate on mainstream pop: in the postwar years, legions of country and blues artists found new outlets for their talent in the fledgling independent label scene.[15]

The other major factor contributing to changing conditions of production was the rise of television in 1950s America. Although television did not contribute to changing musical tastes (American television became instrumental in endorsing those tastes once they had already emerged, as I will later discuss), it was nonetheless instrumental to the rock 'n' roll revolution because of the earthquake it brought to American broadcasting beginning in 1948. As radio lost most of its programming formats to television – as well as its traditional base of white, middle-class listeners – it was forced to reinvent itself in order to survive and it did so by plugging those market segments that television did not reach, mostly black communities in the large industrial cities of the North and West and suburban white youths. And although still operating within the strictly segregated practices of American society at large (there were black radio stations with black DJs targeting a "race" audience and white radio stations with white DJs targeting white youths), the airwaves turned out to be more color-neutral than other cultural outlets.

Besides the technology, music also was changing in the postwar years – especially black music, which witnessed the emergence of R&B as a response to the changing social conditions of urbanized African-Americans. A working-class genre, R&B was a sophisticated convergence of at least three African-American music forms: urban blues, with a heightened role for the electric guitar and a departure from topics of loss and despair typical of rural blues; gospel, with its hand clapping, call and response, rhythmic complexities, melodic improvisation, and percussive accompaniments; and jump band jazz, a style popular at the tail end of the big band era after World War II which promoted a highly entertaining sound, performed by small five- or six-piece ensembles, with prominent saxophone solos and an upbeat swing feeling.[16] Emphasizing accents on the second and fourth beats of the measure (the so-called "backbeat"), played primarily on the snare drum, R&B was conducive to body movement, and emerged as quintessential African-American working-class dance music.[17] New Orleans virtuoso Fats Domino's 1956 hit "Blue Monday" celebrated R&B as free-time fantasy, a style that set the tedium of weekday labor against the excitement of weekend leisure. As the song starts out deploring the working week – "Blue Monday, how I hate Blue Monday/Got to work like a slave all day" – the mood changes as the weekend approaches:

> Saturday mornin', oh Saturday mornin'
> All my tiredness has gone away
> Got my money and my honey
> And I'm out on the stand to play.

More optimistic than depression-era blues, R&B's worldview was still firmly rooted in real-life experiences of hard drinking (as in Stick McGee's "Drinkin' Wine Spo-Dee-o-Dee" of 1948), hard partying (as in Roy Brown's "Rockin' at Midnight," of 1948), celebration of women and romance (as in Ray Charles' 1954 classic "I Got a Woman,") and uncensored sexuality (as in "Big" Joe Turner's 1954 "Shake, Rattle and Roll"), all delivered through vocal virtuosity and onstage showmanship, both gospel legacies, as displayed by stylish tenor lead singers like wailer Clyde McPhatter and crooner Sonny Til. Vocal emotion, slurred pronunciations, and blue notes were carried over from the blues. The instrumental solo, most often by the tenor saxophone, combined the improvised fluidity of jazz with the long slurs and repetition derived from the blues.[18]

By the turn of the 1950s, as R&B bands began to appear on record and those records hit the airwaves, black music began to appeal to audiences beyond its African-American target group. From Cleveland to New York City, from Detroit to Los Angeles, millions of white teenagers became avid listeners of black radio stations and their "race" programming. Cross-racial success on the airwaves boosted record sales for R&B records beyond the limited, and less affluent, African-American market, as whites flocked to the ghetto music stores to purchase R&B records (which were not distributed elsewhere). As George Lipsitz has reported, in 1952 the Dolphin Record Store in Los Angeles sold over 40 percent of its R&B records to whites and in that same year New Orleans record dealers noticed numerous purchases of rhythm-and-blues music by white housewives, some of whom pretended to be running errands for their (African-American) maid or housekeeper.[19]

Taking notice of the exodus of their white audience to the black stations, some DJs on the white radio stations in urban centers began popularizing "race music" across race lines. The best known of this new breed of white DJs was Alan Freed, who had begun broadcasting a night-time show called "Alan Freed's Moondog Show" on Cleveland's WJW in 1951. His broadcasts were syndicated to other stations, and in March 1952 Freed organized a "Moon Dog Coronation Ball" which attracted 18,000 fans to the 10,000-seat Cleveland Arena. The next year another such program was cancelled because 30,000 people turned up to fight for the 10,000 seats available. Freed's Balls showcased R&B artists such as the Buddy Johnson Orchestra, Joe Turner, Fats Domino, the Moonglows, the Harptones, the Drifters, Ella Johnson, Dakota Staton, and Red Prysock to crowds that were composed for two thirds by whites and racially separated by a dividing rope.[20] In 1954 Freed moved to WINS radio in New York City, with the highest annual salary paid to an independent R&B jockey up to that point, and his "Rock and Roll Party," broadcast nightly from 7 to 11 pm, quickly became the city's most popular music show.[21] Nationwide, more white DJs entered the "race music" arena. Bill Randle in Cleveland, Hunter Hancock in Los Angeles, "John R." Richbourgh in Nashville, and George "Hound Dog" Lorenz in Buffalo, NY all contributed to defining what was now a trend: the DJs were now filling the void left by orchestra leaders in the previous decades and had become the crucial link between songs and audiences, the midwives of success in popular music. The "record spinners" established themselves as the hit-makers of the popular music industry and their impact on the rock 'n' roll revolution cannot be overstated.

The sudden success of the new independent music studios and record labels as well as radio stations with the affluent white youth market shaped a new geography of America's music industry. Since they all operated within strictly defined regional markets – for the radio broadcasters, because of the inherent limitations of the medium as well as the strict regulations limiting station ownership in the US; for the independent record labels, because of the impracticable cost and complexities of national distribution for the small local music entrepreneurs – music radio and the indie labels began a model of local music production and distribution that terminated New York City's prewar hegemony of the industry. As a dozen major cities across the nation (Los Angeles, Chicago, Cleveland, Cincinnati, Detroit, Memphis, just to name a few) created "short loops" of production and distribution, they exposed, under the national radar, a new music that had no geographical center, focused on singers and singing groups in the ordering of its economic priorities, valued performer and performance over song and songwriter, targeted a predominantly young consumer group and, even more important, seemed oblivious to the boundaries of race still prevalent in most other domains of society.[22]

As white and black audiences were converging through the ingenious mediation of the record spinners, black and white musics also began converging through several paths of adaptation and assimilation which saw hits "crossing over" from one stream to the other. George Lipsitz has offered a telling inventory of blurring racial lines in popular music, reflecting changing racial attitudes in urban America:

> Bull Moose Jackson's 1949 rhythm and blues hit, "Why Don't You Haul Off and Love Me," copied the original version recorded three months earlier by country singer Wayne Raney, and the efforts of country artist Hank Penny provided the model for Wynonie Harris's successful cover of "Bloodshot Eyes" in 1951. The Orioles placed eight records on the rhythm and blues best-seller lists between 1948 and 1953, culminating in their biggest hit "Crying in the Chapel," written by Artie Glenn, first released as a country song by his son Darrell, and delivered in a decidedly country vocal style by Orioles lead singer Sonny Til.[23]

R&B artists in particular became conscious that in order for their music to cross the race lines, it had to be made more congenial to the white audiences. Artists like Bill Ward, Roy Brown, and Fats Domino began smoothing out some of the "race" elements in their music – the African-based rhythms, the slurred pronunciations – so as to make their records more palatable to white teenagers. Bill Ward and The Dominoes' 1951 hit "Sixty Minute Man," recorded on Federal, one of King Records' subsidiary labels, began the exodus to the white charts. Immediately topping the R&B charts upon its release, the record also made a landmark appearance on the pop charts, becoming the first R&B single to penetrate the white market. In the terminology of the industry, "Sixty Minute Man" became the first "R&B to pop crossover." The song was unmistakably framed with gospel harmony and rhythm, including the instrumentation of piano, drums, bass, guitar, and organ. Nevertheless, "Sixty Minute Man" was completely secular, with a bold and driving bass voicing, in the familiar genre of explicit male praise songs of sexual prowess, its title explicitly referring to extended love-making:

> Look a here girls I'm telling you now
> They call me "Lovin' Dan"
> I rock 'em, roll 'em all night long
> I'm a sixty-minute man

According to rock 'n' roll lore, it was this song that inspired Alan Freed to announce a new era in American music: "Rock and Roll!

That's what it is!" Freed reportedly exclaimed on WJW in 1952 after playing Bill Ward's record. A metaphor for sex in African-American vernacular since at least the 1930s, the phrase "rocking and rolling" had previously appeared in several R&B songs, including Roy Brown's "Good Rockin' Tonight" and The Ravens' "Rock All Night Long" (both dating from 1948). Yet, it was only after Freed's epiphanic proclamation that the phrase took on its definitive meaning. "Rock 'n' roll" came to label a new type of music, a "softer-edged" version of R&B which, in Philip Ennis' words, was "not authentic rhythm and blues, or jazz or pop" and yet had the potential "to communicate the simple but dangerous fact that [Freed] was bringing a black popular 'party' music (risqué lyrics with a strong dance beat) to a mixed audience of black and white teenagers."[24] Much more than jive talk, "rocking" became a label transcending its own semantics: it signaled "the musical crossing of sensitive racial and moral boundaries" while at the same time – by "neutralizing" the naming process through a signifier bearing no specific connotation to an average white consumer – it also masked that very crossing that it was announcing.[25]

Rockers Take the Stage

The first generation of rock 'n' rollers was composed predominantly of back artists whose crossover hits were making white vs. black demarcations in American popular music irrelevant. In early 1954, "Gee" by The Crows, one in the large family of vocal groups of the era, became the first R&B record to hit number one in the pop charts. In that same year, "Sh-Boom" became the first song to make the national pop charts in both its R&B version (by the Chords) and pop version (by the Crew-Cuts). By 1955, black artists were in fact beginning to outsell the white covers and the major labels were beginning to take notice: in 1955 Little Richard's "Long Tall Sally" was the first black original to surpass its cover (recorded by domesticated white rocker Pat Boone) on the national market; and the Platters, who had recorded a number of hits on the independent King label, moved to Mercury in 1955, becoming the first R&B group to make the switch to a major recording company. Concurrently, more black artists began to break through to the popular charts scene with increasingly more distinct crossover elements.

Saint Louis-born Charles Edward Anderson ("Chuck") Berry was a case in point. A skilled performer of hillbilly music (especially Hank Williams' songs) for mixed white and black audiences in the Saint Louis area, Berry blended his R&B roots with country, to produce his first black crossover in 1956, "Maybellene," whose driving beat and chronicles of the 1950s teenage experience (focusing on hot-rodding and romance) made it ideal material for a young white audience. "Maybellene" was quintessential of a style that was as revolutionary in its synthesis of music genres, innovative guitar and performance style as it was conventional in the themes it chose to address.[26] This blending of styles and musical traditions was also a strong element in New Orleans R&B artist Antoine "Fats" Domino. His exotic pronunciation of words, dance-oriented rhythms, and use of dense, swirling instrumental backgrounds reflected the historical interactions between white (especially French) music and black blues in Louisiana and East Texas.[27] Domino reached the pop top-forties in July 1955 with "Ain't That a Shame," and then again the next year with an old big band song from the early forties previously recorded in country versions which he released as "Blueberry Hill." Meanwhile his sound, called R&B up to 1954, was now heralded as rock 'n' roll, granting him access to the American teenage market and a six gold (million selling) records in his career. Less successful in record sales, Chess bluesman Bo Diddley nevertheless capitalized on his syncopated with his bump-and-grind shuffle to rank high in demand at high school dances.

As black artists were increasingly crossing over to the white "pop" audiences, a similar trend became noticeable in the reverse direction, when several country musicians, mostly southern, began to experiment with blending hillbilly and R&B as a response to the new demand from white audiences for up-tempo, beat-driven music. This new sound, which was no longer white and yet not altogether black, found its pioneer in a western swing musician from Michigan called Bill Haley.[28] Although he lacked "the youthful charisma and sexual swagger" to emerge as rock 'n' roll's first teenage heartthrob, Haley made a conscious effort to integrate his country roots with R&B music and became instrumental in pushing rock 'n' roll up another rung in popular attention.[29] In 1951, Haley covered, with his group the Saddlemen, "Rocket '88," an R&B hit originally recorded by Jackie Brenston and written by Ike Turner, two African-American artists in Sam Phillips' stable at Sun. Haley's version, recorded for Philadelphia's Holiday Records, became a regional hit in the Northeast and set the tone for a string of R&B-influenced recordings which included "Rock the Joint" (1952) and "Crazy Man Crazy" (1953), both recorded on the independent Essex label (also based in Philadelphia). Although it never made the hit parade, "Rock this Joint" was quintessential rock 'n' roll in its infancy: an R&B-derived tune, which the Saddlemen, an outfight right out of country music who donned sideburns and cowboy boots, performed with accordion and steel guitar. Between "Rock this Joint" and "Crazy Man Crazy," Haley underwent a major transformation: gone were the sideburns, cowboy boots and country sound, replaced by tuxedoes and a powerful rock 'n' roll ensemble, now renamed The Comets, consisting of drums, bass, two electric guitars, and tenor saxophone, propelling "Crazy Man Crazy" to his first national hit parade appearance in 1953.

Although R&B-inspired, Haley's records were far from being copies of any particular black style or band. Haley's voice was unmistakably white and the repetitive choral chants followed the tradition of a white musical style known as "western swing," an up-tempo rendition of country music, expressly developed for dancing crowds and epitomized by bands such as Bob Wills and His Texas Playboys. The novel feature of Haley's style was its rhythm, drawn from black music but dominating the arrangements much more than it did in R&B records. As Charlie Gillett has suggested, "with Haley, every other beat was heavily accented by the singers and all the instrumentalists at the expense of the relatively flexible rhythms and complex harmonies of dance music records cut for the black audience."[30]

In a typical move that would define rock 'n' roll's commercial trajectory, Decca (one of the majors) signed Haley in the wake of his national success. In April 1954 the group assembled at New York's Pythian Temple studios for their first Decca session, recording "Rock

Around the Clock," a song written by a pair of white middle-aged music-business veterans and originally recorded (just one month before) by Italian-American group Sonny Dae and His Knights. Although it sold a healthy 75,000 copies, the record failed to make much of an impact. It was the decision to use "Rock Around the Clock" behind the opening credits of the 1955 Richard Brooks' movie *Blackboard Jungle* that secured the song, and Bill Haley, a place in the history books. In 1955 "Rock Around the Clock" rose to number 1 in the pop charts and stayed there for eight straight weeks. It has since sold 30 million copies, more than any other rock single.[31]

Later in 1954 Bill Haley hit the charts again with a cover of Joe Turner's R&B hit "Shake Rattle and Roll." Haley's version of Turner's song became in many ways the blueprint of the white crossover record. Haley's version departed from the R&B original in several ways: it cleaned up the black original by removing its sexual innuendo (Turner's gaze at woman's naked body in the line "Way you wear those dresses, the sun comes shinin' through [...] I can't believe my eyes, all that mess belongs to you," becomes with Haley the image of distant femininity: "Wearin' those dresses, your hair done up so right/ You look so warm, but your heart is cold as ice"). It also stripped away many musical effects from the original R&B recording – the slurred pronunciations, the complex and harmonious backing – while adding guitar work and other effects from hillbilly music which still generated a raw, emotional excitement in a thumping and shouting delivery that sounded like "a powerful and liberating force" for the white teenage audiences.[32]

In Haley's wake, a host of white rockers including Gene Vincent and Eddie Cochran emerged in the second half of the decade, catalyzing shared musical experiences which cut across race and class boundaries to merge into a "seventh stream" which would eventually condense blues, country and popular music into a new, definitive, long-lasting component of American music.

From Presley to "Elvis"

It is precisely at this juncture, both stylistic and historical, that Elvis Presley enters the picture. Presley was one in a cohort of white southern hillbilly rockers out of Sam Phillips' stable of artists at Sun, or directly inspired by it, which also included Carl Perkins, Jerry Lee Lewis, Buddy Holly, and the Everly Brothers – all of whom contributed to forging a brand of country-rooted rock 'n' roll, emphasizing a guitar-oriented string sound and which came to be known as "rockabilly."[33] An ideal point of convergence between the black and white working class music traditions, rockabilly was the definitive force that shook the 1950s American music industry to its roots. Presley's youthful, handsome, almost feminized persona allowed him to shape an iconic look which, together with his pioneering music formula, contributed to thrusting his character into the arena of mass culture stardom. His three-way crossover exploits (he was able to sell pop, country and R&B-gospel tunes across all three music markets) made him the epitome of a decade in American popular music when a monolithic industry had to reshape itself, in the wake – instead of at the helm – of youth culture's new tastes and trajectories.

Although his national success came following his transition to a major label, RCA – a move dictated by his commandeering manager Colonel Tom Parker – Presley's musical revolution was shaped in the twelve months he spent at Sun Records in Memphis, from July 1954 to July 1955, when he became the instrument in Sam Phillips' vision of a "white man [with] the Negro sound and the Negro feel." While at Sun, Presley released five singles, all based on the same formula: a blues song backed up by a country and western song – songs that his audience was likely to have heard before, but which Presley performed in ways that were utterly new.

Presley's first Sun record combined Memphis bluesman Arthur "Big Boy" Crudup's 1946 "That's Alright Mama" and "Blue Moon of Kentucky," a song that had been recorded by country music legend Bill Monroe in 1947. Both sides presented a previously unheard mix of a "clean and austere" country backup, provided by guitarist Scotty Moore and bassist Bill Black, to which Presley superimposed an exuberant vocal delivery which was softer and more ballad-like on the blues side and more pop-oriented on the country side. Basically, Presley turned the conventions of both genres around, in a deliberate stylistic reversal, or displacement, which Phillips had envisioned as the new highway to pop. According to Greil Marcus, Presley's breakthrough was first of all cultural: he reached "beyond his community," Marcus has argued, not so much imitating black singers, but rather embracing "the nerve to cross the borders he had been raised to respect." Once that step was taken, he was able to deliver songs in which he "moved back and forth in a phrase" from country to blues, from white to black, in a completely new manner that "thrilled some, and threatened others."[34] Indeed Elvis Presley didn't "sound like nobody." He commanded a style that, according to Gillett, was "high and clear, breathless and impatient," with varying rhythmic emphases that were exceptional for a white singer. It was a sound suggesting "a young white man celebrating freedom, ready to do anything, go anywhere, pausing long enough for apologies and even regrets and recriminations, but then hustling on towards the new."[35]

The next four Sun records built, in a crescendo pattern, on this breakthrough intuition. In September 1954, Presley recorded a Roy Brown blues classic, "Good Rockin' Tonight," which he backed with a country rendering of "I Don't Care if the Sun Don't Shine." Marcus has defined "Good Rockin'" a "cataclysmic" event, reflecting "the new confidence of a young man who knows what it means to satisfy an audience, to take them beyond their expectations," a record "charged with an authority that no other country rocker ever approached."[36] After two more singles with good regional sales (Sun was too small a label to afford nationwide distribution), in August 1955 Presley recorded his two last Sun sides, a country number, "I forgot to remember to Forget," backed by "Mystery Train," a dark blues Junior Parker had originally released two years before. To many critics, "Mystery Train" might as well be regarded as the epitome of Presley's career, the song that best of all defined his place in American music, the definitive proof that rockabilly, and rock 'n' roll, were in fact the result of a deep dialog between white and black cultures and not a mere formula for pop success. As Marcus has shown, "Mystery Train," co-written by Junior Parker and Sam Phillips, was a veritable roller-coaster into the American music's past: reaching back to a Carter Family song of the 1930s entitled "Worried Man Blues," it "submitted" to the mood of its predecessor which blended white gospel and the blues in a tale combining intimations of an unfathomable human destiny, human helplessness, and uselessness of action. Whereas on the earlier Sun records Presley had, in Marcus' words, "left home with the blues and come black on the flipside" (i.e. through country music), on "Mystery Train" Presley delivered a blues that was rooted deep down in his own cultural lore, a blues he could make his own and at the same time upend through his own rebellion:

> Inspired by the feeling of going up against the old meaning of the tune, or determined to beat out Junior Parker, the black man, or simply thrilled by the music, Elvis sings this song with shock: he rebels against it. There is so much fire in his singing, so much personality and soul, that he changes the meaning of the song without smoothing it over. There is a tremendous violence to the record: "Train I ride," Elvis sings, but he sounds as if he's going to run it down. "It took my baby," Parker had moaned (riding us back to the days when a black locomotive was the symbol of a force no one could resist, of fate on wheels): "It's gone do it again." "Well," Elvis declares, "it took my baby – BUT IT NEVER WILL AGAIN – no, not again."[37]

Fully capturing the agon of Presley's anxiety of influence, "Mystery Train" closed the circle of white music's problematic misprision of its African-American other, whereby misreading his predecessors Presley created whole new avenues of imaginative space for himself and for the new sounds he was minting.

Fully defining Presley's and rock 'n' roll's future trajectories, his Sun sides were the precondition for the transition from Presley to "Elvis," i.e. to the fabrication of the long-lasting myth of the inception of rock 'n' roll. To accomplish this feat, the full shebang of mass culture had to be mobilized. The transition, in late 1955, to RCA, which made him a national and international star, and his televised appearances, beginning in January 1956 on the Tommy Dorsey Show, made Elvis the icon of popular culture we revere today. Especially defining in this context were Elvis' appearances on the Ed Sullivan Show in late 1956 and early 1957, which packaged his persona into an audio-visual commodity to be sold within the realm of mass culture. And a rebellious commodity it was, in its problematic mixing of gender and race elements which proved highly upsetting to the middle class consensus. Elvis' highly sexualized "pelvis" gyrations, which Sullivan censored by instructing his camera crews to film Elvis from the waist up, as well as his feminized look and gender subversiveness, which inverted traditional modes of visual reception by placing the male figure as the object of the gaze, all contributed to threatening the seemingly solid edifice of containment-era gender roles.[38]

Elvis' sudden departure to Hollywood and the movies, beginning in 1956 – Colonel Parker turned Elvis into a goldmine, in which he shared 50 percent of the profits – delivered his musical breakthroughs to newer cohorts of musicians coming in his wake and crystallized him into the "image," much more than the sound, of the rock 'n' roll revolution. Although Elvis remained a bestseller for RCA records well into the mid-1960s and beyond, between 1956 and 1969 (when his bondage to Hollywood finally expired) Elvis' best energies were captured by his star roles in 31 movies, and the music he recorded after 1957 belonged almost exclusively to the more sedate atmosphere of schmaltz.[39] Elvis' meteoric appearance on the rock 'n' roll horizon, from 1954 to 1956, his waning in Hollywood, his 1968 comeback and subsequent Las Vegas twilight and premature death in 1977 at age 42, all epitomize Elvis' larger-than-life contribution to the music and to the idea of youth music as rebellion and tormented dialogue with elders and tradition, seen as defining and constraining at the same time.

Tim Parrish has likened Elvis to a version of Emerson's "man of parts," the quintessential American phenomenon who links America to its two divergent, and yet coexistent, destinies, slavery and the pursuit of happiness, in a continuum that forces the appraisal of both through a sense that "what we have been is not what we are."[40] A testament to the hybridity of American identity, rock 'n' roll speaks of the need to view America pragmatically, in a perspective according to which identity is process, not entity. Rock 'n' roll confirms that American culture is, as Carolyn Porter has contended, a collision of "cultural forcefields," discrete "borderlands" which historically have shifted from moments of total exclusion to moments of collision and mutual activation, moments during which new identity-altering paradigms are activated.

Although rock 'n' roll did not make the civil rights movement any lighter or less painful, nor did it alter in any way the Fordist process of production and consumption of the middle class consensus, it emerged in many ways as Cold War America's leading cultural narrative at home and abroad. Domestically, rock 'n' roll enabled, as Medovoi has shown, the creation of a Fordist "counterimaginary" which allowed youth to see itself as simultaneously within, yet implicitly critical of, the Cold War consensus.[41] Abroad, it fostered a mythology of America as a harbinger of mass cultural models which official culture resisted, charging American influence as "decadent nonculture," an enemy of bourgeois respectability and social stability, yet promoted it as a Cold War weapon of cultural expression within a liberal democracy.[42] Either way – and like the civil rights movement – it kept Western culture off balance, on guard, and opened the path to the future.

Notes

Notes also function as chapter-by-chapter bibliographical references. For brevity, whenever one single source is used throughout a paragraph, only one note is placed at the end of that paragraph.

INTRODUCTION

1 Robert Frank, "Statement," in Vicki Goldberg, ed., *Photography in Print: Writings from 1816 to the Present* (Albuquerque: University of New Mexico Press, 1988), p. 401.
2 Quoted in Sarah Greenough, Stuart Alexander, and National Gallery of Art, *Looking In: Robert Frank's* The Americans (Washington-New York: National Gallery of Art, 2009), pp. 314–323.
3 Robert H. Bremner and Gary W. Reichard, eds., *Reshaping America: Society and Institutions, 1945–1960* (Columbus: Ohio State University Press, 1982), p. ix.
4 On the divergent cultural imaginaries of 1950s America, see Beatriz Colomina, AnnMarie Brennan, and Jeannie Kim, *Cold War Hothouses: Inventing Postwar Culture, from Cockpit to Playboy* (New York: Princeton Architectural Press, 2004).
5 Bremner and Reichard, *Reshaping America*, p. ix.
6 Kevin Mattson, *Intellectuals in Action: the Origins of the New Left and Radical Liberalism, 1945–1970* (University Park: Pennsylvania State University Press, 2002), p. 24. See also Richard H. Pells, *The Liberal Mind in a Conservative Age: American Intellectuals in the 1940s and 1950s* (New York: Harper & Row, 1985); Paul A. Carter, *Another Part of the Fifties* (New York: Columbia University Press, 1983), pp. 168–197; Russell Jacoby, *The Last Intellectuals: American Culture in the Age of Academe* (New York: Basic Books, 1987).
7 Arthur Schlesinger, *The Vital Center* (Boston: Houghton Mifflin Co., 1949), p. 1.
8 Warren Susman, "Did Success Spoil the United States? Dual Representations in Postwar America," in May, ed., *Recasting America: Culture and Politics in the Age of Cold War* (Chicago: University of Chicago Press, 1989), p. 19.
9 Alan Nadel, *Containment Culture: American Narrative, Postmodernism, and the Atomic Age* (Durham: Duke University Press, 1995), p. 3.
10 Jean-François Lyotard, *The Postmodern Condition: a Report on Knowledge* (Minneapolis: University of Minnesota Press, 1984), p. 19. H. Porter Abbott, *The Cambridge Introduction to Narrative* (Cambridge-New York: Cambridge University Press, 2008), pp. 3–7.

11 Roland Barthes, "The Discourse of History," *Comparative Criticism* 3 (1981): 7–20; Nadel, *Containment Culture*, p. 3.
12 On the 1950s as "distinctive culture," see William Graebner, *Coming of Age in Buffalo: Youth and Authority in the Postwar Era* (Philadelphia: Temple University Press, 1990); Loren Baritz, The Good Life: the Meaning of Success for the American Middle Class (New York: Perennial Library, 1990); David Halberstam, *The Fifties* (New York: Villard Books, 1993). On the opposing front, see Hannah Arendt, who has argued that the postwar period was an undefined, mostly transitional stage set at some point "between past and future." Hannah Arendt, *Between Past and Future; Eight Exercises in Political Thought* (New York: Viking Press, 1968).
13 See Eric Frederick Goldman, *The Crucial Decade: America, 1945–1955* (New York: Knopf, 1956).
14 See James B. Gilbert, *Men in the Middle: Searching for Masculinity in the 1950s* (Chicago: University of Chicago Press, 2005), and Bremner and Reichard, *Reshaping America*.
15 Quoted in Greenough et al. *Looking In*, p. 176.
16 Jack Kerouac, Introduction to Robert Frank, *The Americans; Photographs* (New York: Grove Press, 1959).

CHAPTER 1

1 Howard Zinn, *A People's History of the United States* (New York: Harper, 1980), p. 416.
2 See, among others Robert H. Bremner and Gary W. Reichard, eds., *Reshaping America: Society and Institutions, 1945–1960* (Columbus: Ohio State University Press, 1982), pp. 101–113; Zinn, *A People's History of the United States*, pp. 416–417; and especially Joyce Nelson, "TV, the Bomb, and the Body," in Garber and Walkowitz, eds., *Secret Agents: the Rosenberg Case, McCarthyism, and Fifties America* (New York: Routledge, 1995), pp. 30–35.
3 See Randall B. Woods, *Quest for Identity: America Since 1945* (Cambridge-New York: Cambridge University Press, 2005), pp. 12–17.
4 President Harry S. Truman's Address before a joint session of Congress, 12 March 1947. Truman's presidential speeches are collected at <www.trumanlibrary.org>, last accessed 31 August 2012.
5 The first operation of Soviet containment in fact took place even before the Truman Doctrine was announced. In the spring of 1946 the Truman administration sent the Sixth Fleet to the eastern Mediterranean to force Stalin to make good on his commitment to end his wartime occupation of Iran. See Woods, *Quest for Identity*, pp. 41–42.
6 Woods, *Quest for Identity*, pp. 52–53.
7 *Ibid.*, pp. 48.
8 *Ibid.*, pp. 48–49.

9 Larry Ceplair and Steven Englund, "Introduction" to *The Inquisition in Hollywood: Politics and the Film Community, 1930–1960* (Berkeley: University of California Press, 1983), pp. xiii–xiv.

10 In later stages of the investigations, HUAC "unfriendly" witnesses would lean on the Fifth Amendment – the constitutional right to remain silent – as a defensive strategy, which the Hollywood Ten regarded as an implicitly self-impeaching strategy, and rightly so, as the Rosenberg trial in the early 1950s would demonstrate. On the HUAC investigations of Hollywood ten see Bernard F. Dick, *Radical Innocence: a Critical Study of the Hollywood Ten* (Lexington, KY: University Press of Kentucky, 1989), pp. 8–9.

11 On the Hollywood Ten, see in particular, Dick, *Radical Innocence*; Michael Freedland, *Hollywood on Trial: McCarthyism's War Against the Movies* (London: Robson, 2007); John J. Gladchuk, *Hollywood and Anticommunism: HUAC and the Evolution of the Red Menace, 1935–1950* (New York-London: Routledge, 2007).

12 Carl Solberg, *Riding High: America in the Cold War* (New York: Mason & Lipscomb, 1973), p. 158.

13 Mickey Spillane, "One Lonely Night," in *The Mike Hammer Collection, Volume 2: One Lonely Night, The Big Kill, Kiss Me Deadly* (New York: New American Library, 2001), p. 169.

14 Edgar J. Hoover, *On Communism* (New York: Random House, 1969), pp. 56–58.

15 Alan Brinkley, *The Unfinished Nation: A Concise History of the American People* (New York: McGraw-Hill, 1993), p. 768.

16 Robert Leckie, *Conflict: the History of the Korean War, 1950–53* (New York: Da Capo Press, 1996), p. 429; and pp. 386–387.

17 Burton I. Kaufman, *The Korean War: Challenges in Crisis, Credibility, and Command* (Philadelphia: Temple University Press, 1986), p. ix.

18 Brinkley, *The Unfinished Nation*, p. 771; 775.

19 Woods, *Quest for Identity*, p. 76; see also p. 74.

20 See p. 46 and following.

21 Brinkley, *The Unfinished Nation*, p. 803.

22 Eisenhower concluded 1960, his last year in office, with a $1 billion budget surplus (see Brinkley, *The Unfinished Nation*, p. 803).

23 Zinn, *A People's History of the United States*, pp. 416–417.

24 See Bremner and Reichard, *Reshaping America*, p. 107–111; 119–120.

25 Brinkley, *The Unfinished Nation*, p. 779.

26 The first Soviet atomic test, code-named "First Lightning," occurred on August 29, 1949.

27 Douglas T. Miller and Marion Nowak, *The Fifties: the Way We Really Were* (Garden City, NY: Doubleday, 1977), p. 44. For a study of "national security," see Laura McEnaney, *Civil Defense Begins at Home: Militarization Meets Everyday Life in the Fifties* (Princeton, NJ: Princeton University Press, 2000), p. 4.

28 Miller and Nowak, *The Fifties*, p. 44.

29 For one of many studies of the social and cultural impact of nuclear development in the period, see McEnaney 2000, and Beatriz Colomina, Annmarie Brennan, and Jeannie Kim, *Cold War Hothouses: Inventing Postwar Culture, from Cockpit to Playboy* (New York: Princeton Architectural Press, 2004). On civil defense ideology, see McEnaney, *Civil Defense Begins at Home*.
30 The top secret research during World War II which led to the development of the Hiroshima and Nagasaki bombs.
31 See William E. Leuchtenburg, *A Troubled Feast: American Society Since 1945* (Boston: Little, Brown, 1983), p. 25.
32 Zinn, *A People's History of the United States*, p. 429.
33 Miller and Nowak, *The Fifties*, p. 45.
34 Dwight D. Eisenhower, Farewell Address, 17 January 1961. President Eisenhower's speeches are collected at: <www.eisenhowermemorial.org>, last accessed August 31, 2012
35 Joyce Nelson, "TV, the Bomb, and the Body," in Garber and Walkowitz, eds., *Secret Agents: the Rosenberg Case, McCarthyism, and Fifties America* (New York: Routledge, 1995), pp. 30–45; quotations are from p 36.
36 Blanche Weisen Cook, "The Rosenbergs and the Crime of a Century," in Garber and Walkowitz, eds., *Secret Agents*, p. 26.
37 George Lipsitz, *Class and Culture in Cold War America: "A Rainbow at Midnight"* (New York: Praeger, 1981), p. 159; 136.
38 Ellen Schrecker, "Before the Rosenbergs," in Garber and Walkowitz, eds., *Secret Agents:*, p. 127. See also Virginia Carmichael, *Framing History: the Rosenberg Story and the Cold War* (Minneapolis: University of Minnesota Press, 1993), especially Part I.
39 As Ellen Schrecker has pointed out, "this statement or some variant thereof appears routinely in almost every report the FBI disseminated during the early Cold War years" (Schrecker "Before the Rosenbergs," p. 138).
40 See Schrecker, "Before the Rosenbergs," p. 127.
41 See Weisen Cook, "The Rosenbergs and the Crime of a Century," pp. 23–29; Lipsitz, *Class and Culture in Cold War America*, pp 135–146.
42 For a discussion of *Invisible Man*, see p. 165 and following.
43 David Castronovo, *Beyond the Gray Flannel Suit: Books from the 1950s that Made American Culture* (New York: Continuum, 2004), p. 37.
44 James Wolfe, "'Ambivalent Man:' Ellison's Rejection of Communism," *African American Review* (Winter 2000): 621.
45 Castronovo, *Beyond the Gray Flannel Suit*, p. 39. See also M. Keith Booker, *The Post-utopian Imagination: American Culture in the Long 1950s* (Westport, CT: Greenwood Press, 2002).
46 Arthur Miller, *The Crucible* (Harmondsworth: Penguin, 2000), p. 38.
47 On literary representations of the Cold War, see also Robert Detweiler, *Uncivil Rites: American Fiction, Religion, and the Public Sphere* (Urbana: University of Illinois Press, 1996), pp. 13–66.

48 E. L. Doctorow, *The Book of Daniel: a Novel* (New York: Random House, 2002).
49 Paul Levine, "From the *Book of Daniel* to the Film of *Daniel*," in E.L. Doctorow, *Three Screenplays* (Baltimore: Johns Hopkins University Press, 2003), p. 21.
50 *Ibid.*, p. 16.
51 John G. Parks, "The Politics of Polyphony: The Fiction of E. L. Doctorow," *Twentieth Century Literature* 37.4 (Winter, 1991), pp. 454–463.
52 Parks, "The Politics of Polyphony," p. 457.
53 Quoted in Paul Levine, "From the *Book of Daniel* to the Film of *Daniel*," p. 16.

CHAPTER 2

1 Alan Brinkley, *The Unfinished Nation: a Concise History of the American People* (New York: McGraw-Hill, 1993), p. 778.
2 Randall B. Woods, *Quest for Identity: America Since 1945* (Cambridge and New York: Cambridge University Press, 2005), pp. 121–123.
3 *Ibid.*, p. 124.
4 Brinkley, *The Unfinished Nation*, p. 779.
5 *U.S. News & World Report* is quoted in Andrew L. Yarrow, *Measuring America: How Economic Growth Came to Define American Greatness in the Late Twentieth Century* (Amherst: University of Massachusetts Press, 2010), p. 102. In *The Unfinished Nation*, Alan Brinkley points out that there were approximately 30 million Americans (out of 160 million) living in poverty in the 1950s (*The Unfinished Nation*, p. 778).
6 Yarrow, *Measuring America*, p. 103.
7 *Ibid.*, p. 103.
8 Brinkley, *The Unfinished Nation*, p. 779.
9 In the early 1960s, Galbraith moved on to work as an adviser to President John F. Kennedy. For an account of Galbraith's years in Kennedy's presidential staff, see John Kenneth Galbraith, and Samuel H. Bryant, *Ambassador's Journal: A Personal Account of the Kennedy Years* (Boston: Mifflin, 1969).
10 John K. Galbraith, *The Affluent Society* (Boston: Houghton Mifflin, 1958), pp. 148–149.
11 *Ibid.*, p. 153.
12 *Ibid.*, p. 253.
13 *Ibid.*, p. 155.
14 Stephen R. Fox, *The Mirror Makers: a History of American Advertising and its Creators* (New York: Morrow, 1984), p. 173.
15 On the history of advertising in America, see also T. J. Jackson Lears, *Fables of Abundance: a Cultural History of Advertising in America* (New York: Basic Books, 1994).
16 Bill Bernbach of the Doyle Dane Bernbach advertising agency, cit. in Mark Tungate, *Adland: a Global History of Advertising* (London, Philadelphia: Kogan Page, 2007), pp. 51–52.
17 Tungate, *Adland*, p. 55.

18 David Halberstam, *The Fifties* (New York: Villard Books, 1993), p. 504.
19 *Ibid.*, p. 505.
20 Vance O. Packard, *The Hidden Persuaders* (New York: D. McKay Co., 1957), p. 17–22.
21 *Ibid.*, p. 29.
22 *Ibid.*, pp. 28–31. In *Mad Men*'s fictional advertising firm of Sterling Cooper, the research department is headed by a woman psychologist who speaks with a heavy German accent and is a fervent advocate of motivational research. An obvious tongue-in-cheek reference to Dichter, her research is discarded by Don, who advocates advertising as a tool to selling not so much products but rather the idea of "happiness."
23 Packard, *The Hidden Persuaders*, pp. 66–74; 95–96.
24 *Ibid.*, p. 161; 164.
25 Ernst Dichter, cit. in Packard, *The Hidden Persuaders*, p. 151.
26 Rod Carveth and James B. South, *Mad Men and Philosophy: Nothing Is as it Seems* (Hoboken, NJ: Wiley, 2010), p. 1. On nostalgic reappraisals of the 1950s, see Mary Caputi, *A Kinder, Gentler America: Melancholia and the Mythical 1950s* (Minneapolis: University of Minnesota Press, 2005).
27 Carveth and South, *Mad Men and Philosophy*, p. 178. On *The Man in the Gray Flannel Suit*, see p. 113 and following.
28 Will Dean, *The Ultimate Guide to Mad Men: The Guardian Companion to the Slickest Show on Television* (London: Random House, 2011), p. 5.
29 *Ibid.*, p. 2.
30 Lizabeth Cohen, *A Consumers' Republic: the Politics of Mass Consumption in Postwar America* (New York: Knopf, 2003), p. 127.
31 "What a Country!," *Fortune*, October 1956, pp. 127–130, 269–278.
32 Halberstam, *The Fifties*, p. 497.
33 Cohen, *A Consumers' Republic*, p. 13.
34 See Yarrow, *Measuring America*, p. 5. On Eisenhower's remark, see Cohen, *A Consumers' Republic*, pp. 160, 164.
35 Cohen, *A Consumers' Republic*, pp. 123–124.
36 Fox, *The Mirror Makers*, p. 173.
37 Cohen, *A Consumers' Republic*, p. 123.
38 See Halberstam, *The Fifties*, p. 488; Dunar, *America in the Fifties*, p. 169.
39 *Ibid.*, p. 488.
40 On "other-directedness," see p. 104 and following.
41 Halberstam, *The Fifties*, p. 488.
42 *Ibid.*, p. 489.
43 See Alfred P. Sloan (John McDonald and Catharine Stevens, eds., *My Years with General Motors* (New York: MacFadden-Bartell, 1965). This book became an instant bestseller, and is still today regarded as one of the finest specimens of business analysis and management.

44 David L. Lewis and Laurence Goldstein, *The Automobile and American Culture* (Ann Arbor: University of Michigan Press, 1983), p. 400.
45 On market segmentation, see p. 135.
46 Quoted in David B. Audretsch, *The Entrepreneurial Society* (Oxford and New York: Oxford University Press, 2007), p. 180.
47 On American youths and automobiles, see pp. 135–136.
48 Halberstam, *The Fifties*, p. 495; see also John A. Heitmann, *The Automobile and American Life* (Jefferson, NC: McFarland & Co., 2009), and especially Lewis and Goldstein, *The Automobile and American culture*.
49 Chevy 1955 ad, in *Life*, 13 August 1956.
50 Cohen, *A Consumers' Republic*, pp. 63–64; 122–124.
51 Halberstam, *The Fifties*, p. 499; 498.

CHAPTER 3

1 The Servicemen's Readjustment Act of 1944, more commonly known as the GI Bill, was an act of Congress aimed easing readjustment to American life for returning World War II veterans. It provided for college or vocational education as well as one year of unemployment compensation. It also provided low or no-interest loans to buy homes and start businesses.
2 On recurring suburban ideals in American culture, see Dolores Hayden, *Building Suburbia: Green Fields and Urban Growth, 1820–2000* (New York: Pantheon Books, 2003); Mark S. Foster, *From Streetcar to Superhighway: American City Planners and Urban Transportation* (Philadelphia: Temple U. Press, 1981).
3 Thomas Jefferson, "Notes on the State of Virginia" in *Thomas Jefferson: Writings* (New York: Library of America, 1984), p. 290.
4 See Kenneth T. Jackson, *Crabgrass Frontier: the Suburbanization of the United States* (New York: Oxford University Press, 1985), p. 205.
5 Source: Myron A. Marty, *Daily Life in the United States, 1960–1990: Decades of Discord* (Westport, CT: Greenwood Press, 1997); U.S. Census Bureau. *Demographic Trends in the 20th Century*. Census 2000 special reports. November 2002.
6 Leerom Medovoi, *Rebels: Youth and the Cold War Origins of Identity* (Durham: Duke University Press, 2005), p. 96.
7 Jackson, *Crabgrass Frontier*, pp. 234–235.
8 Robert Beuka, *SuburbiaNation: Reading Suburban Landscape in Twentieth-Century American Fiction and Film* (New York: Palgrave Macmillan, 2004), p. 8.
9 See Beuka, *SuburbiaNation*, p. 234; D. J. Waldie, *Holy Land: a Suburban Memoir* (New York: W.W. Norton, 1996), p. 6.
10 See Carla Lind, *Frank Lloyd Wright's Usonian Houses* (San Francisco: Promegranate Artbooks, 1994).
11 Clifford E. Jr. Clark, "Ranch House Suburbia: Ideals and Realities," in May, ed., *Recasting America: Culture and Politics in the Age of Cold War* (Chicago: University of Chicago Press, 1989), pp. 171, 174. On Wright's "Usonian home," see Scott

Donaldson, *The Suburban Myth* (New York: Columbia University Press, 1996), pp. 78–90.
12 Clark, "Ranch House Suburbia," p. 178.
13 Michael Johns, *Moment of Grace: the American City in the 1950s* (Berkeley: University of California Press, 2003), pp. 101–102.
14 Lizabeth Cohen, *A Consumers' Republic: the Politics of Mass Consumption in Postwar America* (New York: Knopf, 2003), pp. 209–211.
15 Clark, "Ranch House Suburbia," pp. 182–183.
16 William H. Whyte, *The Organization Man* (New York: Simon and Schuster, 1956), p. 314.
17 *Ibid.*, pp. 314–315
18 Medovoi, *Rebels*, p. 95.
19 Jackson, *Crabgrass Frontier*, p. 208.
20 Lewis Mumford, *The City in History* (New York: Harcourt, Brace, 1961), p. 486.
21 Whyte, *The Organization Man*, p. 310; 311.
22 John H. Kunstler, *The Geography of Nowhere: the Rise and Decline of America's Man-made Landscape* (New York: Simon & Schuster, 1993); Andres Duany, Elizabeth Plater-Zyberk, and Jeff Speck, *Suburban Nation: the Rise of Sprawl and the Decline of the American Dream* (New York: North Point Press, 2000).
23 Alan Finkielkraut, "The Ghosts of Roth. An Interview with Alan Finkielkraut," *Esquire*, September, 1981.
24 Philip Roth, *Goodbye, Columbus and Five Short Stories* (Boston: Houghton Mifflin, 1959), pp. 8–9.
25 Cohen, *A Consumers' Republic*, p. 261.
26 *Ibid.*, p. 257.
27 Dunar, *America in the Fifties*, p. 178.
28 William S. Kowinski, *The Malling of America: an Inside Look at the Great Consumer Paradise* (New York: W. Morrow, 1985), p. 25.
29 *Encyclopedia of Architecture: Design, Engineering, and Construction*, vol. 4 (New York: Wiley, 1988).
30 The first fully enclosed mall, and the prototype of the mall as we know it today, was the Southdale Center, built in 1956 in Minneapolis by Victor Gruen.
31 See Cohen, *A Consumers' Republic*, p. 258.
32 Helen Sheumaker and Shirley T. Wajda, *Material Culture in America: Understanding Everyday Life* (Santa Barbara, CA: ABC-CLIO, 2008), pp. 407–408.
33 See Peter Gibian, "The Art of being Off-Center. Shopping Center Spaces and Spectacles of Consumer Culture," in Gibian, ed., *Mass culture and everyday life* (New York: Routledge, 1985), pp. 238–291.
34 Cohen, *A Consumers' Republic*, p. 262.
35 *Ibid.*, p. 259; 282.
36 In the 1960s there were 33.1 percent of whites living in suburbs as percent of all whites, and 29.2 percent of whites living in suburbs as percent of all Americans. Source: U.S. Census Data, 1960.

37 There were in fact more American women working by the end of the 1950s that at the height of the war, when women had been called en masse to replace men for the war effort in the factories. In *Now Hiring: The Feminization of Work in the United States, 1900–1995*, Julia K. Blackwelder has argued that "as the traditional center of home life and as a moral tutor to her children, the mother of the 1950s found that her role newly scrutinized [...] Employers and bureaucrats thought they had the answer in a redefinition of maternal obligation, a redefinition that included providing for as well as protecting children, a redefinition that ultimately prevailed. Beginning in the 1950s middle-class women took on employment as an extension rather than an abdication of their parental responsibilities." Julia K. Blackwelder, *Now Hiring: the Feminization of Work in the United States, 1900–1995* (College Station, TX: Texas A&M University Press, 1997), p. 148; regarding American women in the workforce, see also American Academy of Political and Social Science, *Adolescents in Wartime* (New York: Arno Press, 1974), p. 44, which claims that there were just under 17 million women employed in 1944.
38 Johns, *Moment of Grace*, p. 97. The twenty-year period from 1945 to 1964 is commonly regarded as the baby-boom era in America.
39 Douglas T. Miller and Marion Nowak, *The Fifties: the Way we Really Were* (Garden City, NY: Doubleday, 1977), p. 155.
40 See David Popenoe, *War Over the Family* (New Brunswick, NJ: Transaction Publishers, 2005), p. 21.
41 See Elaine T. May, *Homeward Bound: American Families in the Cold War Era* (New York: Basic Books, 1988), pp. 140–142.
42 Pat Boone, *'Twixt Twelve and Twenty*, cit. in Miller and Nowak, *The Fifties*, p. 157.
43 See May, *Homeward Bound*, pp. 78–79.
44 Miller and Nowak, *The Fifties*, p. 147–153; Johns, *Moment of Grace*, p. 95.
45 Paul Gallico, "You Don't Know How Lucky You Are to Be Married," *Reader's Digest*, July 1956, pp. 134–136. Paul H. Landis, *Making the Most of Marriage* (New York: Appleton-Century-Crofts, 1955), p. 213.
46 Ferdinand Lundberg and Marynia F. Farnham, *Modern Woman: the Lost Sex* (New York & London: Harper & Brothers, 1947), pp. 170–171.
47 Susman, "Did Success Spoil the United States?" p. 26. For a discussion of *Rebel Without a Cause*, see pp. 154–156.
48 Susman, "Did Success Spoil the United States?" p. 26.
49 David Castronovo, *Beyond the Gray Flannel Suit: Books from the 1950s that Made American Culture* (New York: Continuum, 2004), p. 189.
50 John Updike, *Picked-up Pieces* (New York: Fawcett, 1977), p. 483.
51 John Updike, *Rabbit Run* (London: Penguin, 1995), p. 134.
52 Bernard Shopen, "Faith, Morality and the Novels of John Updike," in Macnaughton, ed., *Critical Essays on John Updike* (Boston: G.K. Hall, 1982), p. 201.
53 Castronovo, *Beyond the Gray Flannel Suit*, p. 188.

54 Richard Yates, *Revolutionary Road* (New York: Vintage, 2005), p. 23.
55 Castronovo, *Beyond the Gray Flannel Suit*, p. 192; 193.
56 May, *Homeward Bound*, pp. 1, 21.
57 For an in-depth reading of Disneyland, see: The Project on Walt Disney, *Inside the Mouse. Work and Play at Disney World* (Durham and London: Duke UP, 1995); Susan Willis, ed., *The World According to Disney*, special issue of *South Atlantic Quarterly*, 92.1 (Durham, NC: Duke University Press, 1991). Sharon Zukin, *Landscapes of Power: from Detroit to Disney World* (Berkeley: University of California Press, 1991). The classic intellectual biography of Walt Disney remains Robert Schickel, *The Disney Version. The Life, Times, Art, and Commerce of Walt Disney* (New York: Simon and Schuster, 1968).
58 Louis Marin, "Disneyland: A Degenerate Utopia," *Glyph* (1, 1977): 54.
59 Emma Lambert, "'Don't Fight it. You Can't Whip Mickey Mouse.' Disneyland's America, 1955–59," in Abrams and Hughes, eds., *Containing America: Cultural Production and Consumption in Fifties America* (Birmingham: University of Birmingham Press, 2000), p. 29; 30; 31.
60 See Beatriz Colomina, Annmarie Brennan, and Jeannie Kim, *Cold War Hothouses: Inventing Postwar Culture, from Cockpit to Playboy* (New York: Princeton Architectural Press, 2004), p. 16–17. The full kitchen debate is at: <http://teachingamericanhistory.org/library/index.asp?document=176>, last visited 31 August, 2012.
61 Lambert, "Don't Fight it," p. 34.
62 *Ibid.*, p. 41.

CHAPTER 4

1 A.C. Nielsen, NBC and CBS, quoted in Leo Bogart, *The Age of Television; a Study of Viewing Habits and the Impact of Television on American Life* (New York: F. Ungar Pub. Co., 1972).
2 On the demise of American radio, see Jim Cox, *Say Goodnight, Gracie: the Last Years of Network Radio* (Jefferson, NC: McFarland & Co., 2002).
3 William Boddy, *Fifties Television: the Industry and its Critics* (Urbana: University of Illinois Press, 1990), p. 116.
4 See William Boddy, *Fifties Television: the Industry and its Critics* (Urbana: University of Illinois Press, 1990), p. 116; J. Fred MacDonald, *One Nation Under Television: the Rise and Decline of Network TV* (Chicago: Nelson-Hall, 1994), p. 42; Andrew J. Dunar, *America in the Fifties* (Syracuse, NY: Syracuse University Press, 2006), p. 234; Lizabeth Cohen, *A Consumers' Republic: the Politics of Mass Consumption in Postwar America* (New York: Knopf, 2003), p 302.
5 MacDonald, *One Nation Under Television*, p. 42–43.
6 Quoted in Cox, *Say Goodnight, Gracie*, p. 13.
7 "TV transforming U.S. social scene: challenges films," *New York Times*, 24 June 1951. Selznick is quoted in Miller and Nowak, *The Fifties*, p. 195. Other data are drawn from Dunar, *America in the Fifties*, p. 234 and Paul Monaco, *A History of*

Notes

American Movies: a Film-by-Film Look at the Art, Craft, and Business of Cinema (Lanham, MD: Scarecrow Press, 2010), p. 141.

8 See Leerom Medovoi, *Rebels: Youth and the Cold War Origins of Identity* (Durham: Duke University Press, 2005), pp. 97–101; Lynn Spigel, *Make Room for TV: Television and the Family Ideal in Postwar America* (Chicago: University of Chicago Press, 1992), pp. 36–44.

9 Spigel, *Make Room for TV*, p. 39.

10 Robert T. Bower, *Television and the Public* (New York: Holt Rinehart and Winston, 1973), p. 143.

11 Dunar, *America in the Fifties*, p. 233.

12 Edward Stasheff and Rudy Bretz, *The Television Program. Its Writing, Direction, and Production* (New York: A.A. Wyn, 1951), p. 25.

13 Spigel, *Make Room for TV*, pp. 144–54.

14 *Ibid.*, p. 143.

15 Dunar, *America in the Fifties*, pp. 234–235.

16 Dennis W. Mazzocco, *Networks of Power: Corporate TV's Threat to Democracy* (Boston: South End Press, 1994), p. 2.

17 See Denis McQuail, *Audience Analysis* (Thousand Oaks, London, New Delhi: Sage, 1997), p. 8.

18 Dunar, *America in the Fifties*, p. 237.

19 McQuail, *Audience Analysis*, p. 14; see also D. W. Smythe, "Communications: Blindspot of Western Marxism," *Canadian Journal of Political and Social Theory* 1 (1977):120–127.

20 See, among others, MacDonald, *One Nation Under Television*, p. 135–136.

21 Miller and Nowak, *The Fifties*, p. 356.

22 For a more detailed treatment of game shows, Brian Geoffrey Rose and Robert S. Alley, *TV Genres: a Handbook and Reference Guide* (Westport, CT: Greenwood Press, 1985); and Kent Anderson, *Television Fraud: the History and Implications of the Quiz Show Scandals* (Westport, CT: Greenwood Press, 1978).

23 Spigel, *Make Room for TV*, p. 141–142.

24 Brett Mills, *The Sitcom* (Edinburgh: Edinburgh University Press, 2009), p. 28.

25 See Spigel, *Make Room for TV*, p. 158.

26 Lynn Spigel, *Welcome to the Dreamhouse: Popular Media and Postwar Suburbs* (Durham, NC: Duke University Press, 2001), p. 31.

27 Spigel, *Make Room for TV*, pp. 145; 157–158.

28 *Ibid.*, p. 159; 37.

29 *Ibid.*, p. 37; 39.

30 Medovoi, *Rebels*, p. 94.

31 See p. 121–122.

32 Spigel, *Make Room for TV*, pp. 42–43.

33 *Ibid.*, p. 152–153.

34 Mary B. Haralovich, "Sitcom and Suburbs. Positioning the 1950s Homemaker," in Morreale, ed., *Critiquing the Sitcom: a Reader* (Syracuse, NY: Syracuse University Press, 2003), pp. 69–70.
35 Haralovich, "Sitcom and Suburbs," p. 72.
36 *The Staturday Evening Post*, 27 April 1957, cit. in Haralovich, "Sitcom and Suburbs," p. 71.
37 Spigel, *Make Room for TV*, p. 154; 60.
38 Morreale, ed., *Critiquing the Sitcom*, p. 60.
39 <http://www.museum.tv/eotvsection.php?entrycode=ilovelucy>, last accessed 31 August 2012.
40 Spigel, *Make Room for TV*, p. 159; 160.
41 *Ibid.*, p. 161.
42 *Ibid.*, p. 161; 164; 167.
43 Marc Eliot, *American Television, the Official Art of the Artificial* (Garden City, NY: Doubleday, 1981), p. 19.
44 Erik Barnouw, *Tube of Plenty: the Evolution of American Television* (New York: Oxford University Press, 1975), p. 169.
45 Horace Newcomb, Cary O'Dell, Noelle Watson et al., *Encyclopedia of Television* (Chicago: Fitzroy Dearborn Publishers, 1997).
46 See pp. 163–164.
47 Barnouw, *Tube of Plenty*, p. 177.
48 *Ibid.*, p. 179.
49 *Ibid.*, p. 182.
50 On Murrow and *See in Now*, see Thomas Rosteck, See it Now *Confronts McCarthyism: Television Documentary and the Politics of Representation* (Tucaloosa: University of Alabama Press, 1994).
51 Barnouw, *Tube of Plenty*, p. 182.
52 On the relevance of television for Eisenhower's 1952 and 1956 presidential campaigns, see p. 24.

CHAPTER 5

1 The notion of the 1950s as the age of conformity has been a leitmotiv of the discourse of the decade and about the decade, in books so diverse as David Riesman's *The Lonely Crowd* (1948), William Whyte, *The Organization Man* (1956), and later myriads of commentaries on the decade, including Robert H. Bremner and Gary W. Reichard, *Reshaping America: Society and Institutions, 1945–1960* (Columbus: Ohio State University Press, 1982); and James B. Gilbert, *Men in the Middle: Searching for Masculinity in the 1950s* (Chicago: University of Chicago Press, 2005).
2 Daniel Bell, *The End of Ideology; on the Exhaustion of Political Ideas in the Fifties* (Glencoe, IL: Free Press, 1960), p. 25.
3 As well summarized by William Henry Chafe in *The Unfinished Journey: America Since World War II* (New York: Oxford University Press, 1986), "it is the theme of

paradox that best describes the postwar era – diversity in the face of uniformity, the creation of close-knit community despite massive mobility, changes in sex roles occurring in the face of the 'feminine mystique,' the emergence of cultural rebels in the midst of chilling conformity" (p. 144).

4 David Riesman, *The Lonely Crowd: A Study of the Changing American Character* (New Haven: Yale University Press, 1950), p. 33.
5 *Ibid.*, p. 33.
6 *Ibid.*, pp. 33–34.
7 See Dennis Wrong, "'The Lonely Crowd' Revisited," *Sociological Forum* 7, No. 2 (Jun., 1992, 1992): 382.
8 Riesman, *The Lonely Crowd*, p. 34.
9 *Ibid.*, p. 35.
10 *Ibid.*, p. 30.
11 *Ibid.*, p. 36.
12 Benjamin Spock, *The Common Sense Book of Baby and Child Care* (New York: Duell, Sloan & Pearce, 1946), p. 185, italics in the original.
13 Nancy P. Weiss, "Mother, the Invention of Necessity. Dr. Benjamin Spock's *Baby and Child Care*," *American Quarterly* 29.5 (1977):543.
14 Riesman, *The Lonely Crowd*, p. 37; 38.
15 Charles Wright Mills, *White Collar: the American Middle Classes* (New York: Oxford University Press, 1951), p. 233.
16 *Ibid.*, p. 63.
17 *Ibid.*, p. 63; 65; 67.
18 *Ibid.*, p. 67.
19 *Ibid.*, pp. 68–69.
20 *Ibid.*, p. 70–75.
21 *Ibid.*, p. 70.
22 Steven Rytina, "Youthful Vision, Youthful Promise, Through Midlife Bifocals: C. Wright Mills' *White Collar* Turns 50," *Sociological Forum* 16.3 (September 2001): 568.
23 Mills, *White Collar*, p. 70.
24 David Riesman, "Review of *White Collar: The American Middle Classes* by Charles Wright Mills," *The American Journal of Sociology* 57.5 (March 1952): 513–515.
25 William H. Whyte, *The Organization Man* (New York: Simon and Schuster, 1956), p. 3; 4; 10.
26 *Ibid.*, pp. 4–5; 19; 20; 6.
27 *Ibid.*, p. 7.
28 *Ibid.*, p. 14.
29 William H. Whyte, "The Consumer in the New Suburbia," in Clark, ed., *Consumer Behavior; the Dynamics of Consumer Reaction* (New York: New York University Press, 1955), pp. 5–6.

30 Roland Marchand, "Visions of Classlessness, Quests for Dominion: American Popular Culture, 1945–1960," in Bremner and Reichard, eds., *Reshaping America: Society and Institutions, 1945–1960* (Columbus: Ohio State University Press, 1982), pp. 163–190.
31 Whyte, "The Consumer in the New Suburbia," p. 6. On advertising, see p. 44–48.
32 See Marchand, "Visions of Classlessness, Quests for Dominion," p. 169.
33 See Steven Cohan, *Masked Men: Masculinity and the Movies in the Fifties* (Bloomington: Indiana University Press, 1997), p. 70. In his close analysis of the novel, Cohan has argued that war memories bring Tom back to "a moment of uncontrollable desire," which function as a psychological counterpart to his present inability to "negotiate the power relations of his new job [...] within the limits of his moral integrity" (p. 70).
34 Sloan Wilson, *The Man in the Gray Flannel Suit* (Cambridge, MA: Da Capo Press, 2002), p. 109.
35 Wilson, *The Man in the Gray Flannel Suit*, p. 109.
36 *Ibid.*, p. 61; 64; 66.
37 *Ibid.*, p. 185.
38 Jeffrey T. Schnapp and Matthew Tiews, *Crowds* (Stanford: Stanford University Press, 2006), p. 209.
39 I have written on the relevance of Western narratives to the Cold War imaginary in Andrea Carosso, "Disney e la (ri)scrittura della Frontiera nell'America della Guerra fredda," in Rosso, ed., *L'invenzione del west(ern). Fortuna di un genere nella cultura del Novecento* (Verona: Ombre Corte, 2009), pp. 96-107.
40 Richard Slotkin, *Gunfighter Nation: the Myth of the Frontier in Twentieth-Century America* (New York: Atheneum, 1992), p. 395.
41 Cit. in Ronald L. Davis, *Duke: the Life and Image of John Wayne* (Norman: University of Oklahoma Press, 1998), p. 142.
42 Stephen J. Whitfield, *The Culture of the Cold War* (Baltimore: Johns Hopkins University Press, 1991), p. 148.
43 *Ibid.*, p. 147.
44 *Ibid.*, p. 147. Friendly witnesses were those who appeared voluntarily in front of the HUAC, and thus were fully prepared to cooperate in the witch-hunt.
45 Slotkin, *Gunfighter Nation*, p. 393.
46 Whitfield, *The Culture of the Cold War*, p. 148.
47 "The New American Domesticated Male," *Life*, 4 January 1954; "The Decline of the American Male," *Look*, 1958.
48 Gilbert, *Men in the Middle*, pp. 2–3.
49 Douglas T. Miller, and Marion Nowak, *The Fifties: The Way We Really Were* (Garden City, N.Y.: Doubleday, 1977), p. 168.
50 In the state of Georgia, an anti-sodomy law criminalized oral and anal sex in private between consenting adults. The U.S. States Supreme Court upheld the constitutionality of that law up until 1986. Sodomy continued to be held as a crime in states such as Texas as late al 2003. Kinsey's 1948 *Sexual Behavior in the Human*

Male was followed in 1953 by a study of female sexuality, entitled *Sexual Behavior in the Human Female*.
51 Miller and Nowak, *The Fifties*, p. 160–167.
52 On working women during World War II, see Maureen Honey, *Creating Rosie the Riveter: Class, Gender, and Propaganda During World War II* (Amherst: University of Massachusetts Press, 1984); Penny Colman, *Rosie the Riveter: Women Working on the Home Front in World War II* (New York: Crown Publishers, 1995); Sherna Gluck, *Rosie the Riveter Revisited: Women, the War, and Social Change* (Boston: Twayne, 1987); Emily Yellin, *Our Mothers' War: American Women at Home and at the Front During World War II* (New York: Free Press, 2004).
53 Steven Mintz and Susan Kellogg, *Domestic Revolutions: A Social History of American Family Life* (New York: Free press, 1988), pp. 161–162.
54 Honey, *Creating Rosie the Riveter*, p. 24. On the ambivalence of public rhetoric on women's roles during the war, see Sherrie A. Kossoudjia and Laura J. Dresser, "Working Class Rosies: Women Industrial Workers during World War II," *The Journal of Economic History* 52 (June 1992): 432. The theory according to which women during World War II "were drawn into industrial labor markets during extraordinary times and then voluntarily retreated to their traditional roles after the war" is now discredited as ungrounded.
55 Stephanie Stephanie Coontz, "What We Really Miss About the 1950s," in Rudnick, Smith, and Rubin, eds., *American Identity: An Introductory Textbook* (Malden, MA: Blackwell, 1997), p. 20.
56 See Miller and Nowak, *The Fifties*, p. 152.
57 Hannah Lees, "What Every Husband Needs," *Reader's Digest*, October 1957, quoted in Miller and Nowak, *The Fifties*, p. 158.
58 Quoted in Miller and Nowak, *The Fifties*, p. 158.
59 The distinction between vaginal and clitoral orgasm went unquestioned through the decade and well until the end of the 1960s, when Anne Koedt's groundbreaking essay "The Myth of the Vaginal Orgasm" appeared in 1968 and challenged many of Freud's assumptions and their reception in society. See Anne Koedt, "The Myth of the Vaginal Orgasm," in Unger and Unger, eds., *The Times Were a Changin': The Sixties Reader* (New York: Three Rivers, 1968), pp. 204–212.
60 Lynn T. White, *Educating Our Daughters. A Challenge to the Colleges* (New York: Harper, 1950), pp. 77–78.
61 Miller and Nowak, *The Fifties*, p. 162. A film of the early years 2000, *Mona Lisa Smile* (2003), directed by Mike Newell, dwells on women's education in 1950s America and its consensus on underachievement and complacent acceptance of society's predefined gender roles.
62 Lynn Spigel, *Make Room for TV: Television and the Family Ideal in Postwar America* (Chicago: University of Chicago Press, 1992), p. 75.
63 *Variety*, 22 September 1948, quoted in Spigel, *Make Room for TV*, p. 78.
64 Spigel, *Make Room for TV*, pp. 85–86.

65 *Ibid.*, p. 92.
66 Jessica Weiss, *To Have and to Hold: Marriage, the Baby Boom, and Social Change* (Chicago: University of Chicago Press, 2000), p. 32.
67 Divorce and abortion rates actually declined in the 1950s compared to previous decades, but the popular media were replete with sensationalist articles warning young women to the moral threat these posed. See Elaine T. May, *Homeward Bound: American Families in the Cold War Era* (New York: Basic Books, 1988), pp. 4–5 and 153–154. Janice Angstrom, Rabbit's wife in John Updike's *Rabbit Run* is an excellent prototype of this growing social malaise.
68 Daniel Horowitz, *Betty Friedan and the Making of* The Feminine Mystique: *the American Left, the Cold War, and Modern Feminism* (Amherst: University of Massachusetts Press, 1998), p. ix.
69 Horowitz, *Betty Friedan and the Making of* The Feminine Mystique, p. ix.
70 Betty Friedan, *The Feminine Mystique* (New York: Norton, 2001), p. 57; 61.
71 *Ibid.*, p. 58.
72 *Ibid.*, p. 60.
73 *Ibid.*, p. 76. Friedan refers here to all the responsibilities of "the perfect mother," who shuttles the children to post-school activities, and then picks up her commuting husband of the "6:45 train" (most suburban families in the 1950s owned only one automobile). This image is well depicted, for example, in films such as *The Man in a Gray Flannel Suit* (1956) and *Far From Heaven* (2002), where women are represented as the home chauffeurs, responsible for putting the one family automobile to the myriads of daily uses dictated by suburban life, from driving the husband to the station to catch his commuter train to picking him up from the same station at the end of the working day.
74 Friedan, *The Feminine Mystique*, p. 62.
75 Lauri Umansky and Michelle Plott, eds., *Making Sense of Women's Lives: An Introduction to Women's Studies* (Lenham, MD: Rowman & Littlefield, 2000), p. 157.
76 Friedan, *The Feminine Mystique*, p. 426; 509.

CHAPTER 6

1 Quoted in Grace Elizabeth Hale, *A Nation of Outsiders: How the White Middle Class Fell in Love with Rebellion in Postwar America* (Oxford & New York: Oxford University Press), p. 80, italics mine.
2 See Matt Theado, *Understanding Jack Kerouac* (Columbia, SC: University of South Carolina Press, 2000), pp. 23–24.
3 See Andrew J. Weigert, J. Smith Teitge and Dennis W. Teitge, *Society and Identity: Toward a Sociological Psychology* (Cambridge: Cambridge University Press, 1986), pp. 1–20.
4 Scholarly notions of the "tranquillized fifties," as well as the full range of 1950s "nostalgia" (especially in film, television and music) which began to surface in the

early 1950s promoted amply unrealistic visions of the decade as an age of carefree social consensus.
5 Leerom Medovoi, *Rebels: Youth and the Cold War Origins of Identity* (Durham: Duke University Press, 2005), p. 55.
6 Weigert, Teitge and Teitge, *Society and Identity*, p. 1.
7 Medovoi, *Rebels*, pp. 7–8.
8 *Ibid.*, p. 10–14.
9 *Ibid.*, p. 7.
10 Elaine T. May, *Homeward Bound: American Families in the Cold War Era* (New York: Basic Books, 1988), pp. 3; 7.
11 W. T. Lhamon, *Deliberate Speed: the Origins of A Cultural Style in the American 1950s* (Washington: Smithsonian Institution Press, 1990), p. 4.
12 *Ibid.*, p. 8. James B. Gilbert, *A Cycle of Outrage: America's Reaction to the Juvenile Delinquent in the 1950s* (New York: Oxford University Press, 1986), p. 13.
13 Gilbert, *A Cycle of Outrage*, p. 23.
14 *Ibid.*, p. 12.
15 Medovoi, *Rebels*, p. 24.
16 See Gilbert, *A Cycle of Outrage*, p. 19.
17 See Dorothy W. Baruch, *You, Your Children, and War* (New York: D. Appleton-Century Company, 1942); Elizabeth F. Boettiger, *Your Child Meets the World Outside. A Guide to Children's Attitudes in Democratic Living* (New York & London: D. Appleton, 1941); and the already discussed Dr. Benjamin Spock's *The Common Sense Book of Baby and Child Care* (New York: Duell, Sloan & Pearce, 1946). For a thorough analysis of democratic education in postwar America, see Henry Jenkins, "'No Matter how Small:' The Democratic Imagination of Dr. Seuss," in Jenkins, McPherson, Shattuc, eds., *Hop on Pop: the Politics and Pleasures of Popular Culture* (Durham, NC: Duke University Press, 2002), pp. 187–208.
18 Gilbert, *A Cycle of Outrage*, p. 17.
19 See p. 121.
20 See Gilbert, *A Cycle of Outrage*, p. 21. On the specific area of girls' rebellion in 1950s America, which this book does not address, see in particular Rachel Devlin, *Relative Intimacy: Fathers, Adolescent Daughters, and Postwar American Culture* (Chapel Hill: University of North Carolina Press, 2005).
21 See p. 148 and following.
22 Gilbert, *A Cycle of Outrage*, p. 17–18.
23 Cohen, *A Consumers' Republic*, p. 318.
24 Eugene Gilbert, cited in Cohen, *A Consumers' Republic*, p. 319.
25 Cohen, *A Consumers' Republic*, p. 319.
26 *Ibid.*, p. 319.
27 Responding to warnings of the growing danger of product competition, Wendell Smith and Pierre Martineau published articles in the *Journal Of Marketing* in 1956 and 1958 to advocate a new marketing philosophy based on consumer segmenta-

tion. Smith argued that in place of a mass markets, goods "find their markets of maximum potential as a result of recognition of differences in the requirements of market segments." (Smith, quoted in Cohen, *A Consumers' Republic*, p. 295). Martineau added to that insight the idea that market segments were always dictated by social class and other criteria.

28 See Gilbert, *A Cycle of Outrage*, p. 22.
29 See John A. Heitmann, *The Automobile and American Life* (Jefferson, NC: McFarland & Co., 2009), p. 177.
30 Heitmann, *The Automobile and American Life*, p. 134.
31 Henry G. Felsen, *Hot Rod* (New York: E.P. Dutton, 1950), p. 17.
32 Lhamon, *Deliberate Speed*, p. 8.
33 Cohen, *A Consumers' Republic*, p. 319.
34 Gilbert, *A Cycle of Outrage*, p. 14.
35 *Ibid.*, p. 13.
36 *Ibid.*, p. 18.
37 *Ibid.*, pp. 16–17.
38 *Ibid.*, p. 18.
39 Medovoi, *Rebels*, p. 24.
40 David Castronovo, *Beyond the Gray Flannel Suit: Books from the 1950s that Made American Culture* (New York: Continuum, 2004), p. 14.
41 Allen Ginsberg, "America" (1956), in *Collected Poems 1947–1980* (New York: Harper & Row, 1984).
42 Jerome D. Salinger, *The Catcher in the Rye* (Boston, New York, London: Little Brown, 2008), p. 224.
43 Christopher Brookeman, "Pencey Preppy: Cultural Codes in *The Catcher in the Rye*," in Jack Salzman, ed., *New Essays on The Catcher in the Rye* (Cambridge: Cambridge University Press, 1991), pp. 58–61.
44 Sarah Graham, *J. D. Salinger's The Catcher in the Rye* (New York: Routledge, 2007), p. 16.
45 *Ibid*, pp. xi–xii.
46 Salinger, *The Catcher in the Rye*, p. 3.
47 Medovoi, *Rebels*, p. 1.
48 Leerom Medovoi, "Democracy, Capitalism and American Literature. The Cold War Construction of J.D. Salinger's Paperback Hero," in Foreman, ed., *The Other Fifties. Interrogating Midcentury American Icons* (Champaign, IL: University of Illinois Press, 1996), p. 269.
49 *Ibid*, p. 271. George Steiner, "The Salinger Industry," *Nation* 199 (14 November 1959):360–363.
50 Castronovo, *Beyond the Gray Flannel Suit*, p. 55.
51 On Trilling, see Castronovo, *Beyond the Gray Flannel Suit*, p. 72. On Simpson, see Jonah Raskin, *American Scream: Allen Ginsberg's Howl and the Making of the Beat Generation* (Berkeley: University of California Press, 2004), p. 15. Norman

Podhoretz, "The Know-Nothing Bohemians," in Donaldson, ed., *On the Road. Text and Criticism* (New York: Viking, 1979), p. 352.
52 Allen Ginsberg, "A Definition of the Beat Generation" (1982), in Phillips, ed., *Beat Culture and the New America, 1950–1965* (New York: Whitney Museum of American Art, 1995), pp. 17–19.
53 *Ibid.*, pp. 17–19.
54 *Ibid.*, pp. 17–19.
55 Raskin, *American Scream*, p. xi.
56 Castronovo, *Beyond the Gray Flannel Suit*, p. 72.
57 In "Tradition and the Individual Talent" (1919), one of the founding essays of modernist aesthetics, T.S. Eliot had argued that "the progress of an artist is a continual self-sacrifice, a continual extinction of personality." T. S. Eliot, *Selected Essays* (New York: Harcourt Brace Jovanovich, 1978), p. 7.
58 Walt Whitman, *Leaves of Grass*, in *Poetry and Prose* (New York: Library of America, 1982), p. 87.
59 Raskin, *American Scream*, p. 121; xiv.
60 *Ibid.*, pp. 65–80.
61 Castronovo, *Beyond the Gray Flannel Suit*, pp. 75–76.
62 Raskin, *American Scream*, p. xx.
63 Castronovo, *Beyond the Gray Flannel Suit*, p. 72.
64 Raskin, *American Scream*, p. 224.
65 Norman Mailer, "The White Negro," in *Advertisements for Myself* (London: Andre Deutsch, 1961), p. 283.
66 Mailer, "The White Negro," p. 283.
67 *Ibid.*, p. 284.
68 See Hale, *A Nation of Outsiders*, pp. 73–74.
69 See Blanche Gelfant, "An Untranquil Novel of the Fifties. Jack Kerouac's On The Road," *RSA Journal* (6.1986): 215–216.
70 Martin Halliwell, *American Culture in the 1950s* (Edinburgh: Edinburgh University Press, 2007), p. 79.
71 On *On the Road* and be-bop, see Halliwell, *American Culture in the 1950s*, p. 79. On Moriarty, see Castronovo, *Beyond the Gray Flannel Suit*, p. 69.
72 Mario Corona, "Jack Kerouac, o della contraddizione," in Corona, ed., *Jack Kerouac: Romanzi* (Milano: Mondatori, 2001), p. xxxv; xxxviii.
73 *Ibid.*, pp. xvi–xviii.
74 Castronovo, *Beyond the Gray Flannel Suit*, p. 64.
75 Corona, "Jack Kerouac, o della contraddizione," pp. xxix–xxx.
76 Medovoi, *Rebels*, pp. 221–224.
77 See Bill Osgerby, "Sleazy Riders: Exploitation, 'Otherness' and Transgression in the 1960s Biker Movie," *Journal of Popular Film and Television* (Autumn 2003): 98–108; David Baker, "Rock Rebels and Delinquents: The Emergence of the Rock Rebel in 1950s 'Youth Problem' Films," *Continuum: Journal of Media and Cultural Studies* (19.1 2005): 39–54.

78 On typical receptions of the film, see John Mundy, *Popular Music on Screen: from Hollywood Musical to Music Video* (Manchester: Manchester University Press, 1999), pp. 105–106; Jon Lewis, *The Road to Romance and Ruin: Teen Films and Youth Culture* (New York: Routledge, 1992), pp. 28–31. Baker's argument is in "Rock Rebels and Delinquents," 44–45.
79 See Warren Susman, "Did Success Spoil the United States? Dual Representations in Postwar America," in May, ed., *Recasting America: Culture and Politics in the Age of Cold War* (Chicago: University of Chicago Press, 1989), p. 27.
80 Baker, "Rock Rebels and Delinquents," p. 46.
81 Medovoi, *Rebels*, p. 38.

CHAPTER 7

1 See James O. Horton and Lois E. Horton, *Hard Road to Freedom: the Story of African America* (New Brunswick, NJ: Rutgers University Press, 2001), pp. 269–271.
2 See Thomas Borstelmann, *The Cold War and the Color Line: American Race Relations in the Global Arena* (Cambridge, MA: Harvard University Press, 2001), pp. 172–221.
3 Juan Williams, *Eyes on the Prize: America's Civil Rights Years, 1954–1965* (New York: Viking, 1987), p. 10. A key focus of the civil rights movement of the 1950s and 1960s, the doctrine of "separate but equal" had been upheld by the Supreme Court as late as 1896 in *Plessy v. Ferguson*, 163 U.S. 537.
4 Douglas T. Miller and Marion Nowak, *The Fifties: the Way we Really Were* (Garden City, NY: Doubleday, 1977), p. 188.
5 Among others, some of the leading the social scientists discussed in previous chapters (and most notably William Whyte and Vance Packard), clearly pointed this out.
6 In 1943, a group of sailors, before leaving Los Angeles, engaged in a fight with the local Mexican-American community, the members of which called themselves "pachucos" and wore "zoot suits" (a suit composed of a long coat and high-waisted, large trousers). Tension rapidly mounted, as the police, supported by public opinion which blamed the pachucos for the outbreak of violence, sided with the sailors and stamped the riots out.
7 The NAACP, established in the early decades of the twentieth century. was the most influential civil rights organization in the U.S. The *Smith v. Allwright* Supreme Court decision in 1944 invalidated the white primary. Sweatt v. Painter and McLaurin v. Oklahoma State Regents for Higher Education, both of 1950, undermined the separate but equal doctrine in the context of higher education. See Michael J. Klarman, *From Jim Crow to Civil Rights: the Supreme Court and the Struggle for Racial Equality* (Oxford-New York: Oxford University Press, 2004), p. 289.
8 George Schuyler, "The Phantom American Negro," *The Reader's Digest* 59, July 1951, pp. 62–63 in Miller and Nowak, *The Fifties*, p. 183.

9 Miller and Nowak, *The Fifties*, p. 202.
10 *Ibid.*, p. 184. The formula referred to had been used in the original 1789 version of the US constitution as a way to determine the population of the states in a way that would downplay the actual number of African-Americans, who counted only for three-fifths of their actual number. This formula had been formally amended in 1868.
11 *Ibid.*, p. 197.
12 *Ibid.*, p. 199.
13 Because of its crucial place in American history, the *Brown v. Board* ruling has spawned endless debate on desegregation in America. Paul Green has argued that the ruling's "legal rhetoric about societal changes [...] sought neither to advance a new social order nor to undermine an old doctrine." Green has underlined how the attitude of the Court was not aimed at shaking the basis of the "separate but equal" doctrine, but rather at maintaining it by advocating the "natural" evolution of society, and therefore of the law, as the rationale behind the necessity of updating it. Paul Green, "The Paradox of the Promise Unfulfilled: Brown v. Board of Education and the Continued Pursuit of Excellence in Education," *The Journal of Negro Education* 73. 3 (Special Issue: "Brown v. Board of Education at 50," Summer, 2004): 268–273; see also William B Harvey, Adia M. Harvey, and Mark King, "The Impact of the Brown v. Board of Education Decision on Postsecondary Participation of African-Americans," *The Journal of Negro Education* 73.3 (Special Issue: "Brown v. Board of Education at 50," Summer, 2004): 328–340; David W. Romero and Francine Sanders Romero, "Precedent, Parity, and Racial Discrimination: A Federal/State Comparison of the Impact of Brown v. Board of Education," *Law & Society Review* 37.4 (December 2003): 809–826; William Henry Chafe, *The Unfinished Journey: America Since World War II* (New York: Oxford University Press, 1986), pp. 153–157.
14 On Byrd, see George Brown Tindall, *America: A Narrative History* (New York: W. W. Norton, 1988), p. 1332. On "private justice," see Horton and Horton, *Hard Road to Freedom*, pp. 276–279.
15 Cit. in Jim Carrier, *A Traveler's Guide to the Civil Rights Movement* (New York: Mariner Books, 2004), p. 70.
16 Chafe, *The Unfinished Journey*, p. 154. See also Tindall *America*, pp. 1330–1332. It took twenty-four more years before Autherine Lucy's expulsion was overturned. Lucy finally earned an MA degree from the University of Alabama in 1992.
17 Ralph Ellison, *Invisible Man* (Londn: Penguin, 2001), p. 3.
18 The term "miscegenation" was current in the nineteenth century to describe having sexual intercourse and begetting children with a partner from outside your racially defined group (in the United States, this referred predominantly to intercourse between a whites and blacks).
19 Robert O'Meally, "Introduction" to Robert O'Meally, ed., *New Essays on Invisible Man* (Cambridge: Cambridge University Press, 1988), p. 5.

20 Saul Bellow, "Preface" to John F. Callahan, ed., *The Collected Essays of Ralph Ellison*, (New York: The Modern Library, 1995), p. xi.
21 Ralph Ellison, *The Collected Essays of Ralph Ellison*, in Callahan, ed., (New York: Modern Library, 1995), p. 471. Henry L. Gates, quoted in John F. Callahan, *Ralph Ellison's Invisible Man: A Casebook* (New York: Oxford University Press, 2004), p. 298.
22 Callahan, *Ralph Ellison's Invisible Man*, p. 295.
23 Ellison, *Invisible Man*, pp. 16. On *Invisible Man*'s modernist palimpsest, see also Herman Beavers, "Finding Common Grounds: Ellison and Baldwin," in Graham, ed., *The Cambridge Companion to the African-American Novel* (Cambridge: Cambridge University Press, 2004), pp. 192–193.
24 Ellison, *Invisible Man*, p. 581.
25 Andrew Hoberek, *The Twilight of the Middle Class: Post-World War II American Fiction and White-Collar Work* (Princeton, NJ: Princeton University Press, 2005), p. 54. Ellison, *Invisible Man*, pp. 577.
26 *Ibid.*, p. 54.
27 Tony Tanner, *City of Words* (London: Cape, 1976), p. 51.
28 Hoberek, *The Twilight of the Middle Class*, p. 54.
29 David Castronovo, *Beyond the Gray Flannel Suit: Books from the 1950s that Made American Culture* (New York: Continuum, 2004), p. 35.
30 Castronovo, *Beyond the Gray Flannel Suit*, p. 39.

CHAPTER 8

1 See Leerom Medovoi, *Rebels: Youth and the Cold War Origins of Identity* (Durham: Duke University Press, 2005), pp. 3–19.
2 On rock 'n' roll as "seventh stream," see *The Seventh Stream: the Emergence of Rocknroll in American Popular Music* (Hanover, NH: University Press of New England, 1992), Philip H. Ennis has described the emergence of rock 'n' roll from the perspective of a "turbulence in the charts" which upset the previous arrangement of the music industry in six distinct genres or "streams" (classical, jazz, gospel, R&B, Country and Western, pop).
3 Peter Guralnick, *Last Train to Memphis: the Rise of Elvis Presley* (Boston: Little, Brown, and Co., 1994), p. 63–64.
4 Phillips, quoted in Peter Guralnick, *Feel Like Going Home: Portraits in Blues and Rock 'n' Roll* (New York: Back Bay Books, 1999), p. 171.
5 On the relevance of Southern culture to the rock 'n' roll revolution, see especially Michael T. Bertrand, *Race, Rock, and Elvis* (Urbana: University of Illinois Press, 2000).
6 On the blandness of postwar pop music in America, see Douglas T. Miller and Marion Nowak, *The Fifties: the Way We Really Were* (Garden City, NY: Doubleday, 1977), p. 293–294.
7 Phillips, quoted in Glenn C. Altschuler, *All Shook Up: How Rock 'n' Roll Changed America* (New York: Oxford University Press, 2004), p. 26.

8 On Elvis and the gospel music tradition, see Greil Marcus, *Mystery Train: Images of America in Rock 'n' Roll Music* (New York: Plume, 1997), p. 142. On Elvis' incursions in black churches, see Guralnick, *Last Train to Memphis*, p. 75. On Crudup, see Elvis interview, quoted in Charlie Gillett, *The Sound of the City: the Rise of Rock and Roll* (London: Souvenir Press, 1971), p. 28.
9 Quoted in Guralnick, *Last Train to Memphis*, p. 63.
10 George Lipsitz, *Class and Culture in Cold War America: "A Rainbow at Midnight"* (New York: Praeger, 1981), p. 216.
11 See Paul Friedlander, *Rock and Roll: a Social History* (Boulder, CO: Westview Press, 2006), p. 16; see also Benjamin Filene, *Romancing the Folk: Public Memory and American Roots Music* (Cultural Studies of the United States) (Chapel Hill, NC: The University of North Carolina Press, 2000), pp. 27–46.
12 Hatch and Millward, for example, have suggested that blues and boogie, the two poles of the tradition of African-American music, "are probably descended from a combination of the 'camp meeting songs' of the Second Great Awakening (ca. 1800), the 'sorrow songs' of the latter slavery period and the 'common-stock' folk songs and ballads of the late nineteenth and early twentieth centuries." David Hatch and Stephen Millward, *From Blues to Rock: an Analytical History of Pop Music* (Manchester-Wolfeboro, NH: Manchester University Press, 1987), p. 34. Geroge Lipsitz has claimed that both musically and lyrically the blues was the product of a "creative tension between European and African harmonies." George Lipsitz, *Class and Culture in Cold War America: "A Rainbow at Midnight"* (New York: Praeger, 1981), p. 198. On the blending of African and European harmonic elements in the blues, see Emmett G., *Encyclopedia of African-American Music* (Santa Barbara, CA: ABC-CLIO), col. 3, pp. 124–125, and Michael Campbell, *Popular Music in America: the Beat Goes On* (Boston: Schirmer Cengage Learning, 2009), pp. 10–11.
13 See Roy Shuker, *Popular Music: the Key Concepts* (London-New York: Routledge, 2005), p. 48–49.
14 On R&B and C&W as working-class music genres, see, among others, Lipsitz, *Class and Culture in Cold War America*, pp. 205–207 and Medovoi, *Rebels*, pp. 97–104.
15 See Albin Zak, *I Don't Sound Like Nobody: Remaking Music in 1950s America* (Ann Arbor: University of Michigan Press, 2010), pp. 9–42.
16 Among the most popular jump musicians of the late 1940s and early 1950s were Louis Jordan and Arnett Cobb.
17 On the black roots of rock 'n' roll, see Preston Lauterbach, *The Chitlin' Circuit and the Road to Rock 'n' Roll* (New York: W.W. Norton, 2012).
18 See Friedlander, *Rock and Roll: a Social History*, p. 18; Herbert I. London, *Closing the Circle: a Cultural History of the Rock Revolution* (Chicago: Nelson-Hall, 1984), pp 13–34.
19 Lipsitz, *Class and Culture in Cold War America*, p. 210.
20 Miller and Nowak, *The Fifties*, p. 165.

21 Christopher H. Sterling, ed., *The Biographical Encyclopedia of American Radio* (New York: Routledge, 2011), p. 145.
22 On the "short-loops," see Philip H. Ennis, *The Seventh Stream: the Emergence of Rocknroll in American Popular Music* (Hanover, NH: University Press of New England, 1992), pp. 176–180.
23 Lipsitz, *Class and Culture in Cold War America*, p. 211.
24 Ennis, *The Seventh Stream*, p. 18.
25 *Ibid.*, p. 19.
26 "Maybellene" also contributed to defining some of rock 'n' roll's dubious industrial practices such as assigning writer credits to DJ-promoters (written by Berry, "Maybellene" was credited to Alan Freed and Russ Fratto, another DJ who had been lending money to Chess, Berry's label).
27 Lipsitz, *Class and Culture in Cold War America*, p. 211.
28 Born in Michigan in 1925, Haley came form a Kentucky family which settled in Chester, Pennsylvania during the Depression years. While still a teenager he became a professional country and western musician and traveled widely in the Midwest, but he eventually quit the road, got married, and returned to Chester, where he worked as a disc jockey, sports announcer, and as a musician at clubs in the black section of town, sharing the stage with to-be blues and R&B legends such as B. B. King, Fats Domino, Lloyd Price, Ray Charles, and Nat King Cole.
29 Friedlander, *Rock and Roll: a Social History*, p. 30.
30 Gillett, *The Sound of the City*, p. 14.
31 Friedlander, *Rock and Roll: a Social History*, p. 32.
32 Miller and Nowak, *The Fifties*, p. 299. See also Ennis, *The Seventh Stream*, p. 213 and Friedlander, *Rock and Roll: a Social History*, p. 30–32.
33 See Friedlander, Rock and Roll: a Social History, p. 42.
34 Marcus, *Mystery Train*, pp. 182–185.
35 Gillett, *The Sound of the City*, p. 28.
36 Marcus, *Mystery Train*, p. 164.
37 *Ibid.*, p. 192.
38 See David Shumway, "Watching Elvis: The Male Rockstar as Object of the Gaze," in Foreman, ed., *The Other Fifties: Interrogating Midcentury American Icons* (Urbana: University of Illinois Press, 1997), pp. 124–143.
39 Between 1956 and 1962, Elvis recorded 31 out of RCA's 39 million-selling records. Between 1956 and 1966 he was responsible for one quarter of RCA's total sales. See Lipsitz, *Class and Culture in Cold War America*, p. 216.
40 Tim Parrish, *Walking Blues: Making Americans from Emerson to Elvis* (Amherst: University of Massachusetts Press, 2001), p. 16.
41 Medovoi, *Rebels*, pp. 94 and following.
42 See Uta G. Poiger, *Jazz, Rock, and Rebels: Cold War Politics and American Culture in a Divided Germany* (Berkeley: University of California Press, 2000), especially chapter 5.

Index of Names

ABC-TV 87, 89, 102
Aladdin Records 177
Algren, Nelson 139, 140
Allen, Fred 84, 98
Allen, Gracie 94
American Dream 20, 35, 40, 55, 74
Anderson, Margaret 95
Arnaz, Desi 97
Bacall, Lauren 21
Baker, David 154
Ball, Lucille 94, 97
Barnouw, Erik 101, 102
Barthes, Roland 11
beat generation 129, 139, 143, 144, 149, 151, 171
Bell, Daniel 103
Bellow, Saul 166
Benedek, Laszlo 152
Bergman, Ingrid 122
Berle, Milton 86
Berlin Airlift 18
Berry, Chuck 183
Billboard magazine 175
Black Arts movement 169
Black, Bill 174, 186
Blake, William 147
Bogart, Humphrey 21, 122
Boone, Pat 72, 182
Bradbury, Ray 34
Brando, Marlon 152, 153
Brecht, Bertolt 20
Brenston, Jackie 184
Bretz, Stasheff 86
Brinkley, Alan 24, 39, 40
Brookeman, Christopher 141
Brooks, Mel 87
Broonzy, "Big Bill" 173

Brown v. Board 100, 158, 163, 164
Brown, Roy 179, 181, 182, 187
Bunche, Ralph 161
Bureau of Labor Statistics 113
Burns, George 95
Burroughs, William 144
Butler, Nicholas M. 146
Byrd, Harry F. 164
Caesar, Sid 87
Cain, James M. 73
Carter Family, The 174, 176, 188
Cash, Johnny 176
Cassady, Neal 144
Castronovo, David 33, 77, 139, 143, 146, 169
CBS-TV 57, 87, 88, 89, 96, 100, 101, 102
Chambers, Whittaker 19
Chandler, Raymond 73
Charles, Ray 179
Chess Records 177
Chicago Tribune 20
China 22, 24
Chords, The 182
Chrysler 53
Churchill, Winston 15
civil rights movement 13, 158, 159, 162, 163, 164, 165, 171, 190
Clark, Clifford E. 63
Cleaver, June 95
Clooney, George 101
Coca, Imogene 87
Coca-Cola 53
Cochran, Eddie 185
Cohen, Elliott 132
Cohen, Lizabeth 50, 51, 70, 135

Cold War 8, 10, 12, 13, 14, 15, 16, 18, 19, 22, 23, 25, 26, 27, 28, 30, 31, 32, 33, 34, 35, 39, 46, 51, 56, 61, 77, 79, 80, 105, 108, 112, 120, 128, 130, 131, 137, 139, 140, 142, 143, 148, 151, 152, 157, 158, 159, 190
Cole, Ed 55
Columbia Records 177
Comets, The 158, 184
Commentary 10
Communist Party of the United States 17, 19, 20, 22, 30, 31, 32, 33, 35
Coney Island 78
Cook, Blanche W. 32
Coontz, Stephanie 123
Cooper, Gary 20, 50, 118, 119
CORE 163
Corona, Mario 150
Corso, Gragory 144
Crew-Cuts, The 182
Crows, The 182
Crudup, "Big Boy" 174, 186
Crystal Cathedral 56
Curtiz, Michael 122, 152
Dae, Sonny 185
Dakota Staton 180
Davis, Joan 94
Dean, James 152, 155
Dean, Will 50
Decca Records 184
Dichter, Ernest 47, 48, 49
Diddley, Bo 183
Disney, Walt 20, 51, 78, 79
Disneyland 12, 37, 77, 78, 79, 80
Dissent magazine 148
Doctorow, E. L. 34, 35, 36
Domino, Antoine "Fats" 178, 179, 181, 183
Dorsey, Tommy 188
Doyle Dane Bernbach 44, 45, 48
Drifters, The 179
Duany, Andres 66
DuMont Television 89

Dunar, Andrew 85
Earle, Harley 55
Ebb Records 177
Eisenhower, Dwight 7, 23, 24, 27, 28, 30, 48, 52, 96, 102, 159, 165
Eliot, T.S. 145, 147, 167
Ellison, Ralph W. 32, 33, 159, 165, 166, 167, 168, 169
Emerson, Ralph W. 189
Ennis, Philip 182
Enola Gay 28
Enright, Dan 90, 91
Erikson, Erik H. 130, 131, 139
Essex Records 184
Everly Brothers, The 186
Fair Deal 22
Farnham, Marynia and Ferdinand Lundberg 122, 123
Faubus, Orval 165
FBI 22, 31
Federal Communications Commission 84
Federal Housing Administration 65
Federal Records 181
Felsen, Henry G. 136
Ferlinghetti, Lawrence 144
Fiedler, Leslie 143
Fifth Amendment 31
Finney, Jack 34
Ford Motor Company 53, 55, 111
Ford, Glenn 157
Ford, Henry 54
Fortune magazine 51, 110
Fox, Stephen 53
Frank, Robert 7, 13, 14
Frawley, William 97
Frazer, James 145
Freed, Alan 179, 180, 181, 182
Freedman, Albert 90, 91
Freud, Sigmund 47
Friction magazine 144
Friedan, Betty 11, 73, 126, 127, 128
Friendly, Fred 101
Fuchs, Klaus 30

Index of Names

Furness, Betty 56, 57
Galbraith, John K. 10, 12, 42, 43, 44
Garcia Lorca, Federico 147
Garroway, David 125
Gates, Henry L. 167
General Electric 84, 111
General Motors 24, 25, 53, 54, 55
Germany 15, 18
GI Bill 53, 59, 60, 61
Gilbert, Eugene 135
Gilbert, James 120, 121, 132, 134, 137, 138
Gilded Age 104, 105, 112
Gillett, Charlie 184, 187
Ginsberg, Allen 139, 140, 143, 144, 145, 146, 147, 151, 152
Gleason, Jackie 96
Glenn, Artie 181
Goodman, Paul 10
Goodwin, Dick 90
Graham, Sarah 142
Grant, Cary 44
Great Depression 83, 122
Great Migration 60, 160, 161, 173, 176
Gruen, Victor 69
Guralnik, Peter 174
Halberstam, David 54, 164
Haley, Bill 158, 183, 184, 185
Halliwell, Martin 149
Hamm, Jon 49
Hammer, Mike 21
Hancock, Hunter 180
Haralovich, Beth 94
Harptones, The 179
Harris, Wynonie 181
Heitmann, John 136
Hemingway, Ernst 149
Heslov, Grant 101
Hiroshima 25, 27, 28
Hiss, Alger 19, 28
Hoberek, Andrew 168
Holiday Inn 56
Holiday Records 184

Holly, Buddy 186
Hollywood 8, 20, 21, 46, 78, 118, 119, 138, 152, 153, 189
Hollywood Reporter 117
Hollywood Ten 21
Holmes, John C. 144
Honey, Maureen 122
Hook, Sidney 10
Hoover, J. Edgar 22, 31, 32
Howlin' Wolf 173
HUAC 12, 17, 19, 20, 21, 34, 100, 119
Hull, Warren 88
Huncke, Herbert 144
Hunter, Evan 156, 158
Huston, John 21
Iron Curtain 12, 15
Jackson, Bull Moose 181
Jackson, Kenneth T. 60, 62, 65
Japan 15, 22
Jefferson, Thomas 59
Jet magazine 164
Johnson, Buddy 179
Johnson, Ella 180
Johnson, Nunnally 116
Kaye, Danny 21
Kazan, Elia 152
Keiser, Marion 174
Kelly, Gene 21
Kennedy, John F. 11, 27, 48, 159
Kerouac, Jack 13, 14, 129, 139, 140, 144, 148, 149, 150, 151, 152, 171
Khrushchev, Nikita 11, 80
King Records 177, 181, 183
King, Martin Luther Jr. 163, 165
King, Riley "Blues Boy" (B.B.) 173
Kinsey, Alfred 121, 133
Korea 12, 19, 22, 23
Kowinski, William 68
Kramden, Ralph 96
Kramer, Stanley 118
Ku Klux Klan 160
Kunstler, James H. 66
Lamantia, Philip 144

Lambert, Emma 79, 80
Lebanon 19
Lees, Hannah 123
Leo Burnett 45
Lerner, Max 161
Levine, Paul 35
Levitt, Abraham, Alfred and William 59, 61, 62, 64
Levittown 28, 61, 62, 68, 162
Lewis, Jerry Lee 186
Lhamon, W. T. 132, 136
Lidner, Robert 154
Life magazine 41, 52, 71, 113, 120
Lipsitz, George 30, 179, 181
Little Richard 182
Loader, Jayne 28
Lorenz, George "Hound Dog" 180
Luce, Henry 8
Lucky Strike 49, 50
Lucy, Autherine 165
Lynes, Russell 113
Lyotard, Jean-François 11
MacDougall, Ranald 26
Mailer, Norman 134, 139, 140, 148, 149, 151
Malenkov, Georgy 101
Manhattan Project 26, 30
Mao Zedong 24, 101
Marcus, Greil 187, 188
Marin, Louis 79
Marshall Plan 18
Marx, Groucho 88
Mattson, Kevin 10
Mazzocco, Dennis 87
Mc Call's magazine 93
McCarran Act 19
McCarthy, Joseph 8, 12, 19, 21, 30, 32, 33, 34, 36, 100, 101
McDonald's 56
McPhatter, Clyde 179
McQuail, Denis 88
Medovoi, Leerom 93, 130, 131, 139, 143, 151, 190
Meyers, William and Dasy 162

Milland, Ray 26
Miller, Arthur 15, 33, 34, 73
Miller, Douglas and Nowak, Marion 25, 88
Mills, C. Wright 10, 108, 109, 110, 112, 113, 114
Millstein, Gilbert 14
Modern Records 177
Modern Woman magazine 71, 73, 124
Monroe, Bill 186
Moonglows, The 179
Moore, Scotty 174, 186
Mumford, Lewis 65
Murrow, Ed 83, 100, 101, 102
NAACP 160, 163
Nadel, Alan 10, 11, 83
Nagasaki 25
NATO 18
NBC-TV 87, 88, 89, 102, 125
Nelson, Joyce 27, 28
New Deal 24
New York Times 14, 67, 85, 132, 144
New Yorker magazine 85
Newsweek magazine 39
Nixon, Richard 11, 28, 48, 80, 102
O'Neill, Eugene 73, 74
Oakley, Richard J. 85
Operation Crossroads 28
Oppenheimer, J. Robert 26
Orioles, The 181
Packard, Vance 24, 46, 47, 48, 113
Parker, "Colonel" Tom 186, 189
Parker, Junior 173, 187, 188
Parks, John 36
Parks, Rosa 164
Parrish, Tim 189
Partisan Review 10, 129
Peacock Records 177
Pearl Records 177
Peck, Gregory 49
Penny, Hank 181
Perkins, Carl 186
Philip Morris 45

Index of Names

Phillips, Dewey 174
Phillips, Sam 172, 173, 174, 184, 186, 187
Platters, The 182
Podhoretz, Norman 10, 144
Poitier, Sydney 157
Porter, Carolyn 189
Potter, David 39, 52
Preminger, Otto 140, 158
Presley, Elvis 13, 171, 172, 173, 174, 186, 187, 188, 189
Procter & Gamble 53
Prysock, Red 180
Radulovich, Milo 100, 101
Rafferty, Kevin and Pierce 28
Randle, Bill 180
Raney, Wayne 181
Raskin, Jonah 145, 147
Ravens, The 182
Ray, Nicholas 74, 152, 154
RCA Records 136, 177, 186, 188, 189
Reader's Digest 49, 73, 123
Red Scare 12, 28, 30, 32, 33, 34, 37, 100, 101
Redford, Robert 89
Richbourgh,"John R." 180
Riesman, David 13, 103, 104, 105, 106, 107, 108, 110, 111, 112, 114, 120, 142
Rodgers, Jimmie 176
Roosevelt, F. D. 16
Rosenberg, Julius and Ethel 12, 30, 31, 32, 34, 35
Roth, Philip 66, 67
Saddlemen, The 184
Salinger, J.D. 138, 139, 140, 142, 143
Sartre, Jean-Paul 76, 148
Savoy Records 177
Schlesinger, Arthur Jr. 10
Schuller, Robert 56
SCLC 163
Selznick, David 85

Seventeen magazine 135
Shopen, Bernard 76
Simon, Neil 87
Simpson, Luis 144
Sloan, Alfred P. 54, 55
Slotkin, Richard 119
SNCC 163
Solomon, Carl 144
Sorokin, Pitrim 133
Soviet Union 15, 16, 17, 18, 25, 27, 30, 31, 131, 143
Spigel, Lynn 86, 91, 92, 93, 94, 98, 99, 124
Spillane, Mickey 21
Spock, Benjamin 72, 106, 107
Steiner, George 143
Stempel, Herbert 89, 90
Stevenson, Adlai E. 24, 102
Stick McGee 178
Sullivan, Ed 188, 189
Sun Records 172, 174, 184, 186, 187, 188
Supreme Court 61, 158, 160, 161, 163, 165
Susman, Warren 10, 74
Taft-Hartley Bill 16, 22
Til, Sonny 179, 181
Till, Emmett 164
Time magazine 95
Trilling, Lionel 10, 144
Truman Doctrine 12, 16, 17, 18, 19
Truman, Harry S. 16, 17, 22, 23, 24, 28, 31, 159, 161
Tungate, Mark 45
Turner, "Big" Joe 179, 185
Turner, Ike 184
Twain, Mark 150
U.S. Constitution 121, 162
U.S. New & World Report 40
United Nations 22, 159
Updike, John 74, 75
Van Doren, Charles 89, 90
Vance, Vivian 97
Vincent, Gene 185

Volkswagen 44
Walker, George 55
Ward, Bill 181, 182
Warren, Robert P. 169
Wattenberg, Ben 162
Wayne, John 20, 119
Weber, Max 111
Weiner, Matthew 48
Weiss, Nancy 107
Wertham, Fredric 137, 138
Weston, Jesse 145
White, Lynn 124
Whitman, Walt 145, 147
Whyte, William 13, 64, 65, 110, 111, 112, 113, 115, 120
Wilder, Billy 73
William, Sioned 83
William, Tennessee 73, 74
Williams, Hank 176, 183
Williams, William C. 147
Wills, Bob 184
Wilson, Charles 24
Wilson, Sloan 59, 103, 114, 120
Wood, Nathalie 155
Woods, Randall B. 18, 24
World War I 121
World War II 10, 11, 15, 18, 22, 23, 24, 25, 26, 27, 42, 43, 51, 52, 54, 59, 60, 61, 66, 83, 103, 105, 110, 122, 132, 134, 142, 145, 147, 160, 166, 172, 175, 176, 178
Wright, Frank Lloyd 63
Wright, Richard 166, 167
Wyle, Philip 95
Yates, Richard 74, 76
Zinn, Howard 27
Zinnemann, Fred 118

Acknowledgements

This book began as a series of undergraduate courses I taught at the University of Torino beginning in 2001. I then upgraded my materials for my American Studies MA students and then upgraded them again into an initial draft for an online American Culture MA class.

Invaluable research support has come from the J.F. Kennedy Institute Library at the Freie Universitaet Berlin, through an initial grant in 2001 and continued support and hospitality over the years, and the Fondazione CRT's Progetto Alfieri, which sponsored valuable research assistance. Special thanks also go to the Melchiori and Solari libraries at the University of Torino, Torino's Fondazione Einaudi, and the Vere Harmsworth Library at Oxford University's Rothermere American Institute.

I have shared discussions on several of these topics with many colleagues in Europe and North America and I thank them for their insights and friendship: Robert Casillo, Ashley Dawson, Sonia Di Loreto, Andrew Gross, Michael Hoenisch and all the colleagues of the European Cluster in America Studies (ECAS), Peter Ling, Giorgio Mariani, Angela Miller, Sharon Monteith, Karen Pinkus, Ennio Ranaboldo, Stefano Rosso, John Paul Russo, Maurizio Vaudagna, and Britta Waldschmidt-Nelson.

I would like to acknowledge several cohorts of my students, whose arguments and feedback have helped me shape my understanding of these materials. I am indebted to my 2009–10 research assistant Luigi Stefanizzi, who has provided background research for some of the chapters, and Lee Herrmann, who has helped reviewing the final manuscript.

Special thanks and love go out to my family, for spurring, supporting and assisting me throughout. This book is dedicated to them.